Comprehensive Computer Essentials

The A to Z of Computers

Chitra Lele

ATLANTIC
PUBLISHERS & DISTRIBUTORS (P) LTD

Published by
ATLANTIC
PUBLISHERS & DISTRIBUTORS (P) LTD
7/22, Ansari Road, Darya Ganj, New Delhi-110002
Phones : +91-11-40775252, 23273880, 23275880, 23280451
Fax : +91-11-23285873
Web : www.atlanticbooks.com
E-mail : orders@atlanticbooks.com

Branch Office
5, Nallathambi Street, Wallajah Road, Chennai-600002
Phones : +91-44-64611085, 32413319
E-mail : chennai@atlanticbooks.com

Printed in India at Nice Printing Press, A-33/3A, Site-IV, Industrial Area, Sahibabad, Ghaziabad, U.P.

Preface

In the early days of civilization, human beings used their hands and fingers as a counting device. Then came the abacus for counting large numbers. And then came a barrage of electro-mechanical devices to handle complex calculations and operations. And now harnessing of the superpower of a modern-day computer has catapulted the world from the days of the humble abacus to the current avatar of hybrid digital devices and portable devices like smartphones and wearables. Most users look at computers as merely calculating devices, but there is more to computers than meets the eye. The book, *Comprehensive Computer Essentials: The A to Z of Computers* will take the readers beyond this myopic view. We all have witnessed the stellar growth of computers, yet the essentials underpinning this dynamic discipline are not noticed or appreciated to the desired extent. An attempt has been made in this book to bring out this aspect so that we are able to learn and appreciate how the future of humanity will increasingly revolve around computer technology, and how, we as enlightened engineers, can contribute to make this virtual connection a mutually beneficial one in the real world.

Over the centuries, the demand for the knowledge of computer science has increased manifold. Computers are the gateway to global growth. Computer science is the fastest growing field in the world. The book discusses the global importance and impact of computers. As it is evident, computers are second to none in terms of their reach and impact, and the number of people joining the 'computer bandwagon' is astonishing.

Apart from discussing fundamental topics like the history, types, generations, applications and programming concepts, the book also provides comprehensive information about the internal architecture of a computer system. Input and output devices along with their types, features, etc. are explained. Various aspects that computer science and computers have a tremendous impact on, right from education to the World Wide Web, and from healthcare to research, are discussed. The intricacies of the Internet are covered in an easy-to-understand manner. Recent developments and future trends (cloud computing, virtual reality, wearables, etc.) in computers are also covered in the book.

The book will be useful for students and teachers of computer science, for those interested in understating the global impact of computers, professionals who are training corporate trainees, and for anyone who wants to be a part of the global growth wave. Besides, it will be a great addition to personal, college, and corporate libraries.

Why have computers, and not some other device or machine, achieved such a status? How are computers integrating our offices homes, and environment? What do IoT, HTTPS, TCP/IP, and HTML stand for? What impact will the revolution of the wired world have on the evolution of mankind? How does miniaturization lead to the development of new products such as smartphones, smartwatches, etc.? Why are computers important in today's times of globalization? This book seeks to answer these as well as many more questions through the three sections: Comprehensive Computer Fundamentals, Inside and Outside, and The Internet, The Future and More.

All the features and tools needed to facilitate quick understanding of computers are provided: figures, images, and tables that clarify concepts, learning tips, spotlight tips, how to and word of caution sections, and questions for reflection. In-depth information of each of the important areas of computers provides students with a good level of proficiency in this dynamic discipline, and will also help them to consolidate their skills.

By the end of the book, you will have gained a significant level of understanding of computers and you certainly will view your laptop or smartphone with a new perspective.

Chitra Lele

Acknowledgements

This book, while an individual work, benefited from the insights and direction of several people. I take this opportunity to express my heartfelt thanks to all those who supported me, in one way or the other, during the completion of this writing project.

What I have learnt over the years comes as a result of being a daughter of wonderful parents—Mrs. Asha Lele and Mr. G.G. Lele. They have been the motivation that has helped me to maintain focus on my goals. Thanks to them for their ongoing support and endless encouragement.

I offer my deep gratitude to the Divine Essence for bestowing on me the strength to follow my heart.

I owe my sincere gratitude to my company colleagues who gave me the time and space to complete this book. Their ceaseless cooperation in adjusting to my project work schedule and writing schedule helped me to maintain balance between these two aspects.

I am grateful to the editorial team of Atlantic Publishers for their constructive comments and unflagging support. Their editorial feedback, design inputs and constant reviews have transformed this writing project into an informative and interesting book.

Special thanks must go to you all, my readers, for investing your time in reading my book.

Last but not least, I beg forgiveness of all those who have been with me over the course of the years and whose names I have failed to mention. I am thankful to them for their support and encouragement.

Chitra Lele

Contents

List of Tables, Figures and Images

A. List of Tables

B. List of Figures

C. List of Images

Part 1
COMPREHENSIVE COMPUTER FUNDAMENTALS

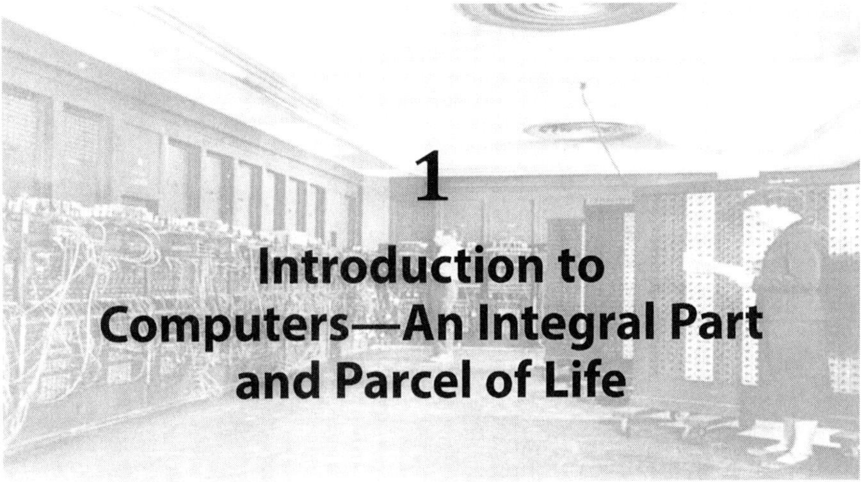

1

Introduction to Computers—An Integral Part and Parcel of Life

Today's world is a tech-driven and an information-rich place. Computers are a part and parcel of everyday life. They are used by everyone, right from home users to large business establishments. A computer is a powerful tool as it is able to perform the information processing cycle operations of input, storage, process and output with reliability, speed and accuracy.

In the past few decades, computers have changed and reshaped our world drastically. Computers have made their impact felt in each and every aspect of our lives—the way we live, the way we work, the way we study, the way we communicate, the way we enjoy, the way we learn and so on and so forth. They offer a quicker way to access information which is by providing Internet access.

They are everywhere and this is not a cliché. In the current era, it is impossible to imagine that someone can live without computers. They are used in almost every field even where it is most unexpected. This widespread impact of computers in modern society implies that computer literacy has become of critical importance.

While almost every household has at least one personal computer, either a laptop or a desktop, but there are no longer the only computers found in a home. Many households have numerous computers embedded throughout their homes like home security systems and entertainment systems. Ordinary homes have become smart homes. Smart homes are becoming more and more common, and all the smart systems, appliances and devices in them are connected through a network and they communicate in a wireless mode.

The term "computer" was originally ascribed to human beings (human computers) who performed numerical calculations and computations using mechanical calculators such as the abacus and slide rule. Later on this term was assigned to mechanical devices as they started doing the job of human computers. The term "computer" was first recorded as being used in 1613 in a book called "The Young Mans Gleanings" by English writer Richard Braithwait. In this book, this term referred to a person who carried out calculations or computations. It is only much later that this term began to be used for a machine that carries out calculations.

Spotlight Tip
As computers become more integrated with our lives, the skills to operate them become more crucial.

1.1 Definition of Computers—An Advanced Programmable Device

A computer is an advanced programmable electronic device that takes raw data as input from the user, stores it for a certain time period, and then processes it using a set of highly organized instructions to produce the final result. This set of instructions is called a program. The final result is also called output, which can be stored on various devices and can be presented in various formats. A computer has the ability to store, retrieve and process data. The term computer is derived from the Latin term "computare," which means "to calculate" or "to think together" or "to count". Data is a collection of raw unprocessed symbols, facts and figures. Information is data that is processed, organized, meaningful, and useful.

A computer is a programmable device that automatically accepts and stores input and data, and performs programmed computations or controls operations on the same. It is also known as a data processing unit as it involves many operations performed on the data fed to the computer system like storing, analyzing, processing, sorting and disseminating.

Modern-day computers essentially follow the concept of the stored program laid out by John von Neumann in 1945. The stored program concept is considered as a von Neumann system with von Neumann architecture. John von Neumann was a Hungarian-American inventor, mathematician and computer scientist, and he was an important figure in the field of computer science. The term "stored program" means that data and a series of instructions for computing and processing a task can be loaded into a computer's memory. Both the data and the instructions that operate on the data are stored in the computer memory itself. This idea was introduced in the late 1940s by John von Neumann, who proposed that a program be electronically stored in binary number format in a memory device. Other engineers like J. Presper Eckert and John W. Mauchly also contributed to this concept. Before the introduction of this concept, data and instructions were considered two separate entities and were thus stored separately.

1.1.1 Characteristics of Computers—From Accuracy to Versatility

1. **Accuracy**—despite the high speed of processing, the accuracy of computers is very high. The degree of accuracy of a particular computer depends on the instructions and the type of processor. Accuracy of results is produced even when computers are used continuously for hours together. They can perform their operations error-free for days at a time. They are reliable and robust.

There is a concept called Garbage In Garbage Out (GIGO), which means if the data fed into a computer is not error-free, it is likely to produce inaccurate results. Errors do occur in computer-based data and information, but a large percentage of these errors are due to faulty human input in terms of a procedural error, program logic error or erroneous data. Errors in the hardware can occur, but due to increased efficiency in error-detecting mechanisms, these seldom lead to inaccurate results.

2. **Reliability**—computers are extremely reliable machines. They are not affected by human factors like boredom or tiredness; hence can carry on their functions repeatedly and relentlessly. Again like accuracy, the reliability factor depends on how reliable the fed input/data is. Reliability is that attribute of a computer that consistently performs according to its specifications. In case of any failure, there are provisions for immediate backup of data, information and programs.
3. **Speed**—computers work at an incredible speed. They can perform millions of instructions and even more per second. Some complex calculation and operations that usually would have taken hours and days to complete, now can be completed in a few seconds using a computer. These speed-driven results enable the user or organization to take timely decisions. Computers are classified on the basis of their speed by comparing their Million Instructions Per Second (MIPS). MIPS is a measure of a computer's raw processing power.

   The speed is determined in terms of microsecond or nanosecond. A microsecond is an amount of time equal to one millionth of a second (10^{-6}). A nanosecond is an amount of time equal to one billionth of a second (10^{-9}). The processing speed is measured in Megahertz (MHz) or Gigahertz (GHz). One gigahertz is equal to 1,000 megahertz (MHz) or 1,000,000,000 Hz. Modern processors run so fast that often gigahertz (GHz) is used as a benchmark.

4. **Storage**—computers can store a mass amount of data and instructions. The storage and memory capacity is measured in Megabyte (MB), Gigabyte (GB), Terabyte (TB), and now even larger units have come into the picture like Petabyte (PB), Exabyte (EB), Zettabyte (ZB) and Yottabyte (YB).

   A megabyte is a multiple of the unit byte for digital information. The unit prefix mega is a multiplier of 1000000 (10^6) in the International System of Units (SI); hence one megabyte is one million bytes of information. One gigabyte is equal to 1,048,576 bytes or 1024 megabytes. One terabyte is 1,099,511,627,776 (2^{40}) bytes, 1,048,576 megabytes or 1,024 gigabytes.

   They can store large volumes of data in storage devices like USB flash drive, hard drive, etc., which have the capacity to store huge amounts of data and also make the retrieval of data an easy task.

5. **Multitasking**—computers can perform several operations, calculations and tasks at the same time. Multitasking allows a user to perform more than one task or process at a time. The computer operating system is able to keep track of where you are in these tasks and jump from one to the other without losing information and data. These tasks or processes share common processing resources like CPU and storage. For example, a user can type a word document and check email concurrently.

   In the case of a computer with single core, only one task runs at any given point in time. True multitasking occurs with a multi core, where the operating system can run multiple tasks simultaneously. With multiple cores, the operating system can execute multiple tasks, processes or applications more efficiently by splitting the different tasks, processes or applications between the separate CPU cores. Multitasking results in better overall throughput and performance.

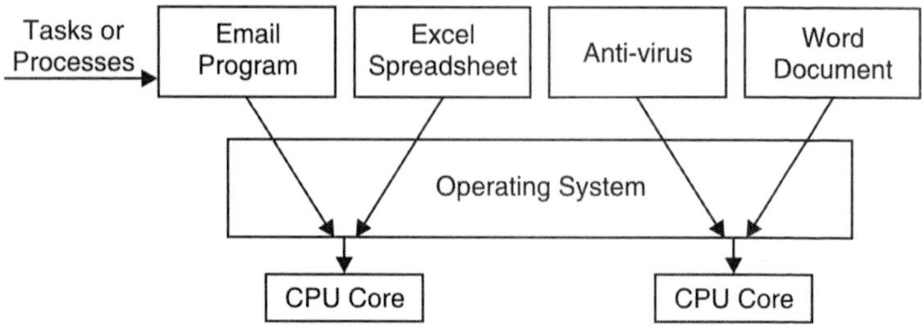

Figure 1: MULTITASKING

6. **Cost Reduction**—computers offer a short-term cost-effective solution and investment for long-term advantage. As computers allow work to be done faster and more efficiently, there is cost savings in terms of employee investment and manpower requirements. There is cost saving in terms of energy, time and monetary resources.
7. **Automation**—computers are automated machines. Once the data and instructions are fed into a computer, it automatically carries out the required instructions and operations without any human intervention. Programs can schedule tasks that a computer can execute without any user interaction or manual intervention.
8. **Diligence**—a computer is not affected by tiredness, monotony and lack of concentration. A computer can continuously work for hours together without making any mistake and without complaining. It can work for a lot of hours with the same speed and accuracy without getting tired.

9. **Versatility**—computers are a versatile machine. They can work with different types of devices and data. They can perform different types of tasks with the same level of ease, both simple and complex tasks. A user can access and perform word processing, imaging, multimedia and communicating tasks from one platform without closing other applications. One moment, a computer is printing the excel worksheet and the next moment it is preparing the results of a finance report, and this transition happens in a seamless manner.

   Though the computers are limited to performing four main functions of receiving inputs from the users or programs, storing and transferring data internally within the CPU, exchanging and sharing the information with the outside world though input-output devices, and performing logical and arithmetic operations, they can still be a versatile device. This is possible because all tasks and activities can be reduced to an interplay between these functions. Because of this versatility factor, computers can be used in various fields for various purposes.

10. **Limitations**—in the previous points, we discussed the plus points of computers, but they have certain limitations too. But the advantages far outweigh the limitations. Although a computer is far better in performance than a human being, it fails in certain aspects: computers need to be programmed in order to perform tasks; they cannot do this on their own and they perform as per the instructions, they do not learn by experience as we human beings do, and they do not have a mind of their own so they cannot take decision themselves.

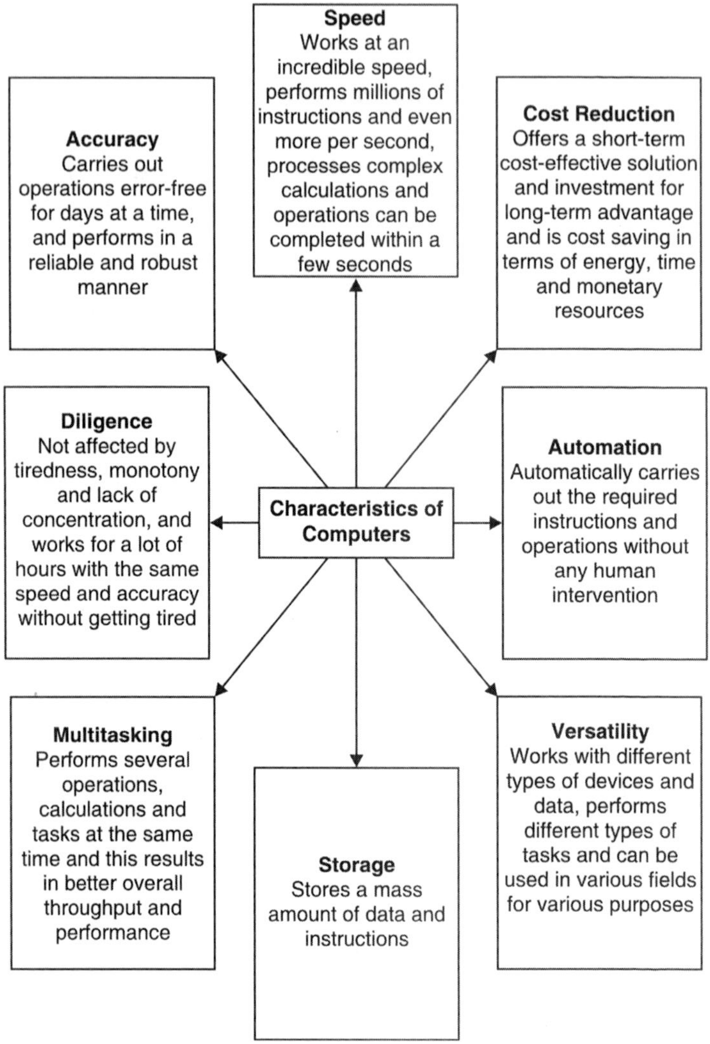

Figure 2: CHARACTERISTICS OF COMPUTERS

1.1.2 Analog versus Digital Computers—From Varying Inputs to Binary Inputs

A lesser-known type of computer is the analog computer (analogue in British English) and it works in a very different way from a digital computer. Analog computers were the first computers to be developed and they provided the basis for the development of the modern digital computers. Today's high-tech digital computers owe a great deal to their analog ancestors.

Analog computers are able to deal with continuously varying inputs for complex phenomena such as voltage changes and temperature fluctuations. They are used to control processes such as those found in paper making, oil refinery and chemical industry where flow and temperature measurements are important. They are also used in scientific applications and in hospitals too. The development of transistors made electronic analog computers practical, and before digital computers had developed sufficiently, analog computers were commonly used in industry and science. Analog computers work with analog signals. These are signals that can take up any value along a scale, can include every conceivable number, even irrational numbers, such as ∏ (Pi). Some of the olden day analog computer examples include slide rules, monographs and astrolabes.

Image 1: ANALOG COMPUTER

Image Source: https://en.wikipedia.org/wiki/Analog_computer#/media/File: Analog_Computing_Machine_GPN-2000-000354.jpg

Analog computers can work both mechanically and electronically. During the late 18th century and early 19th century, the development of analog computer reached its heights. During the World War II and Korean War, these advanced mechanical analog computers were used for encryption and gunfire assistance. Thereafter, development of transistors gave a boost to the development of electronic analog computers which were quite popular and used commonly in science and industry.

The basis of the working of the analog computers is modeling. In an analog computer, the output can be connected to an oscilloscope and results can be seen on it. An oscilloscope is an instrument to observe the change of an electrical signal over time. It provides a graph of a signal's voltage over time. Analog computers measure and compare quantities in a single operation. The output derived from an analog computer is generally in the form of readings on a series of dial or a graph on strip chart.

Analog computers are more flexible than digital computers because of the way in which they represent data, but when it comes to precision or reliability, digital computers are ahead in the race. Analog computers represent data as output voltage signals, and have sets of analog meters and oscilloscopes to display these voltage signals. An analog signal's voltage may be constant or vary with time.

The first electronic digital computers were developed in the early 1940s. They were large devices that needed large amount of power; hence they were expensive. Thereafter, smaller computers were designed but they lacked the versatility of their earlier large counterparts. With the advancement of semiconductor technology, the building blocks of the large computers were replaced with small, less power consuming devices, and from there onwards, there was no looking back for digital computers.

Digital computers work with digits to represent numerals, letters or other special symbols, and perform logical operations and calculations using inputs represented as digits. They represent data as having one distinct value or another with no other possibilities.

Digital computers process data which is in binary format. Digital computers operate on inputs which have two discrete states on or off and the output is also in the same form (on or off). On is represented by a 1 and an off is represented by a 0. They process data which is based on the presence or the absence of an electrical charge (binary 1 or binary 0). These two binary codes or digits 1 and 0, stand for yes and no, true and false. Most of the computers available today are digital computers.

The primary difference between an analog computer and a digital computer is the way in which they process and handle the data. With improved technology, digital computers can emulate the behavior of analog computers, whereas analog computers have limited ability to emulate digital computers. Analog computers generate a lot of noise and this affects their accuracy. Analog computers are used for specialized purposes. Today with advancement in technology, many digital computers are performing the functions of analog computers.

Analog computers are faster than digital computers. Analog computers lack memory whereas digital computers store information. The results of digital computers are more accurate than that of analog computers.

A hybrid computer is a type of computer that has the functionalities and characteristics of both an analog computer and a digital computer within a single unit; it offers the best of both types of computers. It is a computer that has the accuracy and memory of a digital computer combined with flexibility and speed of an analog computer. It offers a cost-effective method of performing complex simulations, scientific calculations and specialized operations. A hybrid computer has tremendous computing speed enabled by the parallel configuration provided by the analog subsystem. The analog subsystem provides efficient processing of differential equations, while the digital subsystem deals with the logical operations.

A hybrid computer is used where both kinds of data need to be processed, continuous and discrete, for example, in petrol pump devices there is a processor that converts fuel flow measurements into quantity and price values. Hybrid computers are used in robotics, hospital intensive care units, defense and radar systems, etc.

Table 1: Differences between Analog and Digital Computers

Analog Computers	Digital Computers
Memory is stored in the form of wave signal.	Memory is stored in the form of binary bit.
Analog technology records waveforms as they are.	Samples analog waveforms into a limited set of numbers and records them.
Analog computers work on continuous values.	Digital computers work on discrete values.
Needs a large power supply.	Needs only negligible power.
Have noise in their circuitry and it is carried along with the data.	Have relatively lower levels of noise and it is easier to separate out noise from the data.
Applications include specialized fields like medical and science fields.	Applications include almost all fields of life.
Analog hardware is not flexible.	Digital hardware is flexible.
Analog computers are used for measuring and calculating analog quantities (continuous) like speed, temperature, etc.	Digital computers are used to perform mathematical and logical operations.
Examples of analog computers are speedometer, thermometer, tire pressure gauge, etc.	Examples of digital computers are laptops, smartphones, etc.

1.2 Importance of Computers—An Integral Part of the World Landscape

The 21st century has witnessed the information technology revolution and computers are the hub of this revolution. The ability to process data and disseminate information across the world in a matter of seconds is what makes computers so fascinating. According to the *Houston Chronicle* (it is the largest daily newspaper in Texas, USA), computers are important because of their ability to improve efficiency, save money and facilitate communication between people across the globe. Computer means much more than a PC.

Without computers and their network, the whole world would freeze, would go into a hang. Apart from their basic importance in terms of huge data storage capacity and speedy processing, computers play an important role in worldwide communications in the form of the popular World Wide Web (WWW). The WWW and its modern tools provide access to different sources of information and facilitate worldwide interactive communication.

There are thousands and thousands of uses in which computers are used, right from performing simple mechanical operations to operating complex unmanned space probes. These uses are increasing day-by-day, which is why computers are so important, and are an integral part of the world landscape. In the coming days, computers are going to be even more pervasive, because technology is advancing at break-neck speed.

Before the internet and the computer revolution—it would take an average of 5-7 days to deliver and receive a letter by post. Now it takes only a few seconds. Especially in the business domain, this fast delivery of information is of crucial importance. No matter what a business does, computers can be leveraged to help business do what it does more efficiently, and this results in significant time saving and cost saving. This makes it a much needed tool of transformation for every business, small or large, and for any domain be it education, government, banking, etc.

Computers also help businesses across the globe to save time, hence save money too. Depending on their usage and service application, they can be classified in various categories. In the business world, they can perform simple operations like ticketing and billing transactions to complex functions like banking and telecommunication. Just one look around and you will realize how entrenched the role of computers is in the business world in particular and in the society in general. They handle the airplane and railway reservations. They are used for inventory storage and analysis. Data mining and analysis is done by them. They are not only found in posh offices, but also in every small business setup including stores, drive-ins, etc. Computers are heavily relied on in the entertainment and media industries. In other words, the conventional paper and pen are becoming extinct in the corporate world.

The Internet and its collaboration tools like email, file-sharing programs and instant messaging facilitate fast communications. As computers are able to store large amounts of data and that too in various formats, it becomes easier to search and extract data based on various criteria and this data can be presented by computers in various formats like comprehensive reports, video presentations, etc.

Without computers and their networks, everything would be a mess and everything would go wild.

1.3 History of Computers—From Abacus to IPhone

One of the earliest machines designed to help people in calculations was the abacus. Even prior to the advent of microprocessors and integrated circuits, there were certain prominent engineers, scientists and inventors that worked relentlessly and helped lay the groundwork for a path-breaking technology that has since drastically reshaped our world and our lives.

In the 20th century, advances in technology led to the introduction of ever-evolving computing machines we see today, including portable devices like laptops and IPhones.

1.3.1 Pre-history of Computers—Numbers, Slide Rule, and Much More

The first computers were people. In the beginning, mankind used fingers and toes for calculation and also used stones and sticks as markers. This became the basis for the base 10 numbering system. As time went by and mankind progressed further and further on the path of evolution, mankind invented the concept of numbers and as these numbers became complex, mankind began to invent devices and machines to deal with these complex numbers.

Although major technological leaps occurred in the last two decades, the true history of computers stretches back more than 2,500 years to the Abacus, also called a calculating tool. It has become undoubtedly the most important invention of human history. Abacus is known to be the first mechanical calculating device and it was first developed in the 10th century B.C. It was used to perform calculations by sliding counters along rods or in grooves.

John Napier, a Scottish mathematician and inventor, invented logarithms in 1614. He is responsible for one of the most significant developments in calculation devices, Napier's Bones. They were a set of rods with multiplication tables written out on them.

Edmund Gunter, a London scholar, invented the logarithmic scales also known as Gunter's Rule. The slide rule is a very simple analog computer. This simple wooden ruler was a key development in the history of computing devices. It uses logarithmic and other scales to assist in numerical and trigonometric calculations.

Blaise Pascal, a French scientist, invented the Pascaline in 1642. It was a wooden box that could only add and subtract by means of a series of gears and wheels. This device was also called the numerical wheel calculator and was one of the world's first mechanical adding machines.

The language in which computers used to execute processor instructions originated in 17th century in the form of the binary numerical system and it was developed by German philosopher and mathematician, Gottfried Wilhelm Leibniz. This language was based on decimal numbers using only two digits and it was inspired from the classical Chinese text "I Ching," which discussed the universe in terms of dualities or polarities like light and darkness. While there was no practical use of this language, Gottfried Leibniz believed that it was possible for a machine to someday use this binary system. Much later, in 1847, George Boole, English mathematician, introduced a newly devised algebraic language built on Gottfried Leibniz's work. Boole's "*Boolean Algebra*" was actually a system of logic, with mathematical equations used to represent statements in logic. Though there was no immediate and obvious usage for Boole's algebra at the time, Charles Pierce, another mathematician spent decades researching and expanding the system and eventually concluded in 1886 that the calculations can be carried out with electrical switching circuits. And over time, Boolean logic did play an instrumental role in the design of electronic computers.

In 1801, Joseph Marie Jacquard, a French weaver and merchant, created a way to automate steam-powered loom by using punched cards to automatically weave fabric designs. The cards contained rows and columns of holes arranged in different patterns to produce different textile designs. The presence or absence of a hole determined whether a thread was allowed to pass or not. Early computers would use similar punched cards. Jacquard's punched cards can be considered as today's read-only storage.

A few years later in 1822, Charles Babbage, an English mathematician and inventor, credited as "Father of the Computer," proposed a steam driven calculating machine the size of a room, which he called the *Difference Engine*. This machine would be able to compute tables of numbers, such as logarithm tables, but this machine was never completed as it was canceled by the British government in 1842. Babbage's next project was called the Analytic Engine which was based on the punch card mechanism. He named the two main parts of this device: the "Store" and "Mill". Both these terms are used in the weaving industry. The Store was where the numbers were stored and the Mill was where the numbers were "woven" or processed. In modern times, these two terms relate to the modern-day parts of memory unit and central processing unit.

In 1890, Herman Hollerith, an American inventor, developed the electromechanical punched card tabulator, successfully adopted from Jacquard's punched cards for the purpose of computation. This tabulator was the basis for the idea of data processing and over the years it also laid the foundation for International Business Machines Corporation (IBM). Hollerith's punched card system was used by the US Census bureau for the 1890 census. It completed the task in just three years and saved the government 5 million dollars.

1.3.2 Recent History of Computers—Electronic Computing, IPhones and Much More

During the late 1940s and early 1950s, with the advent of electronic computing machines, the phrase "computing machine" gradually gave way simply to "computer".

The World War II period was a crucial period in the history of computing, when powerful gigantic computers began to appear. The onset of World War II created a large need for computer capacity, especially for the military. John W. Mauchly, John P. Eckert and their team decided to build a high-speed electronic computer to meet this need. This device is known as the ENIAC. The US military desired a mechanical calculator more optimized for scientific computations. But solving such equations was extremely tedious and manual task, and the US military searched the country for manual operators, but could not find the adequate number. Faced with this situation, the US military was willing to invest in projects to automate this type of computation. One early success was the Harvard Mark I computer which was built as a joint project by Harvard and IBM in 1944. This was the first programmable digital computer made in the US, but it was not a purely electronic computer.

One of the primary programmers for the Mark I was a woman, Grace Hopper, who invented the first high-level language, 'Flow-matic' and this language eventually became COBOL. Building computers in this period had been incredibly expensive because they required so much hand assembly.

Image 2: HARVARD MARK I

Image Source: http://www.cs.kent.edu/~rothstei/10051/HistoryPt3.htm

The microelectronics revolution—the evolution of microelectronics gave a boost to the computer industry due to its small size. The hand-crafted wiring and assembly was replaced by mass-produced integrated circuit. This method of integration was a major improvement over the manual assembly of the circuits using electronic components. According to research figures, in last 30 years, computer performance per dollar has improved more than a million fold. Vacuum tubes were a considerable advance on relay switches. Then came the period of transistors. Like vacuum tubes, transistors could be used as amplifiers or as switches, but were much more advanced in all aspects. Although transistors were a great advancement on vacuum tubes, one key difficulty remained. Systems that used thousands of transistors still had to be hand wired to connect all these components together, and this process was error-prone, laborious and costly. Packaging these transistors into a single package was the next logical step and this is how integrated circuits were born; they did solve the problem but not completely as some degree of hand wiring/assembly was still required. Further developments made it possible to include the connections between the components in an integrated circuit thereby automating the entire process.

The forefather of modern-day all-electronic digital computers is usually considered to be Electronic Numerical Integrator and Calculator (ENIAC), which was built at the University of Pennsylvania between 1943 and 1945. By the end of 1950s, computers were no longer devices exclusively owned by universities and government laboratories. 1970s saw a prominent rise in the mainframe segment. In the decade of 1980s, things changed drastically. Today, we carry more computing power on our iPhones and smartphones than was available in the early devices and models. Smartphones and iPhones—it is nearly impossible to imagine modern life without them.

1.4 Computer Generations—From First to Fifth

The history of computers is often discussed in reference to the different generations. Initially, the generation term was used to distinguish between varying hardware technologies. But nowadays, generation includes both software and hardware. To process data into information, a computer uses software and hardware.

Software (SW or S/W) is a set of instructions and programs that enables a computer to function. Software is divided into two main categories: application software and system software. Application software, also called end-user programs, includes programs like word processor, web browsers, etc. Application software sits on top of system software. Application suite contains multiple application software programs bundled together. System software sits directly on top of a computer's hardware. System software consists of low-level programs that interact with computers at a basic level. The most significant system software is the operating system that manages the functions of a computer system. Other system software examples include compilers, devices drivers, debuggers, etc. Hardware (HW or H/W) is a collection of physical components that contains a circuit board, integrated circuits, mechanical equipment, or other electronics, that make up a computer system. Hardware is what makes a computer function.

There are five definable generations of computers. Each of the five generations of computers is characterized by a significant technological development that fundamentally changed the way computers function and leading to less expensive, more compact, and more powerful machines.

There is no fixed and generally agreed date or period for any of the generations. In fact, the classification of computers generations is more to do with the switching components, memory and technology used to fabricate the processors rather than time period.

Spotlight Tip
With each new generation, the circuitry has become smaller and more advanced than the previous generations.

1.4.1 First Generation—Vacuum Tubes

First Generation—1940–1956—Vacuum Tubes—these early computers used vacuum tubes as circuitry and switching device and magnetic drums and magnetic tapes for memory. These computers consumed a lot of energy, generated a lot of heat and were huge in size, taking up entire rooms, and were high-cost installations, and therefore could be afforded only by very large organizations. The heat generated was often the cause of malfunctions. The programming capability back then was quite low. The commercial appeal of this generation computers was low as each component had to be assembled individually.

A vacuum tube, also called valve or electronic tube, was first developed by John Ambrose Fleming in 1904. A vacuum tube contains electrodes for controlling the flow of electrons and was used in early computers as an amplifier or a switch.

The machine language (the lowest-level programming language understood by computers) was the only way to tell this generation computers how to perform the operations. As this generation computers relied heavily on machine language (machine language was cryptic; hence difficult to understand and program), it was herculean job to program these computers. Punched cards and paper tape were used to feed data and programs and the output/results were produced in the form of printouts. These generation computers could solve only one problem at a time.

Image 3: ENIAC

Image Source: https://en.wikipedia.org/wiki/ENIAC#/media/File:Eniac.jpg

The first generation computers were mainly used for scientific computations. Electronic Numerical Integrator and Calculator (ENIAC) was the world's first successful electronic computer which was developed by two scientists namely J.W. Mauchy and J.P. Eckert at the University of Pennsylvania. Examples of first generation computers are ENIVAC, Electronic Discrete Variable Automatic Computer (EDVAC) and UNIVersal Automatic Computer (UNIVAC-1). ENIAC weighed 30 tons and contained 18,000 vacuum tubes, 70,000 resistors, 10,000 capacitors and 1,500 relays, and required 200 kilowatts of electric power. ENIAC was designed and developed by Army Ordnance to compute World War II ballistic firing tables. When it was announced in 1946, ENIAC was touted by the media as a "giant brain". Apart from ballistics, ENIAC was used for applications like atomic energy calculations, thermal ignition, weather predictions and other scientific uses.

EDVAC is the successor of the ENIAC and was designed and developed by the same designers of ENIVAC. It is one of the first electronic computers that utilized the binary system that first began performing basic tasks in 1951 and as it used binary instead of decimal numbers, this made the construction of arithmetic units much simpler. EDVAC was a stored program machine and used mercury delay lines for memory storage. The UNIVAC was the first commercial computer delivered to a business client, the U.S. Census Bureau in 1951. The UNIVAC was later released as newer version like UNIVAC II and III with various models, such as the 418, 490, 491, 1100, 1101, 1102, 1103, 1104, 1105, 1106, 1107 and 1108.

1.4.2 Second Generation—Transistors

Second Generation—1956–1963—Transistors were used as the electronic component instead of vacuum tubes, and these were the first computers to store instructions in their memory, which moved from a magnetic drum to magnetic core technology. Magnetic cores were used as primary memory and magnetic tape and magnetic disks as secondary storage devices. However, they still relied on punched cards for input and printouts for output. Transistors proved to be a much better alternative to the vacuum tubes.

A transistor is a device composed of semiconductor material like silicon that opens or closes a circuit, or amplifies a signal. Transistors are used to regulate the flow of an electrical current and to switch electricity on and off. Silicon-based transistors are less sensitive to temperature so they cannot easily burn up or heat up. Transistors were invented in 1947 at Bell Telephone Laboratories by Walter H. Brattain, John Bardeen and William B. Shockley, but did not see widespread use in computers until the late 50s. They are the key component of digital circuits, including computers—current day latest microprocessors contain tens of millions of transistors. As a transistor is small in size, the size of this generation computers also reduced greatly.

The stored program concept implied that instructions to run a computer for a specific program were held inside the memory, and could easily be replaced by a different set of instructions for a different program. This concept made this generation computers popular.

The second generation computers consumed less power and gave better performance. They were smaller in size and were of solid state design. The era of miniaturization began during this time period. They were cheaper, smaller, faster and more reliable than the first generation computers. They were less prone to failure as they generated less heat and this feature also resulted in low maintenance costs. This generation computers moved from binary machine language to symbolic assembly language; they used symbolic or assembly language which made programming easier as programming codes could be used instead of difficult binary codes to specify instructions. Alongside high-level programming languages like early versions of FORTRAN, COBOL, etc., were also being developed during this time. Other significant developments of this period are index registers for controlling loops and floating point units for the real number calculations. New careers like analyst and programmer were introduced during this period.

Their first major use was for the atomic energy industry. The first large-scale machines to take advantage of the transistor technology were the early supercomputers, Stretch by IBM and Liverpool Atomic Research Computer (LARC) by Sperry-Rand. They both were developed for atomic energy laboratories. Throughout the early 1960s, there were a number of commercially successful second generation computers used in universities, business setups and government from companies like IBM, Sperry-Rand and Control Data Corporation.

Some of the major commercial machines of second generation computers were IBM 1401 and IBM 7090. IBM 1401 was the first member of the highly successful IBM

1400 series. IBM 7090 was one of IBM's first transistor-based computers. Other transistorized computers include CDC Computers Designed by Seymour Cray and others at Control Data Corporation (CDC).

Image 4: TRANSISTORIZED SECOND GENERATION COMPUTER
Image Source: http://www.techiwarehouse.com/engine/a046ee08/Generations-of-Computer

1.4.3 Third Generation—Integrated Circuits

Third Generation—1964-1971—Integrated Circuits, (IC), also called chips or microchips, was the hallmark of this period. This generation computers used integrated circuits in place of transistors. The IC was invented by Jack Kilby at Texas Instruments and Robert Noyce of Fairchild Semiconductor. An integrated circuit is a semiconductor wafer that can hold anywhere from hundreds to millions of transistors, resistors, and capacitors. It can function as an oscillator, amplifier, microprocessor or computer memory. The IC combined electronic components like capacitors, diodes, and many other components and circuitry onto a small silicon disc, which was made from quartz. An integrated circuit is often classified by the number of transistors and other electronic components it contains. The following Table 2 shows this classification.

Table 2: Integration Classification

Integration	Number of Components
Small scale integration (SSI)	Up to 100 electronic components per chip
Medium scale integration (MSI)	From 100 to 3,000 electronic components per chip
Large scale integration (LSI)	From 3,000 to 100,000 electronic components per chip
Very large scale integration (VLSI)	From 100,000 to 1,000,000 electronic components per chip
Ultra large scale integration (ULSI)	More than 1 million electronic components per chip

Image 5: THIRD GENERATION INTEGRATED CIRCUITS

Image Source: http://edutry.blogspot.in/2014/07/third-generation-of-computer1964-1975.html

The development of IC made computers smaller in size, reliable and faster. These features made this generation computers accessible to common people. They were able to reduce computational time from microseconds to nanoseconds. Less human labor is required at assembly stage. Computers for the first time became accessible to general public because they were smaller and cheaper than their predecessors.

The most noticeable achievement of third generation is the development of operating systems. These computers used operating system, monitor and keyboard. These new developments enabled this generation computers to run many applications at once with a central program that monitored the memory. In this generation, remote processing, time-sharing, multi-programming operating systems were used. Maintenance costs were low as the hardware failure was low. They were easily portable as compared to their ancestors. They generated less heat and consumed less power. High-level languages like C-family (C, C+, C++, C#, Objective-C), BASIC, Pascal, etc., were also being developed at this time.

Graphical User Interface (GUI) also was started from third generation onwards. GUI is a human-computer interface that uses icons, windows and menus to carry out commands like move a file from one folder to another. GUI-based operating systems are much easier to learn and use because arcane commands are not needed to be memorized.

Examples of third generation computers are IBM 370, IBM 360, B6500, PDP-8, PDP-11 and NCR 395.

1.4.4 Fourth Generation—Microprocessors

Fourth Generation—1971-2010—they are the extension of third generation technology and the microprocessor was the highlight of this generation. Three basic characteristics differentiate microprocessors and they are bandwidth (the number of bits processed in a single instruction), clock speed (determines how many instructions per second are executed by a microprocessor and it is measured in units of cycles per second, which is called a Hertz [Hz]), and instruction set (a set of basic instructions in machine language that a microprocessor understands and executes).

In this period, the size and the cost of computers reduced drastically, and the speed and memory (primary storage capacity) increased substantially. What in the first generation occupied an entire room could now fit in the palm of the hand. Large-scale integration or LSI (1,000 devices per chip) and very large-scale integration or VLSI

(10,000 devices per chip) happened during this period. Some major examples of such integration are Intel 4004 chip. Intel 4004 chip, developed in 1971, took the integrated circuit one step further by locating all the components of a computer on a tiny chip. Due to this condensed power, computers became available to general consumers. They were no longer developed exclusively for large business or government contracts. IBM introduced the personal computer (PC) for use in offices, schools and homes in 1981. This generation computers were equipped with user-friendly software packages that offered even non-technical users a wide range of services.

Disks were used as a means of secondary storage. Advance input and output devices were used. Graphical User Interfaces were also developed during this generation. Magnetic core memories were replaced by semiconductor memories. Concurrent programming languages and personal computer operating systems like MS-DOS and MS Windows were also developed during this generation. High-level languages like C, DBASE, C++, etc., were used in this generation.

This generation computers were more reliable, powerful, fast and compact; these factors triggered the Personal Computer (PC) revolution. Portable computers were introduced during this time period. Advancement in technology made this generation computers cheaper and better in quality than all other previous generations of computers. These computers consumed less power in comparison to the previous generations.

As this generation computers became more powerful, they could be linked together to form networks, which also led to the development of the Internet.

1.4.5 Fifth Generation—Artificial Intelligence

Fifth Generation—Present and Beyond—Artificial Intelligence (AI)—as of the 21st century, we are already in the fifth generation phase. This generation is based on AI software and parallel processing hardware; a new super-breed of computers. These generation computers are also called artificial intelligence computers or expert systems. The development of parallel processing replaces von Neumann's single central processing unit design with a system using the power of many CPUs to work as one single system. Another development in this period is that of advancement of superconductor technology, which allows the flow of electricity with little or no resistance, thereby greatly improving the speed of information flow.

Parallel processing is the opposite of serial processing. Serial processing is when computers with one processor access and execute only one instruction at a time, whereas parallel processing is when multiple processors are used to access and execute several instructions at the same time. Until this period processing was limited to pipelining and vector processing.

The main aim of this generation is to build computers that have human-like capability; that is to make logical analysis and take decisions. The aim of the development of this generation is to develop devices that are capable of responding to natural language inputs and are capable of self-organization and self-learning. The process of developing fifth generation computers is still in the development stage. The main aim of fifth generation computing is to develop computers that are able to respond to surroundings using different types of sensors. Nanotechnology and quantum computing will radically change the face of the computer industry.

Very large scale integration has been replaced by Ultra/ Super large scale integration whereby the production of microprocessor chips having millions of electronic components has become possible. They are used in knowledge-based platforms, games, robotics and expert systems. Development of more user-friendly operating systems and object-oriented and functional languages are the other developments of this generation. High-level languages like .Net, Java, etc., are used in this generation. Also visual programming languages (also called natural languages) are popular during this period that provide a visual or graphical interface, called a visual programming environment, for creating source code. Users do not need any specialized knowledge and can interact with computers through words and the voice recognition systems can convert spoken sounds into written words. Some popular languages are Mercury, OPS5 and Prolog.

The fifth generation of computers is still in its infancy but quantum computation and nanotechnology will radically change the face of this generation computers in years to come.

1.5 Functions of a Computer—Input, Storage, Processing and Output

A computer is a multipurpose device. Typically, a computer performs four main functions—input, storage, processing and output. Computers are designed to transform raw data into processed information. They were conceived and designed out of the need to manipulate raw data into usable information. The first computers to use these four functions included the Jacquard's loom and Charles Babbage's Analytical Engine. The first electronic computers to use these four functions included the ENIAC and the UNIVAC. Let us take a look at each function individually.

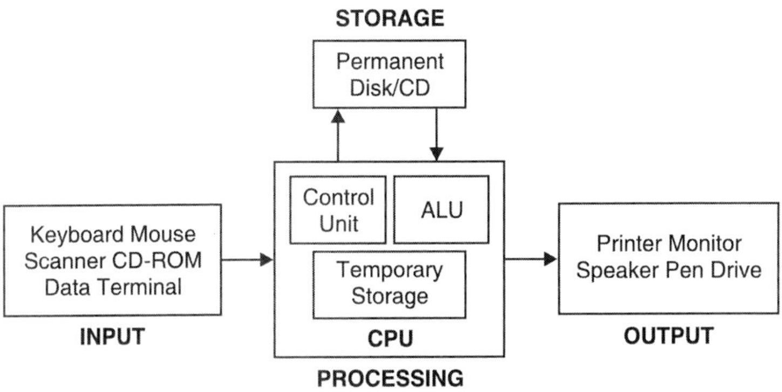

Figure 3: BASIC FUNCTIONS OF A COMPUTER

1. **Accepts Data or Input**—any information, instruction or data that is sent to the computer is called input or data entry. The input can be fed to the computer either through previously loaded software, module, pen drive, CD or through a user input device like mouse, scanner, keyboard, etc. The most basic sort of input would be typing source code through a keyboard. Input is gathered manually, automatically, or a combination of both.

   The application used in the computer will also determine how the data is entered into the system. This can be done manually, automatically, or by a combination of the two. When computers are used for automatic control of machines and processes, computers receive and accept information directly from such machines and processes. Such automatic input can be done by robotics and automated applications.

2. **Storage**—instructions, data or results are also stored/ saved in the computer in such a way that they can be reused later as required.

   A computer can store information internally and externally. There are two broad categories the way in which storage is done. First is the storage of memory in the central processing unit and the second is called the auxiliary memory.

3. **Processes Data or Input**—the process of converting data received by a computer into intelligible information. The brain of the computer is where all the main action happens—the central processing unit.

   The task of performing operations like arithmetic and logical operations is called processing. The central processing unit takes data and instructions from the storage memory unit and performs logic-based decisions, manipulations and calculations based on the instructions given and the type of data provided. It is then sent back to the storage unit.

4. **Produces Output**—output is the exact opposite of input. Any information that has been processed by and sent out from a computer is considered as output. There are various types of outputs like soft copies in the form of Excel reports, PowerPoint slides and Word documents; basically output (video and text) via monitor. Output can be accessed through a computer printer, speaker and monitor. The output can be stored on external devices and drives like DVD or pen drive. These days, data and information can be stored in cloud solutions as well.

   Example: User A is creating a finance report in Microsoft Excel, User A is entering the values (input), the computer will calculate the values based on a formula (processing), then display final figures (output), and after that, User A will save it (storage) on the hard disk.

Spotlight Tip
Not to confuse functions with uses of computers. The functions indicate what computers are designed for and then this in turn can be adapted to various uses and applications. For example, the processing function of computers is very useful in the business scenarios where it can be applied to the analysis of complex data. Functions of computers describe what they are designed for, whereas uses imply the application areas of computers.

With these basic functions, one can use the computer for many purposes, right from typing documents to storing information, and from manipulating this information to producing useful reports.

Computers perform a plethora of functions. Depending on the type of computer, there can be many functions performed by it. For example, a portable computer like a laptop can help you to carry your data and information along with you, which can be used to prepare reports or presentations. A portable computer can help the user to perform office tasks on the go. Handled devices are used for calendar and schedule management.

A computer is used both as a tool of data processing and prediction for decision-makers in the business landscape. Another important function is that of providing a link to link exchange of communication around the world in a short time.

1.6 Questions for Reflection

1. What are the basic operations of a computer?
2. Define data?
3. List the major features for each of the computer generations?
4. What are the main functions of a computer?
5. Why are computers such an integral part of our lives?
6. What is the difference between a calculator and a computer?

2

Organization of Computers—More Basics

Whether it is a personal computer, a workstation or a laptop, most types of computers consist of certain basic elements. These basic internal elements or assembly consists of a motherboard, central processing unit, hard disk drive, central memory and power supply unit, and basic external components like keyboard, monitor and mouse. Having knowledge of all the parts, including components inside the computer case, can help in troubleshooting technical problems.

2.1 Motherboard—Backbone of a Computer

Motherboard, also known as mainboard, logic board or system board, is the printed circuit board containing the principal components of a computer. As the name suggests, a motherboard is the mother to all the other components.

Motherboard is the backbone of a computer and contains all components like memory modules, processor, controllers for devices, and expansion cards (for example, video card, network card and sound card) and ports. A video card is responsible for what is displayed on the monitor. Most computers have a graphics processing unit built into the motherboard instead of having a separate video card. For playing graphics-intensive games, one can add a faster video card into one of the expansion slots to get better performance. A network card (network interface card or Ethernet card) connects a computer to a computer network, usually a local area network. A sound card is responsible for what one hears from the headphones or speakers. Most motherboards have integrated sound, but one can upgrade to a dedicated sound card for higher-quality sound.

Each motherboard has a collection of chips and controllers known as a chipset. The chipset acts as a coordinator and controller to link various devices like memory, USB, etc., and to manage the data flow between CPU, memory and peripherals. It is a collection of integrated circuits that are designed to function together as a unit. It is usually designed to work with a specific family of microprocessors.

A Word of Caution
New motherboards with new chipsets are better and efficient, but there is a downside to this. Older components often are not compatible with new chipsets.

Motherboard has sockets for all the components. It is located on the back side or at the bottom of the computer chassis (system unit or computer case). It controls the functions of different components. It also houses the basic input/output system (BIOS). Motherboard connects directly or indirectly to every part of a computer system. It also has a small battery to ensure that the settings made on the board are retained even when the computer is switched off. This battery serves two purposes: to feed the real time clock and to feed the configuration memory. Errors like CMOS BATTERY STATE LOW, CMOS TIME AND DATE NOT SET, etc., indicate that the battery has become weak and needs to be replaced.

A CPU socket or CPU slot is a connector built into a motherboard where the CPU (central processing unit) goes. It uses a pin grid array (PGA) and PGA is a type of integrated circuit packaging and it is the standard used for most second through fifth generation processors. In PGA, pins on the underside of the processor connect to holes in the processor socket. The motherboard must support not only the form factor or packaging of a CPU, but also its clock speed.

Depending on the motherboard, there may be two to eight memory slots, and sometimes more on high-end motherboards. Tabs at either end of each slot hold the memory module in place and ensure a consistent connection between the memory and the motherboard. Not all random access memory is compatible with every memory slot. The form factor of a memory module describes its size and pin configuration. Most computers have memory slots that can accept only one form factor. Some computers are designed with more than one type of memory slot, allowing a choice between two or more form factors.

Most computers have expansion slots on the motherboard that allow one to add various types of expansion cards (also called peripheral component interconnect cards). The number and type of memory slots and number of connection slots for peripheral devices (speakers, headphones, etc.) are important properties of the motherboard. Additional components can be connected to a motherboard through its expansion slots. In smaller computers like tablets and laptops, the motherboard incorporates the functions of the video card and sound card in order to maintain the compactness of the device. Many modern computers come with motherboards that have built-in sound card, network card and graphics card.

Image 6: THE MOTHERBOARD

Image Source: https://www.lifewire.com/tour-inside-a-desktop-pc-2624588

Some of the main motherboard manufacturers are Intel, Acer, Biostar, MSI, ASUS, ABIT and ACube Systems.

2.2 Central Processing Unit—Heart and Engine

Central processing unit or processor is the heart and engine of a computer. It is the logic circuitry that responds to and processes the basic instructions that drive a computer. Whenever one starts a program, presses a key or clicks a mouse button, one is sending instructions to this component. It is normally a two-inch ceramic square with a silicon chip located inside. All types of devices need a CPU, including laptops, smartphones, desktops, etc. On small workstations and personal computers, the CPU is housed in a single chip called a microprocessor, whereas in large systems, the CPU requires one or more printed circuit boards.

A CPU attaches directly to a CPU socket on the motherboard and it is inserted into the socket pin-side-down and a small lever helps to keep it secure. In some computers, there is a fan (heat sink is an electronic component that incorporates either a fan or a peltier device that helps to dissipate the heat produced by computer parts) on top of the CPU to provide a cooling effect. To dissipate the heat, more advanced cooling options are also available like phase change units and water cooling kits.

Image 7: INTEL PENTIUM PROCESSOR

Image Source: http://www.computerhope.com/jargon/c/cpu.htm

Neither the CPU clock speed nor the core can alone determine a CPU's performance. Along with these two factors, there are several other factors like processor type, cache size and bandwidth that determine performance level. Clock speed is measured in megahertz (MHz) or gigahertz (GHz), and refers to the speed at which the processor can execute instructions. The faster the clock, the more instructions the processor can complete per second. One single-core CPU can only perform one task whereas multi-core CPUs allow multiple programs to run at the same time. Cache is fast memory that the CPU can access as quickly as possible. Generally, the larger the cache is, higher is the performance. Bandwidth is measured in bits (32-bit, 64-bit, etc.) determines how much information the processor can process in one instruction.

The main components of a CPU include the following:

1. **Arithmetic Logic Unit** (ALU) performs arithmetic and logical operations. There can be more than one ALU and these ALUs can also be used for the purpose of maintaining timers that help run the computer.
2. **Control Unit** (CU) extracts instructions from memory and decodes and executes them, coordinating with the ALU and memory unit whenever necessary. It regulates the flow of information through the processor.

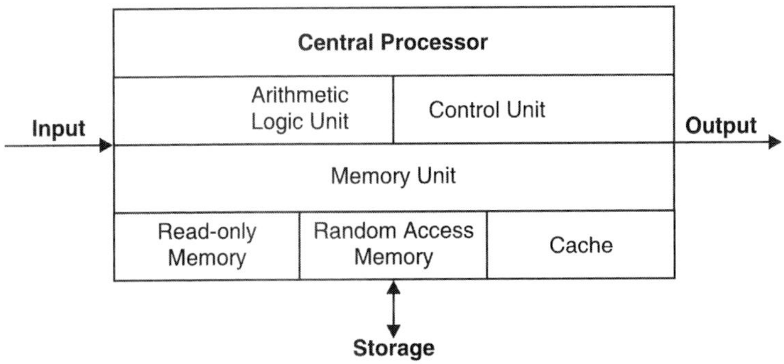

Figure 4: CENTRAL PROCESSING UNIT

3. **Memory Unit/Registers** are temporary storage areas that are responsible for holding the data that is to be processed. This data is further used by CU. There are certain registers used for specific tasks including flags, program counter, etc.

2.3 Hard Drive—Permanent Memory

Hard Drive (HD or HDD or fixed drive) is the permanent or non-volatile memory of a computer where saved files remain intact even when the computer is turned off. It is a sealed unit containing a number of platters in a stack. While Random Access Memory (RAM) is the primary memory device, hard drive is the secondary storage device. Whenever a program is run or a file is opened, the computer copies some of the data from the hard drive onto the random access memory. Whenever a file is saved, the updated data is copied back to the hard drive.

Spotlight Tip
HD stores operating system files and software programs. It also stores and retrieves all types of data like text documents, images, videos, etc. It is set of a few circular disks stacked one on top of the other and a little arm moves over these disks to write to and read from them.

An internal hard drive is connected to the computer using a data cable like SCSI, ATA or IDE, and this data cable connects to the motherboard and it is powered by a power cable that connects to the power supply unit (PSU). A hard drive is kept secure with the use of braces and screws to prevent it from being jarred as it spins at a very high speed.

The sides of a hard drive have pre-drilled, threaded holes for easy mounting in the drive bay inside the computer case. A hard drive is given a letter for convenience sake, and in most computers this will be the letter C; hence it is called the C drive also.

Data is saved to a hard drive as binary digits. Binary digits are also known as bits. A bit is either "on" or "off". In digital format it is represented as 1 and 0. These bits are written on the hard drive using a read-write head. This head is an electromagnet and when an electric current passes through this electromagnet, it creates a magnetic field. This magnetic field then magnetizes the bits that need to be 1s and skips the bits that need to be 0s.

The storage mechanism of a hard drive is based on the principles of magnetism. As data is stored on the hard drive magnetically, it stays on the drive even after the power is turned off. A hard drive is a large shiny circular plate of magnetic material called a platter. The platter is divided into billions of tiny areas and each one of these areas can be magnetized to store a 1 or demagnetized to store a 0. A small hard drive usually has only one platter, but each side of the platter has a magnetic coating. Bigger drives have a series of platters stacked on a central spindle and they have a small gap in between them to avoid friction. The data is stored on a stack of disks that are mounted inside a solid encasement.

There are two read-write heads for each platter, which are mounted on an electrically controlled arm that moves from the center of the drive to the outer edge and back again. The stack of platters rotates at a constant speed. These heads are positioned above and below each platter. This entire process is used to store and read data in an organized manner. Bits of data are arranged in concentric, circular paths or rings called tracks and each track is divided into smaller areas or sections called sectors. All tracks are the same distance from the center of the disk and collectively they comprise one cylinder. A sector is the smallest physical storage unit on a disk, and each sector is normally made up of three parts: the sector header, the error-correcting code (ECC), and the area that actually stores the data. Each disk sector is labeled using the factory track-positioning data. There is a map of sectors that a hard drive maintains in order to find out which have been used and which are still free. Whenever a computer wants to store new data or information, it refers to this map in order to locate the free sectors.

Apart from the platters, read-write heads and spindle, there is yet another important component, the actuator. It is an electronic device run by a motor, and it in turn controls the movement of read-write heads as they navigate their way over the platters. All the heads are attached to a single head *actuator*, also called an actuator arm, which moves the heads around the platters. Older hard drives used a stepper motor actuator, whereas modern hard drives use a servo motor actuator. A stepper motor is an electric motor that converts digital electric impulses into predefined angular displacement. This method of head arm positioning was relevant for earlier times when density of sectors on platters was considerably lower. In a servo motor, the head arm movement is controlled by changing amplitude and polarity of the current through the voice coil in the field of permanent magnet.

A hard drive is divided into one or more partitions, which can be further divided into logical drives or volumes. Though a partition is a mere logical division or section of a hard drive, but it appears as though the division creates multiple physical drives. This partitioning can be done through various partitioning disk management tools. These tools can be used to partition drives, format drives, shrink partitions, assign drive letters, and much more. The partition that has an operating system installed to it is called the primary partition.

While formatting a hard drive, one can define a custom allocation unit size (AUS). AUS is the smallest amount of disk space that can be allocated to store a file. The smaller the allocation unit size, the more efficiently a disk drive can store its information. Formatting is the process of preparing a data storage device such as a hard disk drive, floppy disk, etc., for initial use. There are two different types of formatting—low level and high level. Low level formatting is done by the drive manufacturer before the drive is even sold and it is done to outline sectors and tracks; it is the first step in preparing the drive to store information after physical installation. High level formatting involves the creation of the root directory (highest level directory in a file system in which all other directories and files are stored), file allocation tables (a table that provides a map of the clusters that files have been stored in) and other basic configurations.

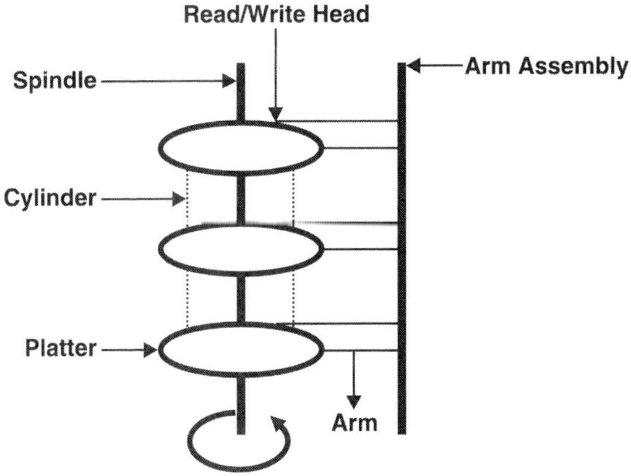

Figure 5: HARD DRIVE COMPONENTS

On the one hand, hard drives can store vast amounts of information in such a small space, but on the other hand, just a small speck of dirt can cause friction in the read-write head and result in the platter crashing and this

How to Repair a Corrupt Hard Drive
There are several ways to repair a corrupt hard drive. HDD Recovery Utility programs are available which can be used to retrieve data. In more serious cases, it is necessary to send the hard drive to a hard drive data recovery service. At times, it is not the hard drive that has failed, but the cables that connect the drive with the motherboard.

is called hard disk crash, head crash or hard disk failure. The head scrapes off the magnetic coating, and data and files on this part of the platter are damaged. Other hard drive failures are caused when head alignment goes off, when the circuitry experiences wear and tear, overheating, firmware faults, power surges, or mechanical or internal faults.

2.4 Power Supply Unit—Also Known as a Power Pack

Power Supply Unit (PSU), also known as a power pack or power converter, is a hardware component that receives power from an electrical outlet and then converts the mains alternating current (AC) to low-voltage steady direct current (DC) power for the internal components of a computer. Everything housed inside the computer case or chassis (motherboard, RAM, CPU, etc.) is powered by the PSU, and any other external peripherals or devices like printers, scanners, etc., have their own power supply source. External power supplies are beneficial because it allows the device to be compact. PSU regulates the voltage level in order to ensure that there is no overheating.

This unit is usually located in a corner of the computer case. It consists of elements like a fan opening to draw air out, a connection for the power cord, a switch to turn on or off the power supply, and a switch to change the power supply voltage.

There are several cables that connect the PSU to the motherboard through an ATX style connector (it is one of the largest connectors inside a computer and it connects power supply to an ATX style motherboard) and to each of the devices by powering them up through various connectors like P4 connector, Berg connector, etc. The motherboard, case and power supply come in different sizes called the form factor. All three must be compatible in order to work together in a proper manner.

The criteria for selecting PSU are reputed manufacturers and brands, efficiency, power output, and the connectors should also be checked for compatibility with a particular computer system. Larger, heavier models are preferable to lightweight units as the larger models have better and bigger connectors, cooling fans and other internal components.

Spotlight Tip
PSU is vulnerable to power surges and spikes and for this reason Uninterruptible Power Supply (UPS) or a surge protector is needed. UPS is a hardware component that provides a backup power source in case of a power surge or outage, and prevents the computer and PSU from being damaged by surges.

2.5 Random Access Memory—Working Place, Temporary Dynamic Storage

Random access memory (RAM), a type of computer memory that can be accessed randomly, i.e., any byte can be accessed randomly instead of sequentially. It is the working place of a computer, where active programs and data are loaded so that any time the processor requires them, it does not have to fetch them from the hard disk. This temporary dynamic storage enhances computer performance. Whenever a computer system is shut down, all the data from RAM is transferred back to the permanent storage hard drive.

RAM is volatile. It is read/write memory that stores data until a computer system is working. As soon as the computer system is switched off, data is erased. RAM is small, both in terms of the amount of data it can hold and physical size.

There are two main types: Static RAM (SRAM) and Dynamic RAM (DRAM). SRAM retains data bits in its memory as long as power is available. The features of SRAM are: it is faster than DRAM and has long life, there is no need to refresh, it is large in size and expensive too, and needs higher power consumption. DRAM is a type of storage that is widely used as the main memory for a computer system.

DRAM capacitors loose charge due to leakage and hence it is a volatile storage device. The features of DRAM are: it needs to be refreshed or given a new electronic charge every few milliseconds in order for the memory state to be maintained.

Table 3: Differences between SRAM and DRAM

SRAM	DRAM
SRAM is usually faster than DRAM since it does not have refresh cycles	DRAM requires the data to be refreshed periodically in order to retain the data; hence slower
SRAM structure is complex	DRAM structure is simpler
As each SRAM memory cell contains 6 transistors unlike a DRAM memory cell, which consists of 1 Transistor and 1 Capacitor, the cost per memory cell is far greater	Cost per memory cell is lesser than SRAM
Data access is faster	Data access is slower
It is static	It is dynamic

2.6 Basic Input/Output System—Also Called ROM BIOS

Basic Input/Output System (BIOS, also called ROM BIOS) is a read-only memory chip located on the motherboard that allows access to and set up of a computer system at the most basic level. It is firmware—a set of instructions that run to help load the operating system. BIOS is low level software as it directly controls the way all the hardware components work. It contains routines that programs access to carry out functions like reading keystrokes, typing characters, etc.

When a computer is started, BIOS instructions are initiated and the first thing they do is run through a series of system checks and diagnostic runs to ensure that every part of a computer system is functioning properly. In the case of anomalies, BIOS reports anomalies with either a code number on the monitor or as a coded series of beeps. When BIOS finds all hardware and attachments are operational then it loads the operating system into a computer's random access memory from a hard disk or diskette drive. It manages and controls data flow between the operating system and attached devices such as the hard disk, mouse, keyboard, etc.

As random access memory is faster than ROM, several computer manufacturers design systems so that the BIOS is copied from ROM to RAM each time a computer is booted. This is known as shadowing. In other words, shadowing refers to the technique of copying BIOS code from slow ROM chips into faster RAM chips during booting up so that any access to BIOS will be faster.

The four main functions of BIOS are POST, Bootstrap Loader, BIOS drivers and CMOS Setup. POST or Power-On Self Test is a diagnostic testing sequence that tests and determines whether all of the hardware and attachments are present and working, and ensures no errors exist before loading the operating system. Bootstrap Loader locates the operating system and if a functional one is found then BIOS will hand over the control to it; a bootstrap loader is a program that is responsible for searching and starting the operating system boot program.

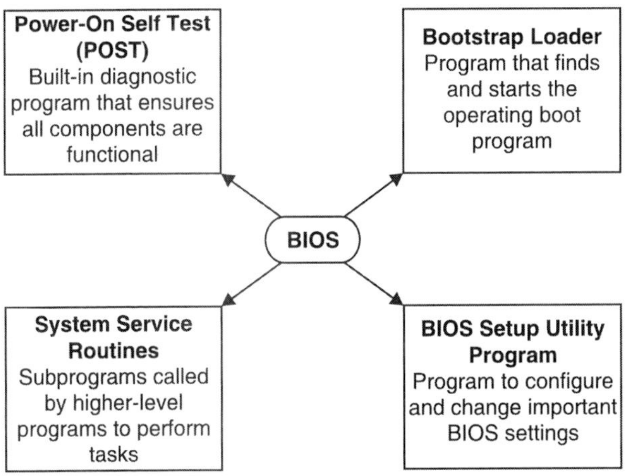

Figure 6: BIOS: BASIC INPUT/OUTPUT SYSTEM

BIOS Setup Utility also stores the system time, the system date and other system configuration settings and information in a battery-powered, non-volatile memory chip, called Complementary Metal Oxide Semiconductor (CMOS). BIOS contains the details about drives, their order of booting, the time and date, and many other features, and it is CMOS that remembers these settings every time a computer is turned on or restarted. It is a tiny memory that holds all BIOS settings, so that a computer won't have to be configured each time you turn the computer on. Various options can be configured through the BIOS Setup Utility like Change the Date and Time, Change the Boot Order, Change Memory Settings, Change CPU Settings, Create a BIOS Password, Remove a BIOS Password, etc.

How to enter BIOS Setup?
There are various ways to enter the BIOS Setup and this depends on the computer or motherboard make and model. Recent computers allow access to this setup using one of the five keys: F1, F2, F10, DEL and ESC.

2.7 Computer Case—Outer Shell

The above discussed elements are housed inside a system unit, also known as cabinet, tower, base unit, chassis or computer case. This unit is the outer shell of a computer and it is what holds all the components together in an organized and compact fashion. The exact location of these components varies from computer to computer, but the overall layout is generally the same.

The number one reason for this unit is that of protection of the internal components from external environment like spills and dust, and having all the components fit together and held together in a compact space. Another reason for using a computer case is to keep everything cool and at the right temperature, and to have a proper airflow over all the internal components. A computer case also facilitates easy transport from one location to another.

The cabinet protects all the components from electrical interference and from dust, dirt and other foreign objects. It also minimizes the noise level as many computers and components have fans that generate noise and having all these components in a confined case minimizes the overall noise level.

The motherboard is usually fixed to the case along its largest surface depending on the form factor and orientation. For example, if a user is using an Extended-ATX motherboard, the user is likely to need a case that is larger than normal. These days, most cases come with slots for more than one fan. While most cases will be able to accommodate a standard size power supply, manufacturers sometimes extend their length to accommodate higher wattages or modular connectors.

A computer case is normally built from aluminum or steel. It usually includes sheet metal enclosures for power supply unit and drive bays. A drive bay is a reserved area where hard drive, floppy drive or tape drive can be installed. The number of drive bays in a computer determines the total number of internal mass storage devices it can have.

There are two main types of computer cases: desktop and tower. Desktop type is in the shape of a rectangular box that sits flat on a desk and normally a computer monitor is placed on top of it. In tower type, computer case sits bedside the keyboard and monitor. Tower cases can be further classified into mini-size, mid-size and full-size tower cases. Mini-size is the smallest, mid-size is the recommended standard size and full-size is the largest and is normally used for high-powered servers.

A Word of Caution
If one does not bother to open and clean the computer case then there is a chance of cobwebs of dust developing inside, due to the presence of cooling fans, computer cases tend to attract dirt and dust particles.

2.8 Types of Computers—Based on Speed, Types of Tasks and Other Factors

When most people hear the word computer, they think of a personal computer such as a laptop or desktop. Computers can be classified in many ways. They come in many shapes and sizes and perform various functions varying in their degree of complexity. Computers differ based on their purpose, data processing abilities and functionality. The power of a computer that an individual user or an organization needs depends on the computing requirements. Factors like greater processing speed and greater capacity to store information will make one computer more powerful than another regardless of the overall physical size. Computers can be categorized based on various factors like speed of processing, types of tasks or the number of users. Other classification categories can include the type of software or hardware used, and also the price factor.

2.8.1 Personal Computer—General Use by a Single User

Personal Computer (PC)—is a computer designed for general use by a single user; a relatively inexpensive computer designed for an individual user. A PC that is not designed for portability is a desktop computer. Desktop computers, Notebook computers, Workstations, Smartphones and Tablet computers are all examples of personal computers as they are designed for use by a single user. Although personal computers are used by single users, they also can be connected together to create networks. PC usually comes with a computer case or tower that holds the main circuit boards and disk drives and a set of peripherals like mouse, keyboard, and monitor.

PC is short for personal computer or IBM PC. The first personal computer manufactured by IBM was called the PC, and increasingly the term PC came to mean IBM or IBM-compatible personal computers. In later years, the term PC applied to any personal computer based on Intel microprocessor or on an Intel-compatible microprocessor. Nowadays, PCs are mainly identified by their use of the Windows Operating System.

Prior to the PC revolution, computers were designed for and could be only afforded by large organizations that connected thin terminals for multiple users to a single large computer, and the resources of this single large computer were shared among all the users. The advent of PC and technology advances began to replace the tradition of terminal computing. PCs first appeared in the late 1970s. By the late 1980s, technology advances made it possible to build a small computer that a single individual could own and use. From the 1980s onwards, PC usage became widespread. In 1975, Ed Roberts, "the father of the personal computer," coined the term "personal computer" when he introduced the Altair 8800. According to the American Computer Museum and Computer History Museum, the Kenbak-1 is considered the world's first personal computer which was introduced in 1971. In 1981, IBM introduced its first personal computer, known as the IBM PC. It quickly became the personal computer of choice. In 1983, Apple introduced Lisa, a personal computer with a graphical user

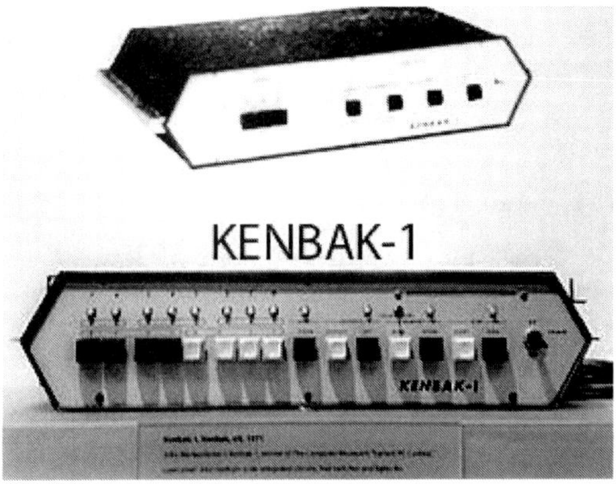

Image 8: KENBAK-1

Image Source: https://en.wikipedia.org/wiki/Kenbak-1

interface (GUI). This development became the basis of Apple's Macintosh personal computer, introduced in 1984. This development also was widely adapted by other PC manufacturers. In 1985, Microsoft launched its GUI-based operating system, Microsoft Windows.

PC is used for several purposes, both business and personal, including internet communications, desktop publishing (DTP), accounting, word processing, playing games, graphics design and much more. The rapid evolution of computer software has enabled PC to be used for email, to play games, to perform complex calculations and to connect to the Internet. Employees use PCs for preparing reports, spreadsheets and presentations. Students can use PCs to connect to the Internet for their studies and research work. The distinction between personal computers and workstations has blurred over the years. High-end PCs offer the same capability and features as low-end workstations. The price of a PC ranges from a few hundred dollars to a few thousand dollars.

2.8.2 Desktop Computer—The Most Common Type of Personal Computer

Desktop computer—the most common type of personal computer is the desktop computer. It is built to be used at a desk or table; it is designed for regular use at a single location on or near a desk or table. It usually consists of a mouse, keyboard, monitor and either a horizontal or vertical tower (also called case, system unit, form factor or base unit). A tower is the enclosure that contains most of the components of a computer, usually excluding the mouse, display and keyboard.

Earlier this tower or form factor contained most of the computer components such as the hard disk, CPU and the RAM, all within this single case that would sit horizontally on a desktop. A monitor would then sit on top of the computer case. Over the years, this tower then became

Spotlight Tip
When it comes to intensive tasks, a desktop computer is preferred to a laptop. For users who value performance over portability, a desktop is the best option. In companies and at homes, desktop computers can be interconnected and can share resources such as scanners and printers by being connected to a local area network. For intensive, high-performance tasks such as games, sound editing, etc., desktop computers are the best option.

the main form of desktop computer and it can be either placed horizontal under the desk or vertical that sits next to a monitor or on the floor. A form factor refers to size and packaging; it refers to size, configuration, or physical arrangement of a computing device.

The first desktop computer was the Hewlett Packard 9100A introduced in 1968. Since then there have been thousands and thousands of desktop computers released. A desktop computer is much easier to customize than a laptop. Throughout the 1980s and 1990s, desktop computers became popular with IBM PC and its clones, followed by Apple Macintosh being the most popular one. While desktops have long been the most popular configuration for PCs, but by the mid-2000s the focus and growth shifted from desktops to laptops.

Desktop computers are much better at handling power consumption and due to their bigger space factor (in comparison to laptops), they come equipped with cooling fans and heat sinks to dissipate heat. Unlike portable devices like laptops, a desktop computer cannot be powered from an internal battery and therefore must remain connected to a wall outlet. When it comes to electrical disturbances like spikes, blackouts, surges and interruptions, desktop computers need a costly uninterruptible power supply unit to provide backup time of 20-30 minutes, whereas in the case of laptops, they can handle such outages easily and they can be used for hours in such disruptive situations.

Laptops come with support for broader range of options for connecting with the Internet, for example, wireless technologies like WiFi, Bluetooth, etc. These options are not available with older desktop models, though this trend is changing as newer desktop computers come integrated with one or more of these connectivity options. Assembly, disassembly and customization of desktop computers, especially for tower configuration, are simple in comparison to laptops.

2.8.3 Laptop—Portable Computer

Laptop—is also called a battery-powered or AC-powered personal computer generally smaller than a briefcase. It is a computer that is portable and suitable for use while travelling and has the same capabilities as a desktop computer. A laptop usually has less disk space than a desktop and also a laptop hard drive is also physically smaller than that of a desktop. This type of computer derives its names from the fact that it allows easy use by resting the device on a person's lap while sitting without the need of a desk or table. Due to its portability, a laptop can be carried in a backpack, briefcase or any other bag. It normally is 3 inches or less in thickness and weighs less than 5 pounds.

In the 1970s, Alan Kay of the Xerox Palo Alto Research Center had a vision for a wireless portable computer roughly the size of a notebook and he termed it as the Dynabook. His proposal never got past sketches and a cardboard model, but it set the stage for the development of a truly portable computer. In 1979, William Moggridge of Grid Systems Corporation created the first functioning portable computer, Grid Compass Computer 1109, and was used by NASA as part of the space shuttle program. The first true laptop computer considered by most experts was the Osborne 1 introduced in 1981.

Image 9: A TYPICAL MODERN LAPTOP

Image Source: By © Raimond Spekking / CC BY-SA 4.0 (via Wikimedia Commons), CC BY-SA 4.0, https://commons.wikimedia.org/w/index.php?curid=45282376

A laptop can be used in a desktop style by connecting a separate mouse, keyboard and monitor. This can be achieved with the help of a docking station or dock. A docking station is a device that allows laptops and other portable computers to be placed for charging, to provide access to a power supply and to connect with other peripheral devices or auxiliary features. The term dock is used to describe the process of connecting a laptop to a docking station. The term undock (or cold dock) is used to describe the process of disconnecting a laptop from a docking station after it has been shut down.

Most laptops have almost the same functionality like a desktop computer. Laptops are definitely costlier than desktop computers, but they have more advantages. Laptops have an all-in-one design advantage, which means they are fully functional even when there are no peripherals connected, as laptops have built-in keyboard, monitor and touchpad (or trackball or pointing stick). Instead of a spacious computer case, a laptop uses a flat design in which all the components fit together in a compact manner. Yet another advantage is that there is a provision in laptops whereby a monitor, mouse, and other peripherals can be connected. This advantage transforms a laptop into a desktop computer.

Laptops are portable devices and the keyboard, memory, hard drive and mouse are integrated in a battery-operation package. You can also use them like a regular PC by using an outside power adaptor; through an AC cord plugged into an electrical outlet. The main feature that attracts users to laptops over desktops is portability. Laptops are usually more expensive than standard computers.

A laptop has a thin display screen that is attached and can be folded flat for portability. A laptop has ports and other interfaces such as USB ports, audio speakers, network interface cards and memory card slots, which are often built into the laptop computer by the manufacturer. A laptop can accommodate a variety of drives to fit in the same bay due to its modular design. Most laptops may not be that good with latest game-intensive applications, but a few specialty high-end laptops, designed for gaming enthusiasts, include more powerful graphics processing unit and additional video memory.

A laptop normally has a specialized power cable called an AC adapter or charger, which is used as an external power supply. The AC adapter helps reduce the size of a laptop by alleviating the need for a standard sized power supply. Every laptop has a battery that allows one to use the device when it is not plugged in. The battery also provides backup power in case the power goes out. A laptop has small fans, heat pipes or heat sinks to help dissipate the heat from the CPU. Some advanced laptop models reduce heat even further with liquid coolant kept in channels alongside the heat pipes.

Spotlight Tip

The following aspects needs to be kept in mind while buying a laptop: memory and processor are the main considerations, then comes the weight (as a laptop gets powerful it becomes heavy), screen size (depends on what purpose a laptop is needed for, for example, for playing games, a large screen is better), and upgradability is yet another major factor.

Laptops may also be referred to as notebook computers, though a notebook computer is normally smaller and lighter than a traditional laptop. Traditionally, the difference between the two is a matter of size and weight, but due to advances in technology, the difference between a laptop and a notebook is mainly what the manufacturer chooses to call its product. Some of the popular laptop brands are Dell, Toshiba, Apple, etc.

2.8.4 Workstation—A High-performance Computer System

Workstation is a type of desktop computer but it has more memory and processing power as it is used for a special task or purpose like scientific or technical applications like medical imaging, CAD, etc. It is a high-performance computer system intended for professional or business use, and it is faster and more capable than a personal computer. It can be used as a server for low level applications. In a typical server workstation model, a computer one uses for work is a workstation. However, in modern usage, the term workstation refers to a high-end computer that performs computationally intensive tasks like advanced data modeling or graphics.

The main features of a workstation are: multiple processor cores, redundant array of independent disks (RAID), Error Correction Code (ECC) memory support and solid state drives (SSD). Multi processor cores indicate more processing ability. RAID uses multiple internal hard drives to store and process data, which means even if one hard drive fails, there is always another one to carry on the work. ECC memory support protects against data corruption by automatically detecting and correcting memory errors. A workstation also contains high-performance graphics card.

The main types of workstations are: Portable, Modular, Network and Ergonomic. A portable workstation allows the user to work from any location thereby giving some degree of time flexibility. It provides mobility as the user can carry out the work through website/s. A modular workstation provides a flexible platform to work.

A PC has enough power to do most tasks such as word processing, email and internet surfing, but a workstation has more power and can do a lot of complex tasks like data analysis, audio creation, animation, visualization, etc. A workstation may also have higher-speed graphics adapter and more connected peripherals. A workstation is for professional users, while a server is more of a utility device.

Spotlight Tip
A workstation-class microcomputer may be used as a server computer that supplies files to client computers.

2.8.5 Personal Digital Assistant—A Handheld Organizer

Personal Digital Assistant (PDA) is also known as a handheld PC or palmtop, and it is a device that provides services tailored to users "on the move". It is a small mobile device and a handheld organizer that provides computing and information storage capabilities and retrieval capabilities for personal or business uses, and it based on a form of touch screen technology. It is considered to be an extension of the PC, not a replacement. It acts as a schedule planner or electronic organizer. PDAs usually come with software to synchronize desktop or cloud server information. Newer machines come with advances in hardware technology to meet

Image 10: PERSONAL DIGITAL ASSISTANT

Image Source: http://www.pcworld.com/article/167231/history_of_palm.html

increasingly intensive processor and memory requirements of applications while maintaining their portability. As PDAs have a small memory footprint, they require operating systems and applications to be lean.

The first PDAs were developed in the early 1990s and had limited functionality and were often not compatible with other electronic systems. As technology advanced, companies developed more efficient and user-friendly models that could also connect to personal computers.

PDA was the precursor to smartphones. The term PDA was first used by John Scully at the Consumer Electronic Show (CES) in 1992 while referring to the Apple Newton. Today, with the popularity and advances in iPhones and smartphones, PDAs are rarely found and used as users are more into using IPhones and smartphones. Many recent PDA models are equipped with phone features, while smartphones have evolved into touch screen devices with personal information management features. Modern PDAs use wireless communications technology and this results in more mobility.

Palm released the first Palm Pilot PDAs in 1996 and this quickly became the standard model for other companies to follow. This device included an electronic cradle to connect to a PC and exchange information with it. Later on in 1998, Microsoft Corporation produced Windows CE, an operating system developed by Microsoft for small footprint devices or embedded systems. This move by Microsoft encouraged several companies to enter the handheld organizer market. Modern-day advancements like Bluetooth allow PDAs to communicate in a wireless mode with other PDAs and with the primary computer.

PDAs come with some kind of personal information management (PIM) software that helps to store contact information, take notes, track and remind appointments, make to-do lists and perform calculations. High-end PDAs are equipped with specialized software applications like web browsing, voice memo recording, multimedia, etc.

Examples of popular PDA devices are HP's Palmtop, Toshiba's Pocket PC, Apple's Newton and Palm's PalmPilot.

2.8.6 Supercomputer—Fastest Type of Computer

Supercomputer—it is the fastest type of computer with a high level of computational capacity and it processes billions or trillions of instructions per second. It has great speed and memory. By definition a supercomputer is exceptional in terms of performance. Supercomputers are very expensive. A little over half-century ago, the smallest computer in the world was a gigantic machine that filled a room—a supercomputer. The first official supercomputer was the CDC 6600, which was released in 1964.

Supercomputer works in an entirely different manner, using parallel processing instead of the serial processing that an ordinary computer uses. It works much more quickly by splitting problems into smaller sections and working on many sections at once, which is called parallel processing. The largest supercomputers have thousands of processors whereas a personal computer has a single processor.

They are used for a wide range of computationally intensive tasks and in scientific and specialized applications like nuclear energy research, molecular modeling, animated graphics, quantum mechanics, weather forecasting, and oil and gas exploration. The first commercially successful supercomputer was the CDC (Control Data Corporation) 6600 designed by Seymour Cray who was an American electrical engineer and supercomputer architect. For several years, supercomputers have been used for mammoth data manipulation, but now they are also being used in mainstream applications like special effects, automobile design, extremely complex animated graphics, testing the aerodynamics of the latest military planes, simulations, etc.

Image 11: SUPERCOMPUTER CDC 6600
Image Source: http://www.computerhistory.org/revolution/supercomputers/10/33/58

A supercomputer has customized computer units called blades, which house multiple nodes (CPUs, GPUs). Each blade contains several nodes, and each node houses CPU, GPU and RAM. Each blade is a server in its own right. These nodes are connected together with a proprietary interconnect. Multiple blades are then stacked together in racks which let tens of thousands of nodes to be packed into a large space.

The main difference between a supercomputer and a mainframe is that a supercomputer uses all its power into executing a few programs as fast as possible, whereas a mainframe uses its power to execute many programs in tandem. Supercomputers are used for complex and mathematically intensive operations, whereas mainframes are mostly used for large data storage and manipulation tasks. Performance of ordinary computers is usually measured and is usually stated in million instructions per seconds (MIPS), whereas the performance measurement for supercomputers is done in floating point operations per second (FLOPS). FLOPS is a measure of computer performance, especially for measuring supercomputer performance, which is used in mathematical, scientific or real-time processing applications.

Desktop computers can perform millions of floating-point operations per second (megaflops), whereas supercomputers can perform at higher speeds of billions of operations per second (gigaflops) and trillions of operations per second (teraflops).

Table 4: Some of the Top Supercomputers

Year	Supercomputer	Peak Speed
2016	Sunway TaihuLigh	93.01 PFLOPS
2013	NUDT Tianhe-2	33.86 PFLOPS
2012	IBM Sequoia	16.32 PFLOPS
2011	Fujitsu K computer	10.51 PFLOPS
2010	Tianhe-IA	2.566 PFLOPS
2009	Cray Jaguar	1.759 PFLOPS

2.8.7 Server—Processes Requests and Delivers Data

Server is a computer, application or device that processes client requests and delivers data to the connected clients as part of the client server architecture over a local network or the internet. A typical client server architecture is a star configuration in which all nodes like computers and peripheral devices of a network are connected to the central hub or switch with a point-to-point connection. A star setup can function separately or as a part of complex network topology.

A server is used to manage network resources. Most networks have one or more servers that handle specialized tasks. There are two main connotations for the term "server"—first one is that it is a combination of specialized software and hardware to serve a particular purpose/specific service, and second one is a system that is configured or setup to serve as such.

Spotlight Tip

While server software is specific to the type of server, the hardware is not as specific, but it is important that the hardware is able to support the demands of the server. In fact, a regular desktop computer can be transformed into a server by adding the apt software. For example, a computer connected to a home network can be used as a print server or file server, or both.

Apart from the corporate network specialized server types, home users too need access to specialized servers and they often interact with them behind-the-scenes, for example chat servers and game servers. A computer system that a server program runs in is also referred to as a server. It can also be a computer system that has been designated for running a specific server application. A server can also serve applications to users on an intranet.

There are two main types of servers: Dedicated and Shared. A dedicated server is committed to a specific task like print server or database server. A shared server can take on the responsibility of several tasks like file server, mail server and print server all at once. Servers are mainly categorized in terms of their purpose. For example, a proxy server is a server that acts as an intermediary for requests from clients seeking services or resources from other servers; it sits in between a user's computer and the Internet. There are servers of varying types. Some of the basic types are web server, print server, file server and database server. A print server has a dedicated printer connected to it, which connects printers to client computers over a network. A file server handles the sharing and storing of files on a network. A database server is a back-end system that provides services related to accessing and retrieving data from a database.

In large organizations, rack-mountable hardware suited for server setups is used. A rack-mounted server is a computer dedicated to be used as a server and designed to be installed in a framework called a rack. A single rack configuration can hold multiple servers stacked one above the other and they often share the same input devices, and this results in space saving and also simplifies cabling.

A server cluster is a group of linked servers and other resources that act like a single system and are called nodes; they work closely together to make a set of services available to clients. The term "cluster" refers to implementation of shared computing resources. Typical examples of server clusters include database servers, print servers and file servers.

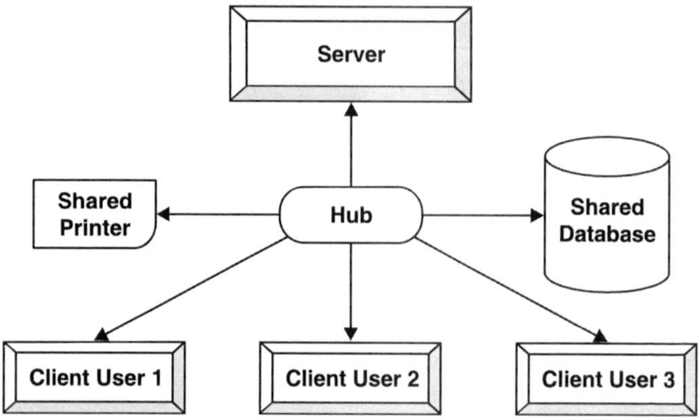

Figure 7: CLIENT SERVER ARCHITECTURE

2.8.8 Mainframe—Also called Big Iron

In computer terminology, large computers capable of handling and processing very large amounts of data at very high speeds are called mainframes, also known as "big iron". They are physically the largest computers. They are capable of processing data at very high speeds (millions of instructions per second) and handling thousands of users and application programs across the world. Their stability, massive computing power and reliability allow these machines to run for a very long time, even for decades. Their ruggedness makes them better to deal with extreme conditions like temperature, humidity, shock and mechanical vibration. They are used for tactical and tactical support operations. Languages for mainframe systems include PL/1, COBOL, FORTRAN, etc.

A mainframe computer has several processor units and these are all housed inside a frame called the Central Processing Complex (CPC) and the CPC frame also contains the main storage. The main processors are called the Central Processor (CPs). Peripheral devices like printers, tapes, disk drives, etc., are connected to a mainframe computer using channels. A channel is an independent data and control path between the memory and input/output devices. It has a large rugged frame or cabinet that houses central processor unit, individual modules or units, memory modules and input/output controller.

Users connect to the mainframe using their terminals and submit their tasks for processing by the mainframe. A terminal is a device that has a keyboard and monitor for input and output, but it does not do its own processing; hence this terminal is called dumb terminal. The processing power of the mainframe is time-shared between all of the users. Regular users never directly handle the mainframe itself. Instead, they interact with a mainframe system using a terminal, which is connected to the mainframe with wires or by a modem. Users use these smaller computers to send request to and get data or information from the mainframe. For examples, users using a commercial e-mail service from their personal computers often connect to a mainframe for their e-mail needs.

A mainframe manages terabytes or petabytes of information in a database and it can also handle large-bandwidth communications. It is typically used by large organizations and governments where huge investment is needed. It is the centralized secure data repository in an organization's data processing center. It is required to run critical applications like Enterprise Resource Planning (ERP), bulk data processing like census, financial transactions, sophisticated reservation systems and complex aircraft design. Mainframe systems are handled and operated by special technicians. Mainframe systems have concurrent or multi-threading capability and this capability helps to free up resources when not in use, which eventually results in less memory usage and higher performance. A mainframe also provides multi-levels of security. A mainframe also performs multiprocessing as it has more than one processor, and due to multiple processors, the risk of losing data and information is minimized and the processor load is also shared.

In the 1960s and 1970s, mainframes dominated the computer landscape. The 80s and early 90s, there were predications that mainframes would disappear from the scene. Mainframe is also referred to as a "dinosaur" not only because of its huge size but because of industry reports going back many years that it is becoming extinct. In 1991 Stewart Alsop, the editor of InfoWorld, predicted that the last mainframe would be retired by 1996. However, in 2008, IBM released a new mainframe, the z10. However, with the incredible growth of the Internet in the mid 90s, though the number of mainframes being used has dropped over the past years, but the amount of work done by them has increased a lot. The World Wide Web is based on the client-server model, where servers on the Internet deliver data-intensive services to millions of users using personal computers as clients. For handling this large data exchange across multiple communication channels is what keeps mainframes alive even today. Another reason for organizations not moving away from mainframes is that mainframes have been continuously evolving around business needs and business has been continuously evolving around mainframes.

Spotlight Tip
Older mainframe systems were large systems; they used to occupy large spaces, almost the size of a room. They were housed in room-sized metal frames; hence the term mainframe. From 1990s, their size has reduced drastically. Latest mainframes come with enhanced features and they can handle petabytes of data.

IBM and Hitachi are the main manufactures of mainframe computers. Although PCs are used by the mass population, mainframes are an important behind-the-scenes part of the business world. Today thousands of people around the globe use these mainframe systems to do wire-transfer, book flights and make credit card purchases. These computers are used by data-intensive industries like retail, banking, travel and insurance.

Image 12: AN EARLY MAINFRAME COMPUTER
Image Source: www.computerhope.com/jargon/m/mainfram.htm

The above image shows an early mainframe computer that took up space as much as that of a room, had a raised floor for power and communication cables, needed many people to operate it, and had special air conditioning and humidity control.

2.8.9 Wearable Computer—Miniature Body-borne Technology

Wearable computer—also known as miniature body-borne computers or wearables is a category of technology devices that can be worn by a user and often include tracking information related to various aspects like temperature, health, fitness, etc. Examples include smart accessories, computer-ready clothing and smart fabrics. In this technology, there is constant communication between users and their devices. This communication has been made possible with the use of sensory devices, and these sensory devices keep track of and record every movement of a user.

Wearables and their interfaces are worn as a head-mounted display or wrist-mounted screen to provide hands-free/eyes-free access and to enable portability, mobility, seamless access and multi-tasking. They are incorporated into items of a person's clothing and personal accessories which can be worn on the body. A number of wearables have been designed for the differently-abled people too. Some examples of devices for differently-abled people are Assisted Vision Smart Glasses, Finger Reader and Braille eBook reader.

Wearable technology has some level of human intelligence built into it. For example, face recognizer devices are already in their initial stages and they could be used for a variety of uses like catching of fraudsters. But privacy concern is a big issue when it comes to data capture of faces.

Spotlight Tip

Wearable technology is easy to carry. Prior to its entry in the consumer market, wearable technology was primarily used in the field of military technology. It tends to be more sophisticated than hand-held technology as it can provide sensory and scanning features like tracking and biofeedback.

Activity-tracking wristbands and smartwatches are the most popular wearable products being used in the real world right now. A smartwatch is a computerized device worn on the wrist and has the ability to do much more than to tell you the time. In other words, it is like having a tiny smartphone on the wrist. For a smartwatch to offer its full potential, it needs to be connected to a smartphone. Once connected, the user can access a spectrum of features, right from displaying notifications to location detection, and from voice search to sending messages on the fly. As smartwatches currently are quite heavily dependent on being connected to a smartphone, it is important to make sure that both the devices are compatible. Main examples are Android and Apple Smartwatch.

Another popular wearable device is Google Glass. Google Glass is a pair of smart eyeglasses; it is an Android-based hands-free device with an optical head-mounted display. It has built-in WiFi and Bluetooth connectivity, and a camera for taking photographs and recording videos. The applications could be endless, right from displaying directions right in front of your face to translation and from real-time updates based on your location to responding to emails via voice dictation.

Wearable technology has been around far longer than most technology experts and enthusiasts realize. As early as the 17th century, Chinese abacus rings allowed wearers to perform mathematical tasks long before calculators were invented. This wearable abacus ring is basically the world's oldest smart ring. The concept of modern-day wearable technology has been around for over half a century. It got its start back in the 1960s and 1970s with the release of the computerized timing devices for winning the gambling game of roulette and first calculator watch respectively. From 2001 onwards, wearable technology started IEEE, Bluetooth and other industry standards, which led to more interfacing under the wireless personal area network (WPAN) and wireless body area network (WBAN) categories. From the year 2011, the wearable market took off to new highs. According to CCS Insight (CCS Insight provides market information, analysis and intelligence) forecast the wearable market is set to expand from 9.7 million device shipments in 2013 to 135 million in 2018.

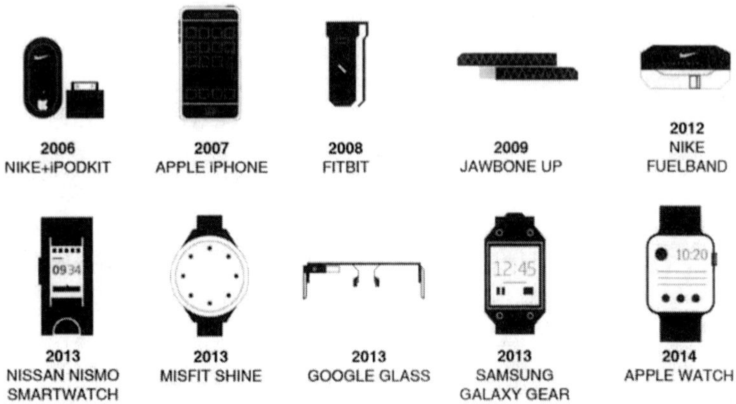

Image 13: WEARABLE TECHNOLOGY TIMELINE

Image Source: https://www.raconteur.net/technology/history-of-wearable-technology

2.9 Questions for Reflection

1. List the components found on a computer's motherboard?
2. What is a chipset?
3. What are the main components of a central processing unit?
4. List the features of the various types of computers?
5. Why are supercomputers used for scientific applications?
6. What is a computer case?
7. List out three application areas of wearable technology?

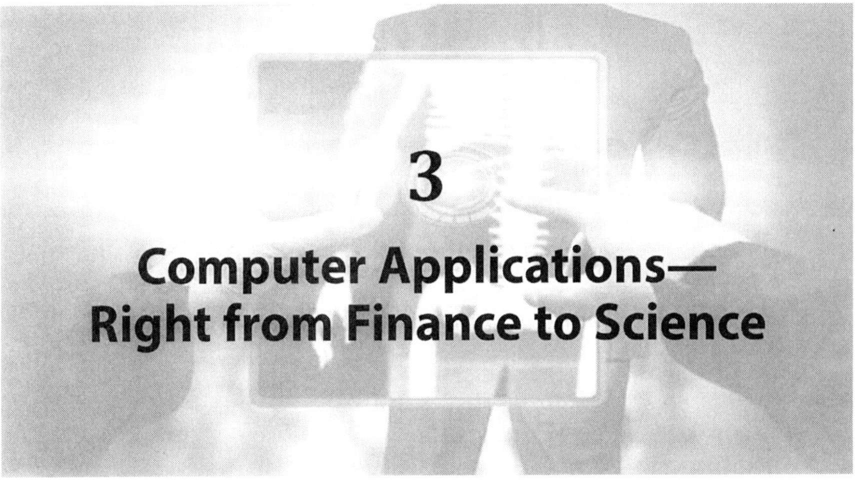

3

Computer Applications—Right from Finance to Science

A computer is a multipurpose system that impacts each and every aspect of life. Computers are making their powerful presence felt in all industries, right from fashion to defense and from E-commerce to finance. All-in-one computers come equipped with components and features that fulfill the needs of various industries and sectors. In less than five decades, computers have influenced practically every corporate field and area of business.

Spotlight Tip
Computers have taken businesses and industries to a whole new level. Computers help everyone to reduce the overall cost of running any setup. Areas of computer applications are: banking, education, computer-aided manufacturing, business, space, entertainment, insurance, tourism and the list goes on.

3.1 Healthcare—Improves the Accuracy and Efficiency of Processes

Up until the turn of the century, patient records were exclusively kept on paper (traditional method), and this was a tedious task. But due to an ever-expanding population and ever-increasing communication between healthcare organizations, this method became obsolete. This is when computers stepped in to solve these problems. Right from a new patient registration form at the front desk to the delivery of medical reports, computers are extensively used in the healthcare industry. With the introduction of advance technology, computers make these tedious and time consuming tasks highly efficient and accurate. They have improved the accuracy and efficiency of the entire healthcare process. Computers provide at-your-fingertips access to a patient's medical history and records.

In 1960s, some healthcare institutions began to include patient care applications in their computer systems. During this era, shared data-processing centers had begun to provide some hospitals with business and financial system processing. Later on in the 1970s, mainframes dominated the early medicalscape with ECG and other diagnostic technologies. In the following decade, administrative uses and imaging emerged on the horizon of the healthcare industry. During the 1990s, there was a shift from the retrospective process oriented systems towards patient-centric outcome-oriented systems. Further developments included tools for communication and clinical research, and better user interfaces to information systems so as to improve and increase clinician usage.

With the availability of large databases and several online record keeping systems, it has become a lot easier for the healthcare industry and medical professionals to access patient records at their fingertips. This instant retrieval also provides quick communication and exchange of patient records and history between medical organizations thereby increasing the life-saving rate. Medical history, insurance forms, billing information, prescribed medications, family history and current health status can be easily accessed and looked up within a short period of time. Due to computer systems, doctors, nurses and clinicians do not have to run down the hall for medical records and test results rather they can spend more face-to-face quality time with their patients. Apart from patient-related information, computers can provide easy access to medical research, data, second opinions and real-time consults. Computer databases maintain patient records and files with utmost security and encryption routines and computers also provide robust backup capabilities.

Computers provide user-friendly interfaces for doctors to connect with more advanced scanning equipment. Apart from this, they are used in all types of image processing like X-rays and CT-Scan. They provide accurate results. Magnetic Resonance Imaging (MRI), Electrocardiogram (ECG) and Computerized Axial Tomography (CAT) would have been impossible without computers. Computers are able to map out two-dimensional and three-dimensional images of activity within the area being scanned. These images allow doctors to analyze and diagnose a patient's problem effectively.

Health informatics is an evolving field that integrates communications, information technology and healthcare to improve the quality and safety of patient care. The concept of electronic health record (EHR) has given a huge boost to this field. EMR is a digital version of a paper chart that contains all of a patient's medical history.

Laboratories are an integral part of the healthcare industry. All the processes are mostly carried out by software like Laboratory Information System (LIS). LIS records, manages and stores data for clinical laboratories, right from patient check-in to result entry and from patient demographics to sample processing. Medical reports can be sent to the patient instantly and also instant correctional feedback can be received from the doctors through the Internet.

Apart from administration applications, computers are used in performing surgeries as well like laparoscopic surgery, also called minimally invasive surgery, where high tech tools and instruments embedded with digital computers are used. Robotic-assisted surgical systems allow surgeons to use computer technology to control and maneuver surgical instruments during minimally invasive surgical procedures.

Live webinars and broadcasts can be used to demonstrate new surgery techniques to doctors worldwide.

There are specialized software programs that help doctors and physicians in their duties, right from sending reminders to alerting them when clinical parameters became abnormal. Computers alert nurses and doctors of fluctuations in parameters that present a danger to the patient's health. Computers allow doctors to monitor patients without being physically present. In critical cases, where lives have to be saved immediately, with the help of advanced computer systems, healthcare professionals can plot a course of action if necessary in regards to treatment without having to do a preliminary procedure. Tablets, due to their versatility, are used in surgical consultations and video-conferencing between doctors. Video-conferencing and web-conferencing can help in training new trainee doctors.

Specialized devices are used to help impaired patients in making their lives better, for example, digital hearing aid technology delivers a more natural, comfortable listening experience. Advanced life support systems like cardiac support, circulatory support, etc., is a set of life-saving clinical interventions and protocols to handle life-threatening medical emergencies.

Portable devices like iPads are increasingly replacing the clipboard and bringing home the medical and health provisions. iPads are becoming popular with the medical student community. Medical students use iPads to access digital textbooks, medical journals and faculty lectures. There are also a variety of apps used by students to download information and share with their peers. iPads are used for filling up questionnaires by patients at admittance and also for feedback surveys taken at discharge that let doctors and staff receive real-time feedback. Doctors are using iPads to collect patient information, prescribe drugs and place orders.

Online resources and databases are helping medical researchers to predict trends in illnesses, outbreaks and treatments with accuracy. Computers are helping researchers and scientists make more informed estimations on disease trends and take preventative measures in controlling disease outbreaks.

Computerized systems provide accurate reading and retrieval of key medical patient parameters like brain readings, pulse rate and heart rate. These parameters can be recorded and monitored continuously by computers so that expert analysis of these up-to-date parameters can provide accurate treatment of patients.

A Word of Caution
The downside of computers in the healthcare industry includes security and costs. Once any hospital or clinic decides to maintain electronic records, issues regarding medical records security and patient privacy can cause a headache to the hospital management. Electronic record keeping costs a lot. Another disadvantage is the lack of standardization and this poses a problem especially when medical records are needed to be transferred from one hospital to another.

3.2 Education—An Invaluable Tool

Computers are an invaluable tool in the field of education. They are being used actively for improving the learning process. Research shows students involve themselves more in learning their lessons and work steadily if they are allowed to use computers during their learning process. They have become the life line of the young generation. Computers provide immediate feedback to the answers elicited. There is better presentation of information through audio-visual aids.

Computer-Based Training (CBT), also called computer-assisted instruction, plays an integral role in preparing educational programs and lectures on a wide variety of topics. A CBT course also called courseware can be delivered through various modes—a software product or training program installed on a computer, through an intranet site, or over the Internet as web-based training or online courses. These modes are all subsets of CBT. This way of learning has several benefits—offers a stimulating environment for learners and students, convenience of learning without investing time and money in travel, complex subjects are offered as manageable learning modules, training can be linked with other training systems, and it can also be tailored to the needs of the learners. Several organizations are also moving from typical corporate training programs to CBT-based training. It is a low cost solution for educating people. A large number of people can be trained easily.

Computer-aided learning (CAL) is used in two main contexts: integrative technology and computer-based learning. Since the 1980s CAL has been increasingly used to describe the use of technology in teaching. CAL helps to make available digital learning content of adequate quality and quantity. With the help of CAL, the time spent on preparing teaching material has reduced considerably.

Computers and the Internet offer students a sea of information for their technical projects and research work. Education is no longer limited to physical classrooms. This avenue of online learning and education is a boon for those who are unable to attend physical schools or colleges. Comprehensive distance learning material and programs can be developed through graphics, webinars, video-based sessions, etc. There are many online educational courses, whereby students are not required to attend classes or be physically present for lectures. This mode of learning also helps working professional to complete their education without any interruption to their work life.

Spotlight Tip
In case of doubts, students can acquire prompt help through e-mails and online discussion. There is also better communication among teachers, students and parents. Students can do and track their projects using computer applications like PowerPoint and Word.

Classroom books and materials can be made more interesting with computer-based learning and websites. Teachers and students can enjoy the perks of interactive learning by integrating classroom texts with videos and other online content. This approach offers teachers the flexibility in their teaching methods and students to participate in active learning. They allow students to progress at their own pace and learn individually or in a group setting. Online libraries and e-books help to guide students in a matter of minutes and save precious time and resources which they can use in other constructive activities.

The modern classroom technology also offers mobile computing solutions that enrich young minds and empower teachers to learn, teach, and explore new dimensions of knowledge in various subjects. New technologies like the interactive whiteboard offers an interactive display that is connected to a projector and computer and apart from classrooms, it is used in several other settings like broadcasting studios and corporate boardrooms.

The instruction aspect of education utilizes computers in several areas like drill and practice, tutorials and problem-solving techniques. For students it is easier to store tons of information on computers than maintaining bulky hand-written notes. Students are able to grasp new technologies at a click of mouse. Computer-assisted instruction (CAI) is an interactive instructional technique in which a computer is used to present the instructional material and monitor the learning that takes place. CAI uses a combination of text and multimedia content in enhancing the learning process.

Computers are useful in various other aspects related to education apart from instruction and learning—online testing and evaluation, maintaining a question bank, storing online sample papers, providing feedback, quick information processing of student records, sample papers and question banks, maintaining records of academic scores, and analysis of test results and scores.

Cutting-edge computer technology like cloud computing can provide greater cost efficiency and flexibility and better learning outcomes in learning setups and also improve learning outcomes at the same time.

Spotlight Tip
Where there is a physical teaching-learning setup, apart from employing computer-based teaching, teachers should also include a healthy amount of face-to-face knowledge exchange with students and also interact with students to elicit their thoughts and to get them actively involved in the learning process.

3.2.1 Challenges and Solutions—Problems and Fixes

In some areas of education, there is a lack of teacher and educators who are willing to integrate technology with education and classroom learning. Training should be held for such teachers and educators where they need to be demonstrated an understanding of how one can communicate with a computer online for sources of teaching and learning, as well as with others in the teaching community and how students using an online network can benefit immensely.

At times, in computer-driven learning setups, a lack of set routine or fixed schedule can often lead to students and learners falling behind deadlines. Due to the lack of timely manual supervision by teachers, students may fall behind in their learning and assignments. A balanced mix of automated learning and face-to-face teacher-student interaction is needed to minimize such problems.

Too much dependency on computers for meeting the learning needs of students can lead to isolation among students. This isolation can in turn lead to lack of motivation. At times, receiving feedback from a physical presence of a teacher motivates a student immensely.

Each and every educational institution and learning academy must fine tune their e-learning strategy from time to time to meet the challenges and ever-changing needs of their students. These timely upgrades are necessary to overcome the problems of isolation and demotivation.

3.3 Publishing—E-books, Online Promotion and More

Computers have completely revolutionized the way books are printed and read. Computers have become a vital marketing tool for publishing houses. They play a big time role in the promotion of books. They are used in the entire book creation cycle, right from typesetting to designing and from printing to promotion. They have transformed the making, reading and promoting of journals, books and magazines.

Digital publishing makes it easier for authors, writers and poets to release their creative and academic works without a traditional publisher's support and services. If the book needs revision, it is easy to revise and make changes to digital files. A change to books or cover designs has become easier as any revision of digital files is quicker and manageable.

Desktop publishing is another area where computers play a vital role. Desktop publishing streamlines the process of disseminating information of all kinds; it helps to make print-ready and publication-ready documents.

Spotlight Tip
Content is everywhere and with the proliferation of smart devices, users have increasing appetite for rich and personalized content that can be accessed anywhere and anytime. And this is where computers come into the picture. Right from content creation and delivery to the content consumption platform, the publishing industry uses the advanced technology of computers.

With devices like Kindle eReaders, smartphones, laptops and tablets, readers are able to download books and magazines to their devices and read their favorite reads wherever they go. Internet has become a vital marketing tool for publishers as well as authors. Publishers e-mail distributors, readers and customers with newsletters about their upcoming book launch events and new releases. Publishers and authors leverage social media for promotion—tweeting about new books, creating Facebook pages or promoting books on GoodReads. Self-published writers and authors use social media to publicize their books or send out digital copies to book reviewers.

Over the years, newspapers also have entered into online publishing where they share an e-format of their newspaper edition. Computers are used in the process of lithography which is used in the publishing of newspapers.

Computers have also fueled the growth of online book retailing. In the past few years, dozens and dozens of online book stores have found an address for themselves on the information highway. Selling books online through various shopping portals helps the publishers to reach out to a wider customer base. They can tap into new markets.

Blogs are a big part of the online publishing industry. Several popular blogs have gone to become popular books again by using digital tools of the computer industry. Computer applications like Word can be used for better and faster book production as it offers several features like automatic correction of spellings and grammar mistakes, and helps to keep track of various edits and versions.

3.3.1 E-Books—Digitized Reading

E-books have become very popular today—all thanks to computers. Digital publishing caters to special-interest magazines and books where hard printing costs are saved.

Digital publishing makes it easier for writers to publish and release their works without a traditional publisher's support and services, and that too in various popular digital formats like AZW (Amazon proprietary format), ePub, MOBI/PRC (MobiPocket) and PDF (Adobe's Portable Document Format) and in a short period of time. Early versions appeared in the late 1990s and by 2000, digitized books became popular as readers were able to read them online or they were printed on demand by the publisher or they could be downloaded on their reading devices or on e-book readers. E-book readers are devices that enable downloading, storing and reading e-books and periodicals. These devices provide various features like making notes, highlighting passages and bookmarking pages. E-books also introduced the concept of books that would never go out of print.

Apart from reading e-books on various digital devices, from personal computers to Kindle E-reader, there are also audio books and digital audio players can be used to listen to these audio books. Smart devices can also be used to access books online through various apps. Browsers also offer apps that support access directly to e-books from the browser and facilitate reading on the go; these apps access e-books and allow readers to read them directly in the browser.

There are several e-book databases and they include the option of searching for phrases or keywords within the books, and some databases include advanced features like hyperlinks, in-built dictionaries and animations. All this is possible due to computers.

3.4 Other Fields—Corporate World, Science and More

Computers are used in the corporate world to automate several tedious tasks such as payroll processing, sales analysis, forecasting, budgeting, etc. Banking, finance and insurance sectors are using advanced computer systems for maintaining their data. Online banking allows customers to perform financial transactions via the Internet. Online banking provides 24/7 access to banking services with ease-of-use-features. In the insurance sector, sophisticated computer systems process much of the industry's routine work. All policy-related data like maturity date, interest rate, next due installment, etc., is stored in large databases.

Computers in the defense and military fields help in the design and development of guided weapons. They also provide simulation software for designing a robust strategy whereby civilian causalities can be minimized. Apart from harsh physical training exercises, the tactical skills of army personnel are honed using computer simulation applications. These simulations help to train soldiers for severe combat situations without actually having to put them in harm's way. Computers are used in military satellites for planning assaults. Army suits with computing features are becoming popular. Computers are used in designing and testing new defense weapons systems.

Marketing departments of organizations, both small and big, leverage the reach of computers to tap into new market areas and to expand their customer base. Computers and the Internet are used for enhancing the various aspects of the marketing department, right from web-based promotion to market research. Marketing on the Internet is relatively cheaper than traditional marketing. Computerized marketing can take the form of in-text advertisements on popular websites, newsletters, e-mail promotion, video advertisements, etc. Marketing research and surveys can be conducted through a website or by using surveying services and apps. Computerized systems can help in marketing feedback and control, report generation and data collection.

Computers enable the finance professionals to keep a tab on key finance policy changes such as price modifications on products and goods. Computer applications like Excel Spreadsheet help the finance department to organize, present and analyze complex finance data and transactions for better decision-making. Maintaining financial data and records is an integral part of business and the large storage capacity of computers meets this critical business need by providing scalable database systems. Computers also provide online access to online financial resources like tax changes, currency exchange rates, etc., through the Internet, which helps the business world to make informed finance-related decisions.

Computer-controlled robots are used to perform many complicated industrial sector jobs and processes. In modern factories, almost every task and process is automated and everything is run by industrial robots. Industrial robots come in all shapes and sizes that perform operations like assembly, welding, lifting, etc.; they perform intelligent operations with minimal human intervention. Computer programs that are used to design the complex models of a product are called Computer Aided Design (CAD). Computer-aided design and computer-aided manufacturing systems are used to both design a product and program manufacturing processes. Computer process control and monitoring systems bring advantages like high reliability and availability, flexibility, simplified operations, quality control, etc. The increasing use of computers in industrial engineering helps in ensuring that there is match between technology and infrastructure.

Supercomputers are used in all major scientific applications, right from molecular biology to meteorology. Computers used in science projects and research-driven products produce better-engineered products; there are fewer errors. Complex data analysis and scientific research often require solving of complex mathematic equations and this is possible with computer systems. They help in checking the accuracy and authenticity of data and this in turn helps in accurate interpretations by the researchers. Scientists use computers for simulation of complex events and processes. Computers are the heart of all modern scientific experiments and discoveries. Scientific research involves experiments and to perform experiments, several types of computerized equipment are needed. They are also used to collect data and prepare results. Modeling tools, statistical programs, etc., help with analyzing information and also presenting it in novel ways to discover new aspects. Computers help the science community in searching the existing research literature (electronic databases of books, journals and bibliographic references) so that it can find the exact gaps to fill. Through computers, it is now possible to share knowledge and learnings from marginalized scholars, researchers and scientists with the rest of the world. Computers help to combine numerical analysis, programming and mathematics for enhancing the research frontier.

3.5 Questions for Reflection

1. What are the advantages of computerized learning?
2. How does the research community benefit from computers?
3. What are the advantages of digitized publishing?
4. How are the various departments of healthcare leveraging the advantages of computers?
5. What is Computer-based Training?
6. List ten application areas of computers?

Part 2
INSIDE AND OUTSIDE

4

Operating System— The Mastermind

An operating system (OS) is a large low-level program that controls and manages the software and hardware components; it is a software program that enables the hardware to communicate and operate with the software. It manages a computer's memory and processes. It is a software program that is required in order to run application programs and utilities. In the initial days of computer systems, user used command line interface OS and now most computers have a graphical user interface OS system that is easy to operate and is user-friendly. There are several different programs running at the same time and they all need to access your computer's central processing unit, memory and storage resources. OS coordinates all of these aspects to make sure each program gets what it needs in a timely manner. OS acts as a manager to allocate the available resources to satisfy the requirements of each process.

Some main examples of OS include versions of Microsoft Windows (like Windows 7, Windows 8 and Windows XP), Apple's macOS and flavors of the open source operating system Linux. The various versions of Microsoft Windows are the most commonly used operating systems. Windows OS is widely used for home and business computers. Apple's macOS comes preloaded on all Macintosh computers. As Linux operating systems are open source they can be modified and distributed by anyone, this is in contrast to Windows and macOS as these are proprietary software programs and they can be modified by their respective companies. Linux is an efficient and fast-performing OS; hence it is used for servers.

Every tablet, desktop computer, smartphone, etc., include an operating system that provides basic functionality for the device. Most computer users use the OS that comes with their computer systems. It is also possible to upgrade the existing OS or even change it completely. OS for mobile devices are specifically designed for mobile devices and some of the popular OS in this category are Google Android, BlackBerry OS and Apple iOS.

When a user turns on a computer, the operating system program is loaded into the main memory; the first program to be loaded after startup. This program is called the kernel. The kernel is the core of an operating system and it acts as a communication interface between the software (user applications) and the hardware (disk memory, CPU, etc.). The kernel is the first program to be loaded during system startup or booting. When an operating system is loaded into memory, the kernel loads first and remains in memory until the operating system is shut down again. Once loaded and initialized, the system program is prepared to run the user programs and permits them to access the machine's hardware resources. The kernel is the heart or the central core of the OS, whereas when additional utilities and applications are added over and above the kernel, then this complete package and platform of libraries becomes the OS.

4.1 Kernel—Core Component

A kernel is the core component of an operating system. It is responsible for several critical functions like task management, process management, interrupt handling, memory management and disk management. There are different design principles governing developing of a kernel architecture. There are various types of kernels: Micro, Monolithic and Hybrid.

A microkernel is a small minimalistic modular part of an operating system kernel which implements its basic features. In contrast to a typical kernel, a microkernel is compact and performs only the basic functions. In a microkernel, the kernel is broken down into separate processes, known as servers. Some of the servers run in kernel space and some run in user space, and servers invoke services from each other by sending messages via inter-process communication protocol. All servers are kept separate and run in different address spaces. As this architecture allows some basic services like file system, device driver management, etc. to run in user space, it helps to reduce the kernel code size and also increases the security and stability of the OS as bare minimum code is running in kernel. The advantages of microkernel architecture are security and stability, and the disadvantages are slow inter process communication can result in poor performance and additional context switches are normally needed. Some kernels have been developed independently for use in any operating system and for parallel computing, for example, Mach kernel developed at Carnegie Mellon University; other examples are L4 and AmigaOS.

A monolithic kernel contains several million lines of code. It is OS architecture/a single large process where the entire operating system, which includes the file system support, device drivers, and the application inter-process communication, is working in the kernel address space. A monolithic kernel is a single large process running entirely in a single address space. The advantages of monolithic architecture are simple design and speed, and the disadvantages are may face stability issue and is difficult to maintain. Examples of monolithic kernel are UNIX and DOS.

A hybrid kernel is an operating system kernel architecture that combines features and benefits of microkernel and monolithic kernel architectures. A hybrid kernel combines the speed, performance and simple design of monolithic kernel with the modularity, stability and execution safety of microkernel. A popular example of hybrid kernel is Windows NT.

Table 5: Difference between Micro and Monolithic Kernels

Micro	Monolithic
Micro kernels are slower	Monolithic kernels are faster
Device drivers reside in the user space	Device drivers reside in the kernel space
Use message queues for IPC	Use signals and sockets for IPC
Microkernels are much secure	Less secure as device drivers resides in the kernel space and when there is a failure in a driver it may lead to a crash
A new feature or patch can be added to a microkernel system without any recompiling	Adding a new feature or patch to a monolithic system means recompiling the whole kernel
Used in Mac OS X and Minix	Used in Unix and Linux

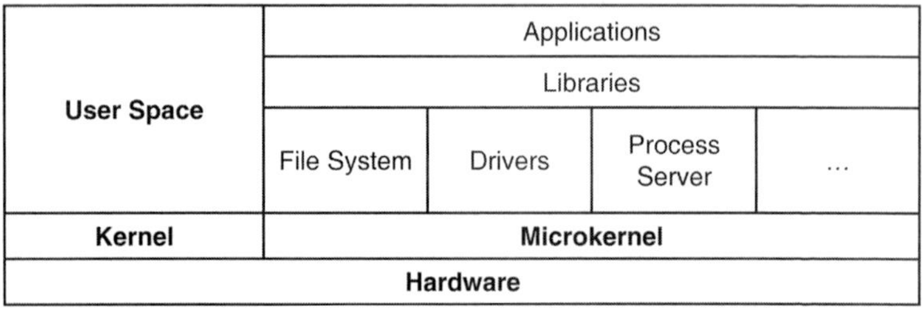

Figure 8: MICROKERNEL OPERATING SYSTEM ARCHITECTURE

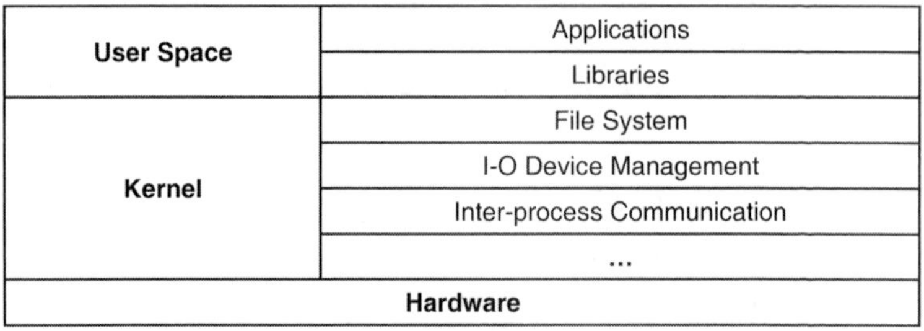

Figure 9: MONOLITHIC OPERATING SYSTEM ARCHITECTURE

Operating system is installed and stored on the hard disk. As the hard disk is a non-volatile memory, OS is not lost when the computer is turned off. As the data access from the hard disk is very slow, therefore just after a computer is started, OS is copied from the hard disk into the random access memory (RAM). The operating system is loaded through a bootstrapping or booting process, and this is done by a program called boot loader. It is automatically executed by the processor when turning on a computer. This program reads the hard drive's boot sector to continue the process of loading the computer's operating system.

BIOS is the first program that runs after start up and it performs some initial tests, and then transfers control to the master boot record (MBR) where the boot loader resides, which then loads the entire OS into the RAM. When the system is turned off, the copy of OS in RAM is lost as RAM is a volatile memory, but the main OS is not lost as it is stored intact in the hard disk. The OS is safe and whenever the system is turned on again, the OS will be ready to be loaded in the RAM yet again.

Each and every computer system needs an OS to run efficiently and effectively. While the most basic and obvious function of the OS is to provide users with an interface with which to work, it controls many other components and subsystems behind the scenes as well. The main characteristics and functions of the OS are:

1. OS is responsible for running all the application programs.
2. OS is responsible for managing all the input and output devices connected to a computer system.
3. OS provides a communication interface between user and computer system such as graphical user interface, menu-driven and command line. A user interface is a means by which users interact with a computer system. It lets users to communicate with the OS so that they can access files, load programs, etc.
4. OS handles the access, storage and retrieval of data from a computer's hard drive. While the actual reading and writing is done by the hard drive, it is the OS that instructs the hard drive what to write and read.

5. OS handles all the system resources such as the central processing unit, memory, etc.
6. OS schedules the various processes and allocates the required memories for these processes.

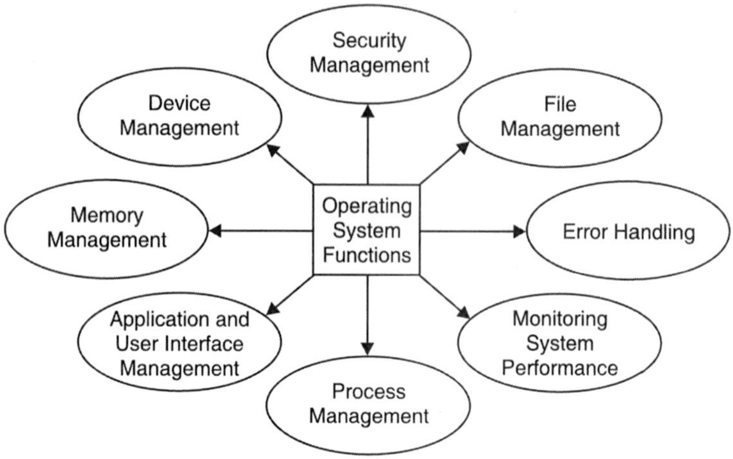

Figure 10: FUNCTIONS OF THE OS AT A GLANCE

4.2 Types of Operating Systems—From Batch to Time-sharing

Operating systems are usually categorized based on their working technique. The common classification is as follows:

1. **Batch:** This kind of operating system is optimized for running jobs without user interaction. The users of a batch operating system do not interact with the computer directly. To speed up processing, jobs with similar needs are grouped together and then run as a batch. This processing is performed by a batch monitor. There is no mechanism to prioritize jobs and there is no interaction between user and computer. An example of batch processing: for instance a large organization may invest in a mainframe loaded with a batch operating system to run its payroll system.

Setting up a batch requires that the following details are ready: how much processor time is allowed for the job; job priority; accounting data, job owner; how to handle job failure; and data file details both for input and output.

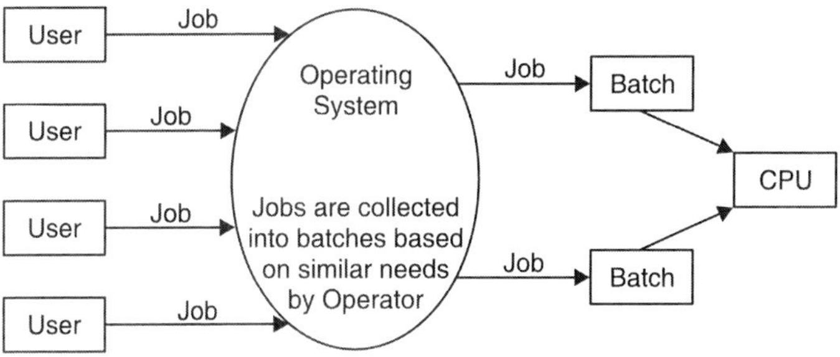

Figure 11: BATCH OPERATING SYSTEM

2. **Distributed:** It is designed to work in a network. It manages a collection of independent computers and makes them appear as a single system; looks like a virtual uniprocessor. The benefits are: resource sharing, reliability and load sharing. All nodes have their own copy of operating system and own memory, and they communicate with each other by exchanging messages over a communication network.

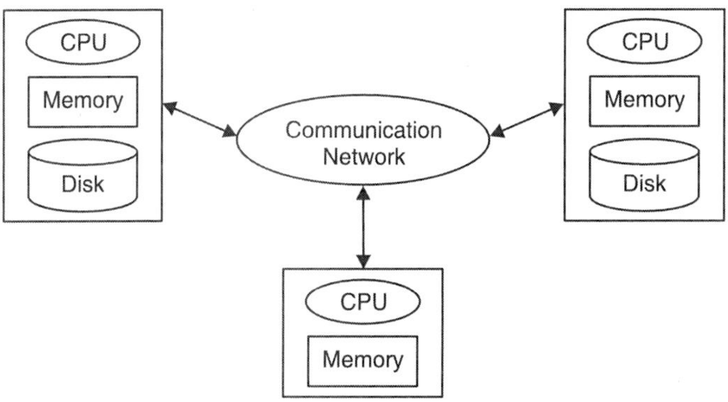

Figure 12: DISTRIBUTED OPERATING SYSTEM

A distributed operating system uses multiple CPUS to cater to multiple applications and users. The main benefits are flexibility, fast processing and low price-performance ratio. More resources can be added easily. A popular example of a distributed OS is the World Wide Web.

3. **Real-time:** It is a multitasking OS designed for real-time applications. A real-time OS is used in setups where a large number of events are processed in a short time. It is often used as a control device in dedicated applications like flight control systems, industrial control systems, medical imaging systems, etc.

   The main features of a real-time operating system are multitasking, a sufficient level of interrupt levels and process threads that can be prioritized.

   A hard real-time OS must operate within the confines of strict deadlines, and missing a deadline is a total system failure. In soft real-time OS, the meeting of deadlines is not compulsory for every time for every task, but process should get processed and give the result. With each failure in meeting a deadline, the system becomes less productive.

4. **Time-sharing:** The CPU is multiplexed among several jobs that are kept in memory and on disk, and the CPU is allocated to a job only when it is in memory. Each process is allotted a particular time span and the process has to finish its execution within that time span. If it fails to complete its execution then CPU control goes to the immediate next process.

   A time-sharing OS manages the allocation of computer resources in time slots/time slices to several programs simultaneously. When a particular time slot is over, the OS passes control over to the next user. The prime focus of a time-sharing operating system is on minimizing the response time.

4.3 Memory Management—Controlling and Coordinating Memory

The function of memory management is the most important function of an operating system and it deals directly with both the main memory and secondary memory. The OS manages main memory and moves processes back and forth between main memory and disk during execution.

The main memory provides storage area for each program that can be accessed by the CPU for its execution; hence for the program execution to occur, it is the task of the memory management unit of the OS to load the specific program into the main memory. The OS loads the program instructions into main memory and then picks up these instructions and maintains a queue for them in order to acquire CPU time for their execution. The memory manager keeps track of the available memory locations: which one is available, which is to be allocated or deallocated.

The OS also decides which pages are required to swap between the main memory and secondary memory. This swapping (memory compaction) process is called virtual memory management; it is an optimization technique that gives a program the impression that it has more memory than actually exists. The need of virtual memory arises from the fact that physical memory is limited. Virtual memory is a section of a hard disk that is set up to emulate the RAM. Virtual memory allows the sharing of memory by multiple processes, allows memory protection and allows many programs to run at once. The kernel translates each virtual address into a physical address (mapping of memory addresses used by a program called virtual addresses into physical addresses in computer memory) before the operation is carried out. There are two main ways of implementing virtual memory management: segmentation and demand paging.

In segmented virtual memory, memory is divided into variable length segments and each segment has a base address + length (an offset within that segment). There are two issues with paging: the pages have fixed size and pages are contiguous, and segmentation resolves both these issues, as it maintains completely independent segments that all start at address 0 up to a maximum value and the address spaces are not linear. As bits of code can be broken up and stored in individual address spaces, segmentation allows the sharing of libraries and procedures between processes.

In paged virtual memory, memory is divided into fixed sized pages and each page has a base physical address. A page table is a data structure maintained by the virtual memory manager component of the OS that maps virtual addresses to physical addresses. The OS stores information like physical page number, modified bit, reference bit, valid bit, access permissions, etc., for each page. While executing a program, if the program references a page which is not available in the main memory because it was swapped out a little while ago, the CPU treats this invalid memory reference as a page fault, and then transfers control from the program to the OS to demand the page back into the memory. Pages are loaded as per demand.

Table 6: Differences between Segmentation and Paging

Segmentation	Paging
Segmentation requires programmer to be aware of memory limits	Paging is transparent to programmers
Address space is not linear	It has one linear address space
It is of arbitrary size	It is of fixed size
It is a logical unit of information	It is a physical unit of information
Fragmentation does not occur	Fragmentation may occur

The main memory management functions performed by the OS are: decides which process should be loaded into the memory when the memory space is available, each process must have enough memory in which it can execute without running into the memory space of other processes, and the different types of memory should be used/allocated properly so that each process can run successfully, and deallocation should also be done properly. The OS keeps track of which part of memory is in use and by whom. The OS employs various techniques to keep track of where and how a program resides in the memory, and also converts logical addresses into actual physical ones.

The OS manages primary memory and moves processes back and forth between main memory and disk during execution. Through memory management, the OS keeps track of all memory locations. A logical address space is generated by the CPU whereas a physical address space is for the use of the memory unit. This concept of a logical address space that is bound to a separate physical address space is central to proper memory management. Logical or virtual address refers to a value that specifies a generic location relative to a program, whereas a physical address is an actual address in the main memory device.

4.4 Process Management—Manages Each and Every Process

A process is a program in execution; a running instance of a program; it is the basic unit of execution in an operating system. Different processes may run different instances of the same program. The OS performs process management by keeping track of each and every process and all of its intermediate states. Each process has a unique number called the process identifier (PID) assigned to it by the OS. A process execution cycle requires memory to hold program code and data, and registers to support execution. Once processes have been created, the OS organizes their execution. This requires interaction between process management and main memory management. Processes are created during system initialization, are created by other processes and are created by user requests. The creation of a process involves assigning unique process identifier, space allocation, process control block initialization, setting up appropriate linkages and creating or expanding other data structures like an accounting file.

Process management is an integral part of OS. The OS performs four main functions in regards to process management: allocate resources to processes, facilitate processes to share and exchange information, process creation, deletion, suspension and resumption, and process synchronization and communication. When a process runs and as it executes, it passes through different states. Some of the common states are: Start/New is the initial state when the process is created and it is just being put together; Ready implies that a process is ready to be assigned to a processor and all ready processes are allocated to a processor by the OS; Running refers to a process that has been assigned to a processor and the processor has begun executing instructions related to it; Waiting refers to a process that is waiting for a resource; and Terminated refers to a process that has finished execution or has been terminated by the OS.

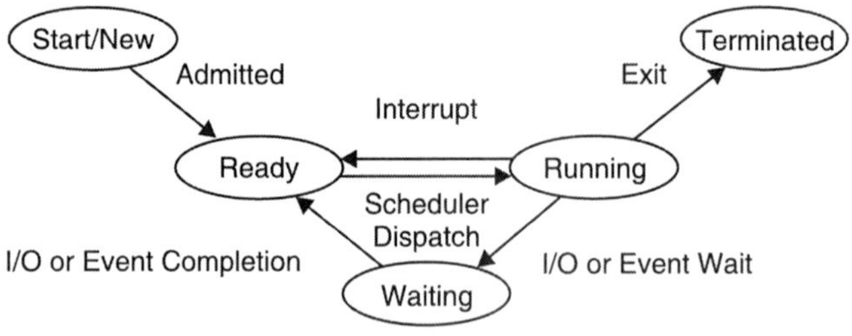

Figure 13: PROCESS STATES

The OS controls and schedules processes for execution by the CPU. The act of determining which process in the ready state should be moved to the running state is known as process scheduling. The main aim of process scheduling is to keep the CPU busy all the time and to deliver minimum response time for all programs. This can be achieved by the process scheduler by applying appropriate rules of swapping processes in and out of the CPU. There are two types of schedulers that the OS can use: Pre-emptive scheduling in which the OS decides to favor another process by pre-empting the currently running process, and non pre-emptive scheduling occurs when the currently running process gives up the CPU in a voluntary manner.

Most modern operating systems support threads. Threads represent multiple execution streams within a single process. A thread is unit of sequential execution. A thread is a single sequence stream within a process. A thread has its own program counter (PC), stack space and a register set. As a thread too has some of the properties of a process, it is also referred to as a lightweight process. A thread is not independent of one another like processes as a result a thread shares with other threads its data section, OS resources, etc. Threads help to improve performance through parallelism. In multitasking environment, the processes need to communicate with each other and to exchange information. These processes are created under a hierarchical structure where the main process is known as parent process and the sub processes are known as child processes.

Context switching is the mechanism of storing and restoring the state (the execution context) of a process or thread so that execution can be resumed from the same point at a later time.

Each program has data and code associated with it. On running a program, the loader reads and interprets the executable file. An executable file is a file that is used to perform various functions or operations on a computer; a particular kind of file that is capable of being executed or run as a program in the computer. An executable file usually has a file name extension of .bat, .com or .exe. It then sets up the process's memory to hold the code and data from this executable file.

A part of the OS called the scheduler is responsible for deciding which program to run when, and it provides the illusion of simultaneous execution by rapidly switching between programs.

4.4.1 Process Control Block—Data Structure for Process Information

A Process Control Block (PCB) is a data structure used for storing information about a process. It is maintained by the OS for every process. The PCB is identified by a process ID (PID). A PCB typically contains PID, states of various registers and flags, memory management information, accounting information, privileges, priority level, process state, program counter and I/O status. Additional fields and components can be added to the PCB, for example, if a system provides facilities with which processes can start up new processes called "parent-child" relationships, then their linking information can be stored in PCB. All this information is used by CPU at run time. The architecture of a PCB is completely dependent on the OS and system requirements; the information stored in the PCB differs from OS to OS. The PCB is maintained for a process throughout its lifetime, and is deleted once the process terminates.

The OS maintains all PCBs in process scheduling queues. The OS maintains a separate queue for each of the process states and PCBs of all processes in the same execution state are placed in the same queue. The OS can use different policies to manage the queues and the OS scheduler decides how to move processes between the queues. The scheduler schedules different processes to be assigned to the CPU based on scheduling algorithms like priority scheduling (each process is given a priority and then the scheduling is done based on this priority), round robin scheduling (a circular queue is setup in such a way that the CPU scheduler goes around that queue and allocates CPU resources to each process for a set time interval), shortest remaining time scheduling (CPU is allocated to the process that is closest to being completed and it can be pre-empted if there is a newer process in the ready queue that has shorter completion time), first in first out (the process that requests the CPU first is allocated the CPU first), etc. In the case of priority scheduling, if two processes have the same priority level, then the process with the shortest CPU burst time is executed first. CPU burst time refers to the duration for which a process gets control of the CPU. When the state of a particular process changes, its PCB is unlinked from its current queue and moved to its new state queue. The following process scheduling queues are maintained by the OS: job queue (set of all the processes), ready queue (set of all the processes in the main memory, ready and waiting to execute) and device queue (set of all the processes that are blocked due to unavailability of I/O device), and all the processes move between these queues. The entries in a queue are pointers to a PCB, which contains all information and state about a process.

4.4.2 Keep Track of the Process—Execution, State, etc.

A process contains the code and the operating system must keep track of the program counter or code location. A process also has a stack and the operating system must track this stack also. It also stores the 'state of process' computation in a process control block (PCB). PCBs and process tables are not the only way for the OS to keep track of what's happening with processes. The memory manager can also hold information as to which process has access to device drivers, pages, etc.

Keeping track of processes involves that the OS ensures that the process code is executed in the normal sequence. Another important aspect is that the OS should preserve the state information even when the process is not being executed, so that it can be restored for the next period of execution. The OS should also have provision to enable special control of processes like debugging support and priority manipulation in regards to processes.

4.5 Device Management—Uniform Interface to Access Devices

Device management is that OS process which manages hardware devices. It provides a uniform interface to access the devices and it also optimizes the performance of these devices. The OS ensures that two processes do not have a "fight" over the usage of a device at the same time.

To avoid this conflict, the OS uses the concept of a queue. For each and every input and output device, the OS maintains a queue that holds the IDs of the processes that want to access a particular device.

There are three types of devices: a block device stores information in fixed-size blocks, each one with its own address; a network device transmits data packets; and a character device delivers or accepts a stream of characters. For handling these device types, a device controller is needed. The I/O manager, together with device drivers, manages all hardware (and software or logical) devices and implements an interface for the rest of the system to use these devices.

The OS through the I/O Controller keeps track of all devices, which is responsible for error correction and for converting serial bit stream to block of bytes. This controller works like an interface between a device and a device driver. This controller has two sub-components: data buffer that OS can read from or write to, and device registers to communicate with the central processing unit. There is always a device controller and a device driver for each of the devices to communicate with the OS. A device driver is OS component responsible for hiding the complexity of input/output devices; it facilitates the OS to access the various devices in a uniform manner. The device driver is a helper program that is responsible for the physical writes and physical reads. A user program can never access a device directly; it can access the device only through a device driver. For example, an executing process might want to write some data to the disk. The program uses an instruction like write (disk, address, data). This instruction is actually a request to the operating system's disk device driver to perform a write. The device driver checks the disk to see if another process is already using the disk. If yes, then the executing process's ID is placed into the queue for the disk, and the executing process is 'Blocked'. If no, then the device driver copies the data and its destination address into the disk's address and data buffers and signals the disk's controller to begin a write operation.

Spotlight Tip
Device drivers are separate from OS so that new features and functions can be added to them without requiring the OS itself to be modified, recompiled and redistributed.

There are two ways of addressing device registers and data buffers. The first way is to assign each device a dedicated range of device addresses in the physical memory, so accessing those device addresses requires special hardware instructions associated with individual devices. The second way is not to distinguish device addresses from normal memory addresses, so devices can be accessed the same way as normal memory, with the same set of hardware instructions (also called memory-mapped I/O). Regardless of these addressing modes, the OS has to keep track of the status of a device and simplest way of doing this is polling. Polling refers to the continuous checking of the controlling device of other devices, processes, queues, etc., and see what state they are in and whether they need attention such as whether they still want to communicate, they still are connected, etc. In polling, CPU repeatedly checks the status of a device for exchanging data.

Device management component of the OS includes four main functions: monitoring of each and every device; determining which process will be assigned which device; allocating the device and finally deallocating the same (both at the process level and job level). Shared devices can be assigned to several processes at the same time by interleaving their requests. This interleaving and conflicts must be handled by the device manager. Dedicated devices are assigned to only one job and they serve this job for the entire time this job is active or until it releases the dedicated device.

The OS manages input and output related to the devices through buffers and queues. These buffers and queues take the bits from a device, hold the bits, and release them to the CPU at a rate slow enough for the CPU to manage. This function is of crucial significance when a number of processes are running and taking up CPU time. The OS system will instruct a buffer to continue taking input from the device, but to stop sending data to the CPU while the process using the input is suspended. Thereafter, when the process needing input is made active once again, the OS will instruct the buffer to send data. This mechanism allows devices like modem, keyboard, etc., to deal with external users or computer systems at a high speed even though there are times when the CPU can't use input from these sources. Buffers, device drivers, queues and start-up commands are essential for the OS to perform device management.

4.6 File Management—Organizing and Managing Data Storage

The OS is responsible for organizing and managing the storage of data on permanent media. The OS also maintains a set of look-up tables that relate file names to locations on storage drives. The OS is also responsible for protection mechanism in order to protect files and folders and to determine how processes users can access the information in files.

A file is a named collection of related information, data, commands or settings that are recorded on secondary storage such as magnetic disks (hard disk or floppy disk), optical disks (CD-ROM) and magnetic tapes. It can be free formed, structured or indexed. A folder, also called a directory, provides a method for organizing files. A file is created using a software program, for example, to create a document, the word software is needed. Some important file management terms: a field is a collection of bytes and it has a type and size, a record is a collection of related fields, a file is a collection of records, and a folder or directory is a special type of file which contains all files and their attributes.

Each storage device on a computer has a drive letter assigned to it. The following table shows a typical allocation of drive letters:

Table 7: Drive Letters and Their Description

Drive Letter	Description
A:	First floppy disk drive
B:	Second floppy disk drive
C:	Hard disk drive
D:	Optical drive
E:	USB drive

Just as processes are an abstraction for processors and virtual memory is an abstraction for memory, similarly a file system is an abstraction for disk. The filesystem or file system is a system used by the OS to organize and keep track of files and all this is done by maintaining metadata for the files and folders. The main aim of a file system is to provide programs with a uniform way of storing and retrieving data. Although the OS provides its own file management system, one can buy and install separate file management systems as well. These external systems provide additional features like better file protection and backup management. A popular example of file system is hierarchical system where directories are used to organize files into a tree structure.

The file manager component of the OS creates the illusion of files and folders, but from the computer's point of view there are only blocks of memory, either allocated or unallocated. The file manager keeps tracks of where files are stored, follows the OS file allocation policies, creates a log of all file usage, uses available storage space for files in an efficient manner and allocates and deallocates files. The file manager allocates file to a user by reading it from the hard disk and then loading it into the memory and also simultaneously updating the log of who is using which file. While deallocating a file, the file manager updates the file tables and rewrites the file (if modified) to the hard disk.

Any process/es waiting to access the specific file will be notified. The OS is responsible for the main operations of a file: create, delete, close, open, write, read, and set attributes. The main implementation goal of the OS is to ensure that operations will have minimal space overhead and as few disk accesses as possible.

File names typically have two parts: name and extension (abc.txt: abc is the name and txt is the extension), and the full name of a file also includes its path, where it is stored. Typical operations that can be done on a file are: create, delete, copy, open, rename, etc. Additional operations include taking backups of files, mapping files onto secondary storage, etc.

The OS stores files as records in memory and many such records make up a single file. There are three main ways in which a file is physically stored in memory: contiguous, non-contiguous and indexed storage. In contiguous storage, records are stored one after another. Although it is a simple method, the downside is that in the case of larger files, there needs to be either free space allocated at the end or the whole file needs to be copied at another location that has adequate space. In non-contiguous storage, the file manager stores the records where there is space available. In this method, there is no easy way to find out the exact location of a record in a file. The file manager will try to put as much as of the record together, but some parts/ bits will be spread out and this extra bits are also called extents. This leads to fragmentation. These extents are linked together with pointers. Non-contiguous storage does not support random access of files, whereas indexed storage does support it as it brings all the pointers together into an index block. In indexed storage, each file is provided with its own index block, which is an array of disk block pointers (addresses). In the case of larger files, there can be multiple indexes.

4.6.1 *Access Mechanism—Direct, Sequential and Indexed*

Normally the OS supports only one file access mechanism, but there are operating systems that also support multiple file access mechanisms. The main file access mechanisms are:

1. Direct Access—the records are accessed directly to where they are physically located on a device.
2. Sequential Access—the records are accessed in some specific sequence, i.e., the information in the file is processed in order, one record after the other.
3. Indexed Sequential Access—this mechanism is based on an index. An index is created for each file which contains pointers to various blocks. The index is searched sequentially and its pointer is used to access the file directly.

4.7 Security Management—Authentication and Authorization

The OS must protect itself from security breaches. OS security is the process of ensuring OS integrity, availability and confidentiality. The OS ensures that each resource is accessed correctly and only by those processes and users that are authorized to do so. The security goals include authentication and authorization, and these are achieved through various methods like access control techniques, file permission, data encryption, password, etc.

Security may be approached in many ways, including installing updated anti-virus software, creating secure accounts with privileges and access levels, and monitoring all network traffic through a firewall. A firewall is a network security device that monitors traffic to or from a network. A firewall can be either a hardware component or software program. One drawback of software firewall is that it is software running on a personal computer operating system. If the underlying operating system is compromised, then the firewall can be compromised as well. OS has certain goals to achieve and certain threats to overcome as far as security is concerned.

Table 8: Goals and Threats

Goals	Threats
Data Integrity	Tampering with Data
Data Availability	Denial of Service
Data Confidentiality	Exposure of Data

Because of the critical role of the OS in the operation of a computer system, security has a fundamental impact on the overall security of a computer system, including security of all applications running within the system. It is the function of OS to ensure that each resource is accessed correctly and only by those processes and users that are authorized to do so. Networking adds to the security problems. For handling network-related security issues, at the OS level, firewall software can be used to either allow or disallow network traffic.

The security kernel of OS is responsible for implementing security mechanisms. It provides security interfaces among the OS, hardware and other components of a computer system.

4.7.1 Access Control—DAC, MAC and More

Access control is the process by which the OS grants or denies resources on a computer or network. Discretionary Access Control (DAC) is a type of access control defined by the Trusted Computer System Evaluation Criteria and the owner of the object (resource to be protected) specifies which subjects (a user trying to access the resource) can access the object. Most operating systems such as Linux, Windows and Macintosh are based on DAC model. Mandatory Access Control (MAC) refers to a type of access control by which the operating system limits the ability of a subject or initiator to access or perform some sort of operation on an object.

The OS access control policy includes the functions of identification, authorization, authentication, access approval and audit. DAC is the preferred mechanism but yet it is vulnerable to Trojan horse attacks; hence a combination approach of DAC and MAC is better. Other access control techniques employed by the OS are rule-based access control and role-based access control. The OS has an access control list for every file and folder that contains a set of permissions associated with an object, it also specifies which subjects are allowed access to an object, and what operations they can carry out on it. An access control list (ACL) is a list of access control entries (ACE). In other words, ACL is a table that tells the OS which permissions and access rights (read, write, execute, etc.) each user or group has to a particular object. With the help of ACL, the OS can perform system-wide security policies for actions such as auditing and logging resource access.

4.8 Other Operating System Functions—Extended System

The operating system also wears the hat of an extended system. It performs several other functions—given below:

1. **System Performance—Analysis and Improvement**

   The OS manages several aspects of system performance. The OS records delays between a request for a service and response from the system. It also ensures that the system is running at peak performance and is able to meet the demands and needs of the users and businesses.

   It keeps track of system performance with the help of short-term and long-term online data for "after-the-fact" analysis of service levels, job delays, resource usage trends and several other performance-related parameters.

   There are several tools used by the OS to monitor system performance and pinpoint performance gaps. There are two main types: real-time and log-based. Real-time tools help to measure the current system state and provide up-to-date information about the system performance. Log-based tools are used to record system performance information for post-processing and analysis, and to find issues and trends in the system performance. Some of the popular tools are Windows Task Manager, Windows Performance Monitor, and Windows Performance Data Log Service. Such type of tools help the OS to perform continuous monitoring and fine tuning of system performance.

2. **Accounting—Resource and Time Usage**

   Accounting involves keeping track of time and resources used by various jobs, processes and users. The OS maintains an activity log for each and every user. It also keeps a record of which user uses which type of resource and for how much time. Usage statistics like number of database operations, CPU time used, etc., is maintained by the OS.

   This log of records is used for accounting purposes. Activity logs may also provide recovery and backup in the event of a system failure. The data and information in the log can be used for trend analysis, billing, statistics, auditing, cost allocation, capacity planning, and also for improving the overall efficiency of a system. These logs can help in making assessments of capacity requirements for future workloads. In multitasking environment, the OS accounting function enhances the system performance by ensuring efficient allocation of resources to each process.

3. **Error Handling—Detection and Correction**

   Error is a condition when the output information does not match with the input data and also errors may occur in the memory, in the CPU and in the I/O devices. In the case of networking, error detection refers to the methods used to detect noise or other interferences introduced into data while it is transmitted from source to destination.

Error detection and correction cannot be handled by normal user programs as these processes and tasks are too critical. Only the OS can keep such conditions in check by monitoring, and in moderate cases, it can adopt altering the area of memory or deallocation of memory for a faulty process, and in extremely critical cases, relinquishing CPU of a process that goes into an infinite loop or in a hang.

The most popular error detection methods are parity and checksum. Parity involves adding a bit to the data that enables the target device to determine whether the data was received correctly; it is used for checking errors in computer-generated data. The parity bit for each unit is set so that all bytes have either an odd number or an even number of set bits. For example, the OS stores data into memory and sets the parity bit using odd parity. Thereafter, when a value is retrieved from memory, the system checks its parity. If the parity is still odd, the system returns the value. If it is even, the system may return the value along with a warning message that the value may have been garbled or corrupted. A checksum is used to ensure the integrity of data after it has been transmitted from one storage device to another or from one computer to another. In the checksum error detection method, the sender uses a checksum generator mechanism/formula to arrive at numerical value based on the number of set bits in the data. Then at the receiver's end, the OS applies the same generator formula to see if this numerical value is the same. If it is the same then everything is fine or else the data/message is corrupted.

To avoid such conditions, the operating system constantly monitors the system for detecting the errors. It produces dumps, traces, error messages and uses other debugging and error-detecting methods.

To avoid hardware problems, the OS constantly monitors the system for detecting the errors and fixing these errors. Examples of such errors include memory overflow, bad sectors on hard disk and many more. Both software and hardware errors must be detected and handled appropriately. Diagnostic and debugging tools help system users and administrators in identifying the cause of the errors. Most operating systems have complex error avoidance or recovery systems like redundant array of independent disks (RAID) and backups.

RAID provides a way of storing the same data in different places on multiple hard disks. By placing data on multiple disks helps in fault tolerance and to increase storage capacity. RAID also lets input/output operations overlap in a balanced way, thereby improving performance. Since multiple disks increase the mean time between failures (MTBF), storing data redundantly also increases fault tolerance. RAID uses the technique of disk mirroring or disk striping, which involves partitioning each drive's storage space into units ranging from a sector (512 bytes) up to several megabytes. RAID appears to the OS as a single logical hard disk. There are various levels of RAID: RAID 0, RAID 1, RAID 2, RAID 3, RAID 4, RAID 5, RAID 6 and Nested RAID levels.

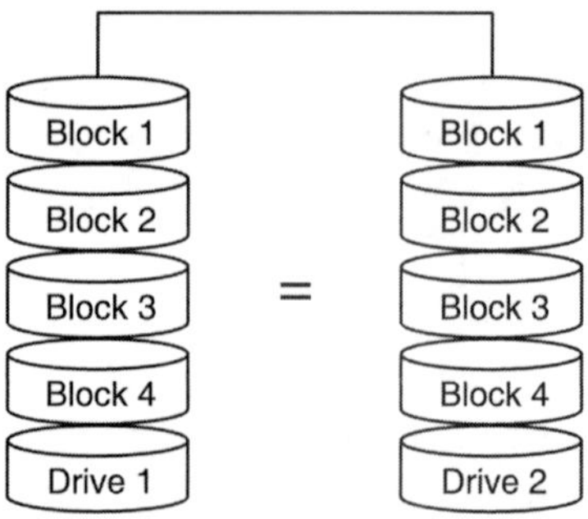

Figure 14: RAID DISK MIRRORING

4.9 Questions for Reflection

1. List the main functions of an operating system?
2. What are the differences between process and thread?
3. What are the different types of operating systems?
4. List the basic functions of process management?
5. What is meant by access control?
6. What is the ready state of a process?
7. What is pre-emptive and non pre-emptive scheduling?
8. What is a kernel?

5

Central Processing Unit—The Brain

The main unit or element inside the computer is the Central Processing Unit or CPU. It is the brain of a computer system that runs the show inside it. CPU is referred to simply as the central processor, but more commonly called processor or microprocessor. It is the unifying system of the computer. The CPU is a highly complex, extensive set of electronic circuitry. It contains all the circuitry that a computer needs to manipulate data and execute instructions. The type of CPU in a computer not only affects its overall performance, but it can also dictate what type of software it uses.

Spotlight Tip
The CPU is responsible for interpreting and executing most of the commands from the software and hardware. All the work that is done on a computer is performed directly or indirectly by the CPU. It is the primary component of a computer that processes instructions. It contains the electronic circuits that make the computer to follow instructions from read only memory (ROM) or from a program in random access memory (RAM).

On personal computers, the CPU is usually housed in a single chip called a microprocessor. The major components of a CPU are the Control Unit, Arithmetic Logic Unit, Memory, Registers and Cache. For many years, most CPUs only had one processor (most CPUs in the past contained a single executing core), but these days they can have more than one processor—a CPU with two processors or processing cores is called a dual-core CPU, with four cores is called quad-core CPUs, with six is called hexa-core or with eight processors is called octo-core. These are multi-core in nature—a multiple core processor has multiple processors within a single processor package. This enables the operating system to run multiple applications simultaneously. Most computers especially for personal use will have a single CPU and that single CPU may have multiple cores. One will find multi-CPU configuration on servers and supercomputers that need as much number-crunching power as they can get.

The two main categories of processors are 32-bit and 64-bit. Over the last several years, CPUs have been moving from 32-bit processors to 64-bit processors. 64-bit processors can manage twice the data than that of a 32-bit processor. A 32-bit processor can process 32-bits of information at a time. A 64-bit processor can process 64-bits of information.

In order to carry out its work properly, a CPU must have two inputs: instructions and data. Instructions tell the CPU what actions need to be performed on the data. The CPU can also read information from external ports such as USB or an extra hard disk.

The CPU operates using an internal clock. This speed is also referred to as frequency. When selecting a CPU, we have to ensure that the motherboard supports the CPU speed. Most motherboards automatically detect the speed. If not, we might have to use jumpers or edit the CMOS to configure the speed.

In addition to clock speed and bandwidth, CPUs are classified as being either complex instruction set computer (CISC) or reduced instruction set computer (RISC). The CISC architecture contains a large set of computer instructions that range from very simple to very complex and specialized, and this approach attempts to minimize the number of instructions per program, sacrificing the number of cycles per instruction. In CISC design, single instructions can execute several low-level operations or are capable of multi-step operations or addressing modes within single instructions. RISC focuses on reducing the number and complexity of instructions. RISC only uses simple instructions that can be executed within one clock cycle. RISC requires less transistors of hardware space than complex instructions, leaving more room for general purpose registers.

Table 9: Differences between CISC and RISC

CISC	RISC
High cycles per second, small code sizes	Low cycles per second, large code sizes
Memory-to-memory: "LOAD" and "STORE" incorporated in instructions	Register to register: "LOAD" and "STORE" are independent instructions
Emphasis on hardware	Emphasis on software
Includes multi-clock complex instructions	Single-clock, reduced instruction only

While other components also play a key role in determining system performance, but the CPU is probably the most important single component affecting the system performance in a computer. The other devices play a supportive role by helping the CPU to reach its full potential.

The speed of a computer depends largely on the speed of the CPU and this speed is in turn based on a number of factors like cache memory and clock frequency. The quality of the CPU determines with how much reliability the computer system will function. Factors like how much energy the CPU needs, determines the level of reliability and stability of a computer system. Moreover, modern processors like Pentium with MMX technology facilitate the use of specialized software thereby enchaining software support which was not usable on earlier systems.

5.1 Logic Gates and Truth Tables—Building Blocks of Digital Circuits

Computers and other digital systems are constructed using logic gates. Arrays of logic gates are found in integrated circuits. They are electronic circuits with two inputs and an output; most logic gates have two inputs and one output. They are the elementary building blocks of a digital circuit. These gates require a power supply. They perform operations on Boolean values. Boolean Algebra has had a massive impact on computers and the language that computers understand is the language of 1s and 0s, which is boolean. Most logic gates have two inputs and one output. There is always a time delay between an input being applied and the output responding.

Logic gates may have more than one input, but generally only have one digital output, except in some special cases. Inputs are driven by voltages having two nominal values, e.g. 0V and 5V representing logic 0 and logic 1 respectively. Output provides two nominal values of voltage, e.g. 0V and 5V representing logic 0 and logic 1 respectively.

A logic gate receives two incoming electric currents, compares them, and then sends a new, outgoing electric current depending on what the result is. The most common gates are: AND, OR, NOT, XOR (Exclusive OR), NAND (NOT AND) and NOR (NOT OR). The AND, OR and NOT Gates are the principal gates, and the rest are hybrid gates. The NOR gate and the NAND gate are called universal gates, as combinations of them can be used to accomplish any of the basic operations and can produce an inverter, an OR gate or an AND gate.

By combining logic gates, a whole range of electronic devices can be constructed, right from flip flops to computer processors.

Spotlight Tip
Using various combinations of logic gates, complex operations can be performed. As integrated circuits become more advanced, the required physical volume for each individual logic gate decreases and then these devices become capable of performing more complex operations at even higher speeds.

A truth table is used to show how Boolean logic works and it helps to understand the behavior of logic gates. It is used to represent the Boolean expression of a logic gate function. The relationship between the inputs and the output can be depicted in a truth table. A and B represent the inputs and Q is the output. All permutations of the inputs are listed on the left and the output of the circuit is listed on the right. Such a table typically contains several rows and columns that show how a logic circuit's output responds to various combinations of the inputs, using logic 1 for true and logic 0 for false.

A truth table is a way of analyzing how the validity of statements, also called propositions, behaves when one uses a logical "and" or a logical "or" to combine them. The basic operations using these propositions in a truth table are:

1. **Negation**—a "not" operation is one that is the complement/opposite of the original value. If *A* is true, then ~*A*/$\overline{A}$ is false. If *A* is false, then ~A/$\overline{A}$ is true.
2. **Conjunction**—an "and" operation where both statements must be true for the compound statement to be true. Conjunction "A and B" is symbolized by A.B or A$\wedge$B. A conjunction is true when both of its combined parts are true; otherwise it is false.
3. **Disjunction**—an "or" operation where both statements must be false in order for the compound statement to be false. Disjunction "A or B" is symbolized by AVB or A+B. A disjunction is false when both of its combined parts are false; otherwise in all other combinations it is true.

5.1.1 Boolean Algebra—Uses Binary Numbers

Boolean Algebra is a branch of algebra in which the values of the variables are the truth values: true and false, usually denoted as 1 and 0 respectively. As it uses only the binary numbers, i.e., 0 and 1, Boolean Algebra is also called as Binary Algebra. It specifies the relationship between Boolean variables which is used to design combinational logic circuits using logic gates. Boolean algebra was invented by George Boole in 1854. Boolean Algebra is the mathematical foundation of digital circuits.

A Boolean variable can have only two values either a binary 0 for "low" or a binary 1 for "high". Complement of a variable is represented by an over line or over bar $\overline{(\ )}$. For example, complement of variable A is represented as $\overline{A}$. For example, if A = 0 then $\overline{A}$ = 1 and if A = 1 then $\overline{A}$ = 0. Logical ANDing of two or more variables is represented by writing a dot between them, for example, A.B or A.B.C and logical ORing of variables is represented by a plus sign (+) between them, for example A + B or A + B + C.

The diagrammatic representation of logic gates and truth tables for the various logic gates is discussed in the following points.

1. **NOT Gate**—the simplest possible gate is called an "inverter" or a NOT gate. It takes one bit as input and produces as output its opposite. In other words, the NOT gate produces an inverted version of the input as the output. For example, if the input is A then the output is NOT A, which is also shown with a bar over A. This gate performs logical negation on its input. In other words, if the input is true, then the output will be false and *vice versa*. It will give a high output if the input is low and *vice versa*. The following is a diagram of the NOT gate. It is a triangle with a circle on the right. The circle indicates negation.

Table 10: Truth Table for the NOT Gate

NOT Gate	
A	$\overline{A}$ = Q
0	1
1	0

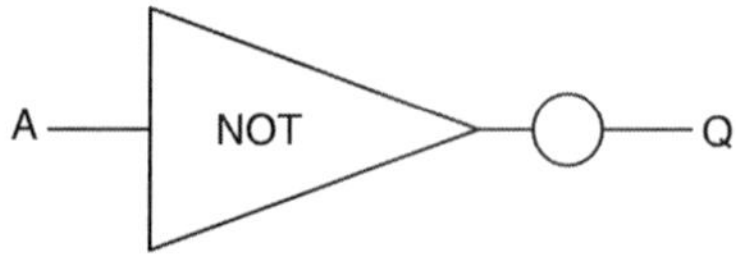

Figure 15: NOT LOGIC GATE

2. **AND Gate**—AND operation is signified by A.B. Other notations are AB and A^B and they are called the intersection of A and B. The output is true when both inputs are true, otherwise the output is false. It is an electronic circuit that gives a high output (1) only if all its inputs are high.

Table 11: Truth Table for the AND Gate

AND Gate		
A (Input)	**B (Input)**	**A.B = Q (Output)**
0	0	0
0	1	0
1	0	0
1	1	1

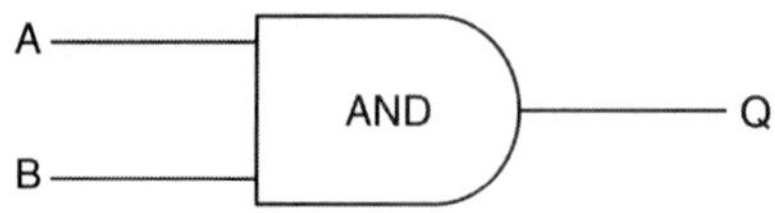

Figure 16: AND LOGIC GATE

3. **OR Gate**—the output is true if either or both of the inputs are true. If both inputs are false, then the output is false. It will give a high output if any of the inputs is high. It implements logical disjunction. The Boolean expression for the OR gate is denoted by a plus sign (+).

Table 12: Truth Table for the OR Gate

OR Gate		
A (Input)	**B (Input)**	**A + B = Q (Output)**
0	0	0
0	1	1
1	0	1
1	1	1

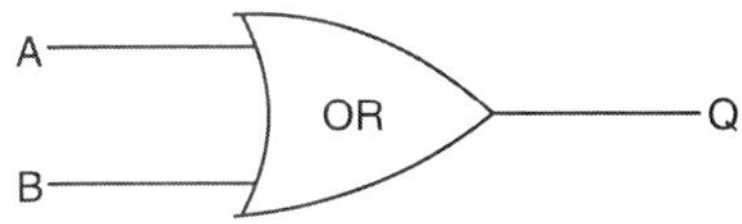

Figure 17: OR LOGIC GATE

4. **XOR Gate (Exclusive OR gate)**—is a digital logic gate with two or more inputs and one output that performs exclusive disjunction. The output of an XOR gate is true only when exactly one of its inputs is true. If both of its inputs are true or both of its inputs are false, then the output is false. It is a circuit which will give a high output if either, but not both, of its inputs are high. The XOR output is represented as $A \oplus B$. An encircled plus sign ($\oplus$) is used to show the EOR operation.

Table 13: Truth Table for the XOR Gate

XOR Gate		
A (Input)	**B (Input)**	**$A \oplus B = Q$ (Output)**
0	0	0
0	1	1
1	0	1
1	1	0

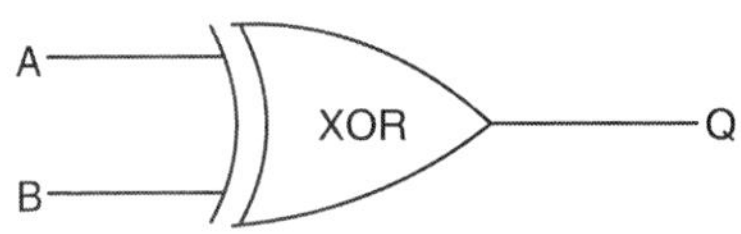

Figure 18: XOR LOGIC GATE

5. **NAND Gate (NOT AND or Negated AND gate)**—is a logic gate that produces an output which is false only if all its inputs are true. Its output is complement to that of the AND gate. The boolean expression of AND gate is A.B whereas that of NAND gate is $\overline{A.B}$. Its behavior is the opposite of AND gate.

Table 14: Truth Table for the NAND Gate

NAND Gate		
A (Input)	**B (Input)**	$\overline{A.B}$ **= Q (Output)**
0	0	1
0	1	1
1	0	1
1	1	0

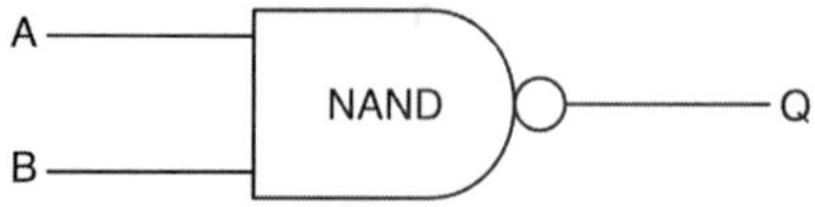

Figure 19: NAND LOGIC GATE

6. **NOR (NOT OR)**—the NOR or "Not OR" gate is also a combination of two separate functions, Not and OR connected together to form a single logic gate function. Its output will be true only when all of its inputs are false. For any other combination of inputs, the output is a logic 0 level. This gate is the reverse or complementary form of the OR gate. The Boolean expression is denoted by a plus sign (+) with an over line ($\overline{\ }$) over the expression: $\overline{A + B}$.

Table 15: Truth Table for the NOR Gate

NOR Gate		
A (Input)	**B (Input)**	$\overline{A+B}$ **= Q (Output)**
0	0	1
0	1	0
1	0	0
1	1	0

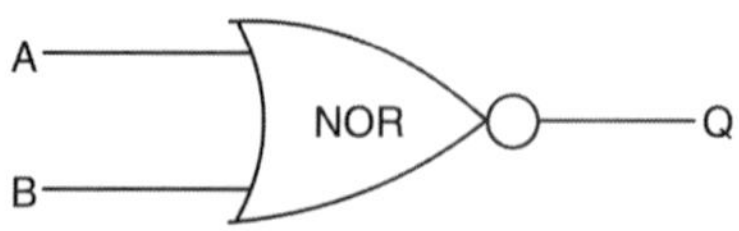

Figure 20: NOR LOGIC GATE

5.2 Main Components of CPU—Memory, ALU, Cache and CU

The CPU has to perform several critical functions like fetch and interpret instructions, fetch and process data, and output the data results. These critical functions need internal memory storage and remembering the location of the instruction to fetch next. For doing all this, the CPU needs the following components.

5.2.1 Memory or Storage Unit—Holds Data and Instructions

Memory is storage component of a computer that holds data and instructions for processing (both before and after processing). Memory can be classified into two types: primary memory and secondary memory. There are two main types of primary memory on the chip: Read-only Memory (ROM) and Random Access Memory (RAM). Secondary storage holds permanent or semi-permanent data on some external magnetic or optical medium like CD-ROM, Flash memory, etc. Secondary storage is not directly accessible by the CPU, as it is not accessed via the input/output channels; it is an external device.

Before an instruction can be executed, data and instructions must be placed in the memory from an input device or a secondary storage device. Once the required data and instructions are in the memory, the CPU performs the following four steps for each instruction:

1. The CU fetches the instruction from memory.
2. The CU decodes the instruction into commands and directs that the necessary data be moved from memory to the ALU. Steps 1 and 2 together are called instruction time or I-time.
3. The ALU executes the arithmetic or logical instruction. It performs the actual operation on the data.
4. The ALU stores the result of this operation in memory or in a register. Steps 3 and 4 together are called execution time or E-time.

The CU finally directs the memory to release the result to an output device or a secondary storage device. I-time and E-time together is called a machine cycle or processor cycle. A machine cycle is the basic operation performed by the CPU. A single machine cycle instruction may be made up of a number of sub-instructions, each of which must take at least one clock cycle. It is called a fetch–decode–execute cycle, in which the CPU retrieves a program instruction from its memory, determines what actions the instruction dictates, and performs those actions.

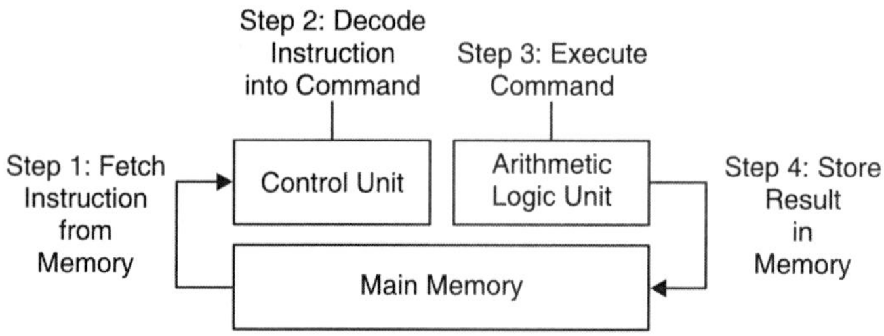

Figure 21: MACHINE CYCLE

The location in memory for each piece of data and instruction is identified by an address. Each location has an address number. These address numbers of the locations remain the same (just like normal mailboxes), but the contents (instructions and data) keep changing. Unlike a mailbox, however, a memory location can hold only a fixed amount of data. In other words, an address can hold only a fixed number of bytes. Each data address is referred to by a name and it is symbolic address. Using these addresses, the CU finds the specific piece of data and instruction.

ROM has been installed on a computer by the manufacturer. Once data has been written onto a ROM chip, it cannot be altered or removed, and it can only be read. This is because the chip is manufactured with a series of fuses. The chip is programmed by burning fuses, which is a permanent process (it cannot be reversed). The open fuses are read as ones, while the burned fuses are read as zeros. ROM is also referred to as non-volatile memory, whereas RAM is also called volatile memory. Data in ROM is permanently stored and is not erased when the computer is shut down. The similarity in both memory types is that they are both directly accessed by CPU. A computer uses RAM to hold temporary data and instructions needed to complete tasks. This enables CPU to access instructions and data stored in memory very quickly.

There are different types of **ROM** including programmable read-only memory (PROM) that is manufactured as blank memory and erasable programmable read-only memory (EPROM). The difference between a PROM and a ROM is that a PROM is manufactured as blank memory, whereas a ROM is programmed during the manufacturing process. To write data onto PROM, a special device EPROM is needed. It is a special type of PROM that can be erased by exposing it to ultraviolet light, and once erased it can be reprogrammed. Another variation is EEPROM (electrically erasable programmable read-only memory) and it requires electricity to be erased.

RAM is a temporary memory as data in RAM is not permanently stored; hence volatile memory. When the computer is turned off, data stored in RAM is deleted. RAM requires a continuous flow of electricity to retain data. Commercially available RAM chips can be plugged-in and plugged-out of a computer's motherboard. RAM can be compared to a person's short-term memory that focuses only on the work at hand at that point in time.

How to Find Out the Amount of RAM
In Windows-based computers, click Start followed by Settings, System and then About. A window will open displaying the amount of RAM available. In Mac computers, one can see the memory by clicking the Mac button in the top left corner of the screen, and clicking About this Mac in the opening menu.

There are different types of RAM including Dynamic Random Access Memory (DRAM) and Static Random Access Memory (SRAM). DRAM must be periodically refreshed. DRAM stores information in a cell containing a capacitor and transistor and because of this design, these cells must be refreshed with electricity every few milliseconds for the memory to retain its contents. The capacitor/transistor can be either charged or discharged and this provides the two states: "1" or "0" for the cell. SRAM is faster and more reliable than DRAM. SRAM does not need to be refreshed like DRAM.

There are many differences between ROM and RAM that have been discussed in the previous paragraphs and recapped in the table below. There are also similarities between these two—both types of memory are used by a computer, and they are both required for the computer to operate properly and efficiently.

Table 16: Differences between ROM and RAM

ROM	RAM
Stands for Read-Only memory	Stands for Random Access Memory
Pre-written, pre-stored	Data/programs are not permanently pre-written or pre-stored
Used primarily in the start up process of a computer, critical programs and it is often used to install the permanent instructions into a computer like the basic input/output system (BIOS)	Used for normal operations after the operating system has been loaded
It is a type of non-volatile memory and does not require a constant source of power to retain information stored on it	It is a type of volatile memory and requires a constant source of power to retain information
Retains data even the when computer is powered off	Cannot retain data when the computer is turned off
Writing data to ROM is a slow process	Writing data to RAM is a much faster process
ROM chips are smaller in size and can store only several megabytes per chip	RAM chips are bigger in size and can store multiple gigabytes (GB) of data per chip

A memory unit has two connotations: the amount of data that can be stored in the memory or storage unit and in what terms the storage capacity is expressed.

Table 17: Storage Units

Unit	Storage	Description
Bit (B)	Binary digit, 0 or 1	It is the smallest unit of data. A bit has a single binary value, either 0 or 1.
Nibble	4 bits	Half a byte (four bits) is called a nibble.
Byte (B)	8 bits	A byte is eight bits.
Kilobyte (KB)	1,024 bytes	A unit of computer memory or data storage capacity equal to 1,024 bytes.
Megabyte (MB)	1,024 KB	One megabyte is equal to 1,024 kilobytes. In the early days of computing, megabyte was considered to be a large amount of data. While CD capacity is measured in megabytes, the capacity of most other forms of media, such as hard drives and flash drives is measured in gigabytes or terabytes.
Gigabyte (GB)	1,024 MB	One gigabyte (GB) is 1,024 megabytes. Examples: A flash memory card in a camera can have storage of 16 GB.
Terabyte (TB)	1,024 GB	A terabyte is 1,024 gigabytes. Used for hi-definition recording or broadcast-quality video.
Petabyte (PB)	1,024 TB	A petabyte is 1,024 terabytes.
Exabyte (EB)	1,024 PB	It is equivalent to 1,024 petabytes. Several hundred exabytes of data are transferred over the Internet each year.
Zettabyte (ZB)	1,024 EB	It is equivalent to 1,024 exabytes or 1,000,000,000,000,000,000,000 bytes.
Yottabyte (YB)	1,024 ZB	It is equivalent to a quadrillion gigabytes, 1,000 zettabytes or 1,000,000,000,000,000,000,000,000 bytes.

5.5.2 Cache—A High-speed Access Area

CPU Cache (pronounced cash), also called CPU memory, is memory that the processor can access directly and quickly without using the regular system RAM. It is normally integrated directly with the CPU chip or placed on a separate chip that has a separate bus interconnected with the CPU. Cache is a high-speed access area that can be a reserved section of main memory or storage device. The two main types of cache are memory cache and disk cache.

Cache is an extremely important component in a computer and it contains active data and information that the CPU accesses immediately and frequently. It is a fast memory that a CPU can access as quickly as possible. It is faster than the system Random Access Memory. This faster memory runs at a refresh rate that is closer to the CPU's clock speed, which minimizes wasted cycles. The job of the cache is to eliminate as many wasted cycles as possible. The faster the CPU is, the more cache is needed to improve system performance. It is used to improve application performance, and to reduce latency and access time. Latency is the delay from input into a system to desired outcome. Cache is closer to a processor core, which stores copies of the data from frequently used main memory locations.

The goal of cache is to make sure that the CPU has the next bit of data it will need already loaded into cache by the time it goes searching for it; this is called a cache hit.

There are three primary types of cache writing strategies:

1. **Write-through cache**—cache performs all write operations in parallel. Data is written to the main memory and the L1 cache simultaneously.
2. **Write-around cache**—similar to write-through cache, but write I/O is written directly to permanent storage, bypassing the cache.
3. **Write-back**—(also called *copy-back cache*) data modifications like write operations to data stored in the L1 cache are not copied to the main memory until absolutely necessary. Write-back gives better performance than write-through because it reduces the number of write operations to the main memory. With this benefit, comes a limitation that data may be lost if the system crashes.

Cache has grown from a single level to as much as three levels on a modern-day CPU. These levels are referred to as L1 for level one, L2 for level two and so on and so forth. The multiple levels help each other to improve system performance. As a CPU processes data in cycles; it can make calculations only as quickly as it can be fed data. If there is no data available then the CPU does not do any processing or calculation and that particular cycle is wasted. This is where the levels come into play to ensure that data is available and exchanged based on the CPU needs. The CPU can talk to its own memory a whole lot faster than it can to the main memory. Hence every time the CPU requests data, it 'caches' a copy to its local memory. This allows it to fetch it much faster whenever the need arises.

Between the CPU and RAM, there are several levels of cache. We can depict these levels as a pyramid. At the topmost level, we have CPU and as we go down towards the RAM, we pass through several levels of cache. The closer a cache level is to the CPU, the smaller and faster will it be. The following figure depicts these points.

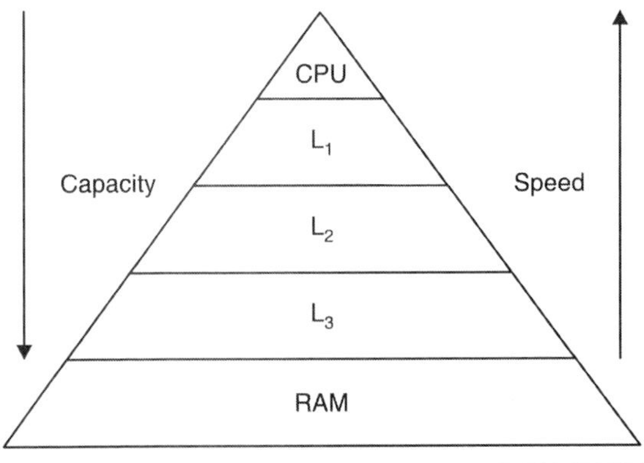

Figure 22: CAPACITY AND SPEED FOR THE MEMORY LEVELS

The L1 cache is small in comparison to other levels, making it faster than the rest. The L2 cache is slightly larger, therefore has some latency. The L3 cache is the largest among all the levels. L3 though it is slower than the earlier two levels, it is still faster than RAM. These levels work hand in hand to improve computer performance. On multi-core systems, each processor normally has its own L1 cache. Some processors might have two L1 caches, one for data and one for instructions. The L3 cache feeds the L2 cache, and the L2 cache feeds the L1 cache, which in turn feeds the CPU. When a request is made to a system, CPU has some set of data and instructions to execute, which it fetches from the RAM. Thus to reduce delay, CPU maintains a cache with some data and instructions which it anticipates it will be need. L1 cache is first searched and if the data and instructions are not present in the L1 cache then it looks in the L2 cache, and subsequently L3 level is searched. If it is not present in any of the cache levels, CPU will finally fetch the instruction from main memory and place them in cache. This is called a cache miss. The number of cache levels and their sizes depends on the architecture.

Caching provides many benefits: cache memory makes the main memory appear much larger and faster than it really is. It helps to speed up the process of fetching data and instructions. It consumes less access time as compared to main memory. It improves the memory transfer rates.

A Word of Caution
The disadvantages of cache memory are: cache memory has limited storage capacity and it is very expensive.

Apart from hardware cache like CPU cache, there are also other types of hardware cache like GPU cache, disk cache and web cache. A disk cache is a mechanism to speed up the process of reading from or writing to a hard disk. A disk cache is also referred to as cache buffer or disk buffer. A disk cache is an integrated part of the hard disk and is a standard feature of most hard disk drives. The size of disk cache ranges from 128 MB in standard disks to 1 GB in solid state disks. A disk cache stores the most recent and frequently used data and programs. When a computer needs these same data or programs, the operating system first reviews and searches the disk cache. If the data or program is found there, the operating system and memory quickly deliver the data to the program. A disk cache can also be soft disk cache when it's implemented on the RAM rather than the host hard disk. Web browsers use cache to improve performance for frequently accessed web pages. This cache represents temporary storage location on a computer for files (cascading style sheet, multimedia content, html files) downloaded by a browser to display websites. When a user revisits a web page, a browser checks which content was updated in the meantime and only downloads updated files or what is not already stored there in the cache. This loads the accessed page faster as the server load reduces and the bandwidth usage on both the server side and client side reduces. Web caching saves the network from the burden of additional traffic.

5.2.3 Control Unit—Manages and Coordinates All the Units

A Control Unit (CU) is considered to be the most complex part of CPU and it is driven by the processor clock. It is responsible for directing the flow of instructions and data within the CPU. A control unit works by receiving input information that it converts into control signals, which are then sent to the central processor. Then the processor tells the attached hardware what operations to carry out. The signals to be generated at a certain moment depend on various factors like the condition and status flags of the processor, the actual steps and instructions to be executed and external signals received on the system bus. Most resources are managed by the CU.

The CU unit does not execute program instructions; rather it directs other parts of the system to do so. It must communicate with both the arithmetic/logic unit and memory. The CU basically fetches instructions of programs from the main memory to initiate sequences of microoperations. The operations executed on data stored in registers are called microoperations. For each instruction, the control unit causes the CPU to go through a sequence of control steps, and in each control step, the control unit issues a set of signals which causes the corresponding microoperations to be executed. One clock pulse triggers the activities related to one control step, and for each clock pulse, the CU generates the control signals corresponding to the microoperations to be executed in that respective control step.

The task performed by any microoperation falls in one of the following categories: perform an arithmetic or logic operation using registers for input and output; transfer data from one register to another; transfer data from a register to an external interface (system bus); or transfer data from an external interface to a register. In order for the execution of a microoperation to occur, one or more control signals have to be issued; they allow the corresponding computation or data transfer to occur.

The purpose of CU is to run the whole computer. It manages and coordinates all the units of the computer. CU performs this using the instructions stored in RAM and ROM. It receives instructions that are stored in RAM and ROM and controls the operations of other components or devices through these instructions.

Spotlight Tip
To carry out its work, a CU needs to communicate with both the arithmetic/logic unit and memory. The CU tells the computer's memory, arithmetic logic unit and input and output devices how to respond to program instructions.

The CU does not take inputs, processes or stores data, or gives out outputs—what it essentially does is that it controls these operations when they are performed by their respective components or devices. In other words, the CU controls the complete workflow of the CPU. The functions of CU vary from CPU to CPU; the CU functions depend on the internal architecture of the CPU.

To generate the control signals in a proper sequence, several techniques exist to do so. Most techniques fall into two main categories. There are two types of control units:

1. **Hardwired**—when the control signals are generated by hardware using conventional logic design techniques, the CU is said to be hardwired. This type of CU is implemented through the use of a combinatorial and sequential circuit that generate complete timing which corresponds with execution of each instruction. As the name implies, the microinstructions are hardwired into the computer.

   The design is based on a fixed architecture—the CU is made up of logic gates, digital circuits, flip-flops and encoder and decoder circuits that are wired in a specific and fixed way. The CU is a combinatorial circuit; it gets a set of inputs (from IR, flags, clock, system bus) and transforms them into a set of control signals. If the instruction set is changed then a change in wiring is required. Hardwired control units are generally faster than microprogrammed but less flexible as hardwired design is difficult to modify.

2. Microprogrammable (microprogrammed) control units—the main advantage of this type of CU is its simple structure. An alternative way of generating the control signals is that of micro-programmed control.

   A microinstruction cycle handles timing in a simple way. Therefore, the design is easier to modify and flexible. However, it is slower than hardwired design as additional time is spent in decoding microinstructions and synching them.

Spotlight Tip
Hardwired CU is faster but costlier; control functions are implemented in hardware; it is not flexible to accommodate new system specification; and has a complex design process. Microprogrammed CU is slower but cheaper; control functions are implemented in software; more flexible to accommodate new system specification; and has a simple design process.

A recap of the functions performed by the CU is as follows:

1. The CU implements the microprocessor instruction set.
2. It determines the sequence in which programs and instructions are executed.
3. It extracts, decodes and executes instructions from the memory, and gathers required data and operands to perform these instructions.
4. Then sends the necessary signals to the ALU to perform the necessary operations like multiplication, addition, etc.
5. Then it performs receiving and sending results of operations of ALU to primary memory.
6. It also performs fetching programs from input and secondary memory and brings them to the primary memory.
7. The CU sends results from the ALU stored in the primary memory to output.

5.2.4 Arithmetic Logic Unit—Intelligence Center

Arithmetic Logic Unit (ALU) is the fundamental building block of the central processing unit in a computer; this is where the intelligence center of a computer system is located. It is also known as an integer unit (IU).

ALU can add and compare numbers and it makes decisions by determining if a number is greater, less or equal to the other number. It is used to perform arithmetic operations like division, subtraction, multiplication and addition, and logic operations like AND/OR/NOR/NAND/NOR calculations. Examples of logical operations are comparisons of letters, special characters and numbers. It is designed to perform integer calculations—besides addition and subtraction, it performs multiplication of integers. Division and other non-integer calculations (floating point numbers or fractions) are normally performed by the component called Floating-Point Unit (FPU). The ALU design varies from processor to processor: in some processors ALU also performs floating point operations too.

Spotlight Tip
In some computer systems, the ALU is divided into an AU and LU. The AU performs the arithmetic operations, and the LU performs the logical operations.

Simple ALUs will perform operations like boolean logic, integer arithmetic (add or subtract) and shifts. The basic ALU operates on integers rather than floating point numbers. Two numbers (operands), A and B, are given as the input of the ALU, and also an instruction called an 'opcode,' such as 'add', 'subtract', 'multiply', 'divide', 'compare'. Along with the output/result (Q), a set of status flags are set which can include 'Carry', 'Zero', 'Negative', 'Overflow'. The ALU carries out the requested operation on A and B and produces an output result. One operand for the ALU is always contained in a register. The other operand may be in a register or may be part of the machine instruction itself. The result of the operation is then put into a general purpose register. More complex ALUs will handle a wider range of integer operations (multiply and divide), floating point operations and mathematical functions (sine, square root, log, etc.).

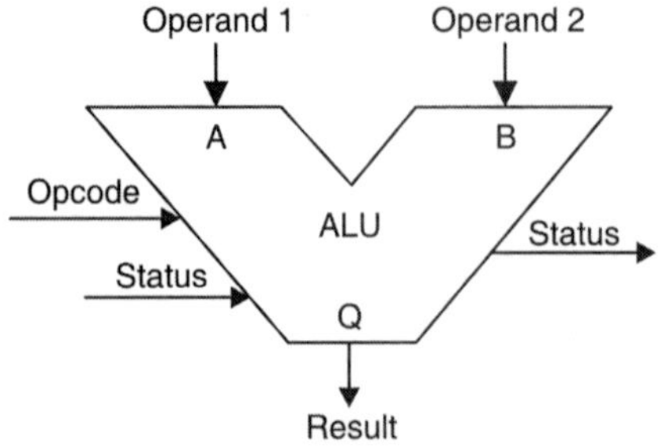

Figure 23: ARITHMETIC LOGIC UNIT

FPU also called math coprocessor is a specialized part of a computer system specially designed to carry out operations on floating point numbers. FPU is used to perform high-level mathematical operations like roots, trigonometric functions, bitshifting, algorithms and long division in a fast and accurate manner. FPU is used with math-intensive programs and applications like databases, spreadsheets and graphics. While early FPUs were standalone processors, most are now integrated inside a CPU. You can usually add FPU by inserting the FPU chip on the motherboard. Older central processing units used an external FPU chip, but now most CPUs have built-in FPU. The instruction set of the FPU chip is different from that of the primary CPU. For the computer system to work efficiently, a program must be able to detect the existence of a FPU and then execute instructions that are FPU-specific.

There are three ways of executing FPU operations: (a) through an add-on FPU (b) through an integrated FPU where operations may be divided between simpler and more complex operations, and for simpler operations the hardware may be used and for more complex operations software may be used and (c) through floating point library or floating point unit emulator.

Some examples of CPU-FPU combinations are Intel 8086 (CPU) and 8087 (FPU) and Intel 286 (CPU) and FPU (287). CPUs like Intel Pentium II/III/Celeron/Xeon and Intel Pentium/Pentium MMX have built-in FPU.

As integer and floating point performance can vary significantly, most CPU benchmarks include both types of calculations. Integer processing speed is typically listed as "integer performance" and is labeled "SPECint". SPECint is maintained by the Standard Performance Evaluation Corporation (SPEC). FPU calculation speed is often listed as "floating point performance" and can be measured in FLOPS (floating-point operations per second).

In more complex architectures and systems, the ALU is divided into two units: the arithmetic unit (AU) and the logic unit (LU). It is the size of the word that the ALU can handle determines the word-size of a processor. For example, a 32-bit processor is one with a 32-bit ALU. Using a combination of logic gates and flip-flops, ALU operations can be performed in less than a microsecond.

5.2.5 Registers—Temporary High-speed Storage Areas

A CPU contains multiple index registers, also known as address registers or registers of modification. A register is a temporary high-speed storage area which is responsible for accepting, storing and transferring data and instructions that are to be processed immediately by the CPU. A register helps to speed up the CPU operations by providing quick access to commonly used values. All data and instructions must be represented in a register before they can be processed. For example, if two numbers are to be added, both numbers must be in a register and the result is also held in a register. A register may hold a storage address, or any kind of data or an instruction. Some instructions specify registers as part of the instruction. Registers are measured by the number of bits they can hold, for example, "16-bit register" or "32-bit register".

Normally, the movement of data and instructions in and out of the registers is completely transparent to programmers and users. Only assembly language programs can work with registers. In high-level languages, the compiler is responsible for translating high-level operations into low-level operations that access registers. At higher levels of hierarchy, memory is faster, smaller and more expensive.

Registers are at the top of the memory hierarchy and are the fastest way for the CPU to process and manipulate data and instructions. Registers perform a variety of functions. There are two main categories: general purpose and special purpose. General purpose registers are used to store data and intermediate results during program execution. Special purpose registers hold program state like stack pointer, program counter and status register.

1. **Accumulator**—a register that is located in ALU and in which short-term, intermediate arithmetic and logic results are stored. It is used to 'accumulate' the result of the currently running instructions.
2. **Program Counter** (PC)—a register (also known as Instruction Pointer Register) that holds the memory address of the next instruction to be fetched. When a program is running, the program counter will often just be incrementing as it addresses one instruction after the other. But in certain cases, there may be a JUMP instruction that causes the sequential flow of the program to jump to another part of the program.
3. **Memory Address Register** (MAR)—a register that holds the memory addresses of data and instructions to be fetched from memory. It is used to access data and instructions from memory during the execution phase.
4. **Memory Data Register** (**MDR or Memory Buffer Register**)—a register of CU that contains the data to be stored in the computer storage or the data after a fetch from the computer storage. This register acts as buffer letting the CPU and memory to act independently without being affected by minor differences in operation.

5. **Instruction Register**—a register that holds the current instruction to be executed. The CU takes instructions from this register, decodes and executes them by sending signals to the appropriate component to carry out the operation.
6. **FLAGS Register (FR)**—the purpose of the FLAGS register is to indicate the status of the CPU. There are two kinds of FLAGS: Control and Status. Control enables or disables certain operations of the CPU. Status reflects the result of an operation carried out by the CPU.
7. **Input/Output Address Register (I/O AR)**—a register that is used to specify the address of a particular I/O device.
8. **Input/Output Buffer Register (I/O BR)**—a register that is used to exchange data between the I/O modules and the CPU.

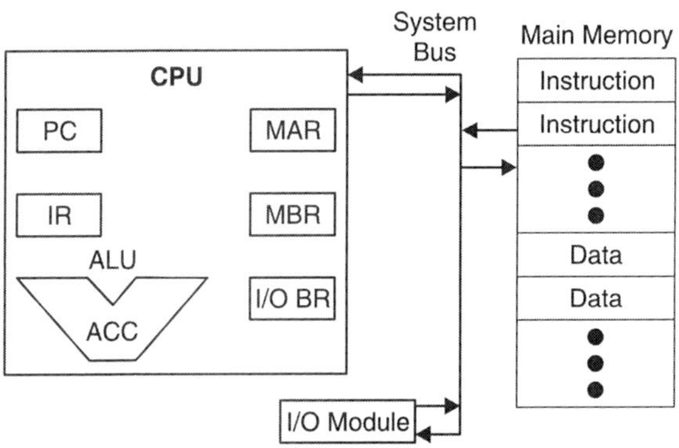

Figure 24: CPU REGISTERS

The number of registers that a CPU has and the size of each register (number of bits) determine the power and speed of the CPU. Registers are normally measured by the number of bits they can hold, for example, a 16-bit register means it can store 16 bits of data or a 32-bit register means it can store 32-bit of data.

5.3 Buses—Electrical Pathway between Devices

A computer bus is a common, shared electrical pathway between multiple devices. A bus has multiple wires (signal lines) through which information flows from one computer component to another. Each wire in the bus carries a single bit of information, which means the more wires a bus contains, the more information it can address. For example, a bus enables the CPU to communicate with the memory. An active device that can initiate its own bus transfer between memory and peripheral devices is called a bus master. A passive device that waits for request/command is called a slave. In a simple system, only the CPU can be bus master but this means that all communications between slave I/O devices must involve the CPU. More sophisticated systems allow other devices or multiple CPUs to take turns at controlling the bus. For example, a network controller card can access a disk controller directly while the CPU performs other operations which do not require the bus. Master is the one who initiates the bus transaction by issuing a command and address, and slave is the one who responds to the master's command by sending data (or receiving data from the master). Most bus masters are connected to the bus by a bus driver/digital amplifier and bus slaves are connected by a receiver. For devices that can function as both master and slave, a bus transceiver is needed.

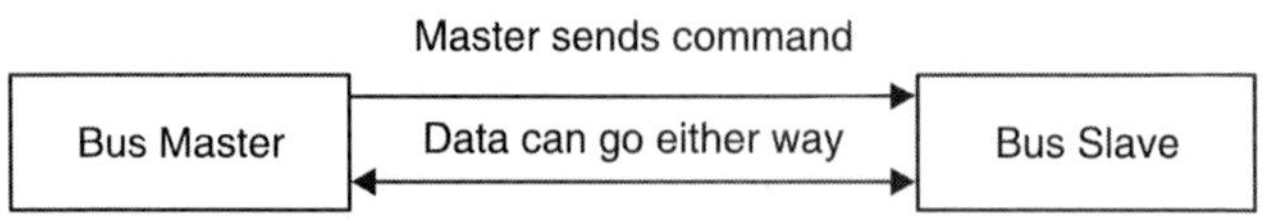

Figure 25: BUS MASTER AND BUS SLAVE

The bus protocol is set of well-defined rules controlling how buses work; it determines the transactions that are supported and the timing of their cycle, and also handles allocation of resources. The basic building block of most

> **A Word of Caution**
>
> A bus is capable of being a parallel or serial bus. A serial data bus carries only one bit at a time while a parallel bus supports multiple data bits over the channel. It may seem that a parallel bus is the best option, but it may not be so. Even though a parallel bus transfers more data per unit it does so simultaneously, which means that all the data arrives at the same time and synchronizing this data is a complicated process.

bus protocols is the four-cycle handshake. The handshake ensures that when two devices want to communicate, one is ready to send and the other is ready to receive. A pair of wires is dedicated to the handshake: *enq* (enquiry) and *ack* (acknowledgement), and extra wires are used for the data transmitted during the handshake. When device 1 raises its output to signal an *enq* (enquiry), it is essentially telling device 2 that it should get ready to listen for data. When device 2 is ready to receive, it raises its output to signal an acknowledgment. At this point, both devices 1 and 2 can transmit or receive. Once the data transfer is complete, device 2 lowers its output, signaling that it has received the data. After seeing that *ack* (acknowledgement) has been made, device 1 lowers its output. The clock component provides synchronization to the bus components.

Benefits of buses include: a single set of wires can be shared in multiple ways, devices/peripherals can be moved between computer systems that use the same bus standard and new devices can be easily added. Disadvantages include: the maximum bus speed is majorly limited by the number of devices on a bus, the length of a bus and the need to support a variety of devices, and the bandwidth of a bus can limit the maximum input/output throughput and this could cause a communication bottleneck. The throughput of a bus is measured in bits per second or megabytes per second.

The main functions of buses:

1. A bus has address lines that match those of the CPU. This allows data to be sent to or taken from specific memory locations.
2. A bus provides the system clock signals to synchronize the peripherals attached to it with the rest of the system.
3. A bus supplies power to various peripherals connected to it.
4. A bus transfers data between computer peripherals connected to it.

5.3.1 Types of Buses—Internal and External

There are two main types of buses: System or Internal and Expansion or External.

1. **System or Internal**—a bus that connects the major components inside a computer. It is used for internal communication purposes. It connects various components inside the case such as CPU, memory and motherboard.

   This bus is a single bus that combines the functions of a data bus to carry information, an address bus to determine where it should be sent, and a control bus to determine its operation/processing.

   The data bus carries data and addresses between the processor and the memory or peripherals. It is bi-directional as it is possible to transfer data both to and from the processor and memory and devices. A data bus contains the contents that have been read from the memory location or are to be written into the memory location. The address bus determines the location in memory that the processor will read data from or write data to. Each of the addresses corresponds to one memory location or one I/O device. The control bus regulates which direction the write and read information need to go. The control bus has control line for read instructions and a control line for write instructions. When the CPU writes data to the main memory, it transmits a signal to the write command line. The CPU also transmits a signal to the read command line when it needs to read. The power bus is used for the power supply to different parts of a computer.

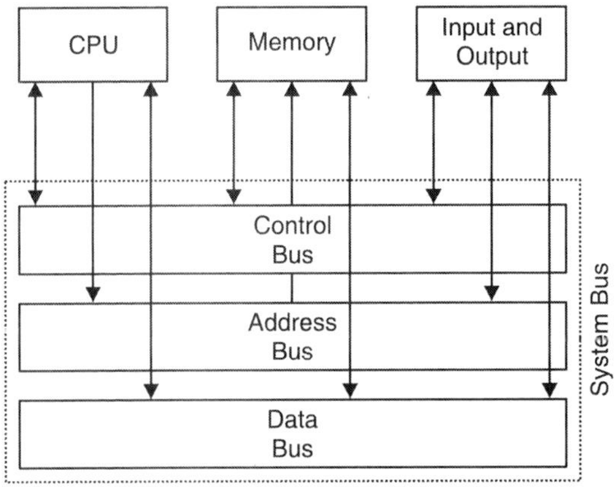

Figure 26: SYSTEM BUS

2. **External or Expansion**—a bus or set of wires that connects external memories, outer peripherals or components to a computer. It is slower than a system bus. It provides an input/output pathway for transferring data and information between internal hardware, CPU or RAM and external devices such as sound card, network card or graphics card. Being external to a computer system, external buses are much slower than internal buses. Expansion slots on the motherboard act as "on ramps" to the external bus; the lines on a bus end at an expansion slot, where they connect to pins that in turn connect to lines on an expansion card inserted in the slot.

There are various types of external or expansion buses: Industry Standard Architecture (ISA),

Accelerated Graphics Port (AGP), Peripheral Component Interconnect (PCI), Universal Serial Bus (SB), and many more.

5.4 Steps in Instruction Execution by CPU—Fetch, Execute and Interrupt

The following steps are involved in executing an instruction by CPU. However, not each of them is required for all the instructions. A basic instruction execution cycle can be broken down into the following steps: Fetch cycle and Execute cycle, and in an advanced instruction cycle, another step is involved: Interrupt cycle. Since many programs can be very large, and since CPU has limited memory, programs are stored in memory (RAM). However, CPU does its processing on the CPU. So, the CPU must copy the instruction from memory to the CPU, and once it's in CPU, it can execute it.

1. **Fetch (Instruction)**—the execution cycle starts with fetching an instruction from the main memory. The instruction at the current program counter (PC) will be fetched and will be stored in the instruction register (IR).
2. **Decode (Instruction) and Fetch (Operands)**—during this cycle the encoded instruction present in the IR (instruction register) is interpreted by the decoder.
3. **Fetch (Data)**—the execution of an instruction may require reading data from memory or from I/O module.
4. **Perform ALU operation (Process Arithmetic or Logic Operation)**—it is here where the two operands in the fetched instruction will be operated on the given operator in the instructions. Such as, if the instruction was to add two numbers, then here the addition will happen. ALU takes two values and outputs one, i.e., the result of the operation.
5. **Access memory**—there are two kinds of instructions that access memory: LOAD and STORE. LOAD

copies a value from memory to a register and STORE copies a register value to memory. Any other instruction skips this step.

6. **Update Register File**—the output or result of the ALU is written back to the register file; hence the register file is updated. The result could also be due to a LOAD from memory. Some instructions don't have any output or result to store. For example, BRANCH and JUMP instructions do not have any results to store.
7. **Update the Program Counter**—at the end of the execution of the current instruction, we need to update the program counter (PC) to the address of the next instruction, so that we can go back to step 1 where the CPU will fetch the instruction. However, the program counter might need to be set to another memory address instead of the next one if the instruction was BRANCH or JUMP.

5.5 Questions for Reflection

1. What is a CPU core?
2. What is the purpose of logic gates?
3. What is a hybrid logic gate?
4. Which steps are involved in a machine cycle?
5. List three differences between RAM and ROM?
6. What are the cache levels?
7. What is a hardwired control unit?
8. What is the difference between ALU and FPU?
9. What is a system bus?

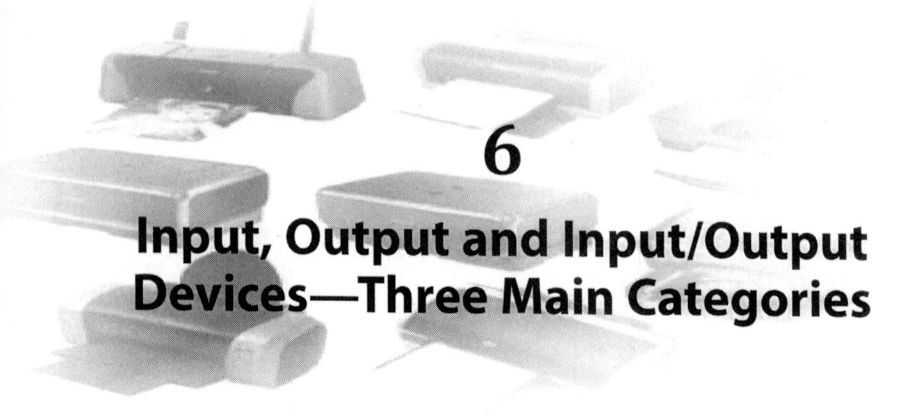

6

Input, Output and Input/Output Devices—Three Main Categories

A computer system has many devices and peripherals connected to it. There are three main categories of these devices: input, output and input/output (I/O). An input device is any device used to send data or information to a computer system for processing. An input device translates analog data into an electronic or digital form for a computer to recognize and understand. An output device is any device used to send data from a computer to another device or user. An output device can produce the final product of machine processing into a form usable by the user; an output device translates information stored in the computer and presents it in a way that humans can understand it. Typical output devices in a computer system are the monitor, speakers and the printer. An input/output device can send data (input) to a computer or another device and also receive data (output) from a computer or another device. We will discuss the main input devices, output devices and input/output devices in this chapter.

Table 18: Input, Output and Input/Output Devices

Input Devices
Keyboard
Mouse
Microphone
Scanner
Optical Character Reader
Barcode Reader

Cont...

Output Devices
Monitor
Printer
Speaker
Plotter
Input/Output Devices
Network Card
CD Burner
DVD Burner
Audio/Sound Card
Modem
Disk Drive
Headset
Facsimile

These devices play an integral role in the Input, Output, Processing, Storage data flow. The first step in the data flow is input. This is when data to be processed by a computer is fed into it. And this input can occur in many ways through a keyboard, mouse, barcode reader, etc. These input devices help to convert data from analog to digital format. Processing is the next stage of this flow. Processing refers to preparing the data for the task or operation to be performed. Processing can refer to tasks such as searching, analyzing, reporting, calculating, sorting, etc. Data is mostly stored either permanently or temporarily. It can be stored permanently on non-volatile storage devices (hard disk drives, optical drives, etc.) or temporarily in memory. After the data has been processed, it is ready for the output stage. This data is presented in the appropriate format, for example, graphs, sounds, printouts, and for displaying the output, several output devices like monitor, speaker, printer, etc., can be used.

6.1 Keyboard—The Most Common Input Device

Keyboard is the most common input device and it looks similar to an electronic typewriter, but has additional keys and features for performing additional functions. It is the primary device used to enter text, characters and commands into a computer. The data and instructions are input by pressing keys on the keyboard.

There is no standard computer keyboard as different keyboards differ somewhat in the placement of function keys, shift keys, return key and control keys. Many different keyboard layouts like Dvork, AZERTY and XPeRT are available, but the most common layout is referred to as a 'QWERTY' keyboard after the keys on the left-hand side of the top row of letters. Some keyboards, especially those on laptops, will have a slightly different layout. Most keyboards have anywhere between 80 and 110 keys. For touchscreen devices like smartphones, KALQ keyboard layout has become popular as it has been optimized for rapid two thumb typing.

Image 14: QWERTY KEYBOARD LAYOUT

Image Source: http://www.computerhope.com/jargon/k/keyboard.htm

Some of the popular keyboard brands are Logitech, Microsoft and Razer. Typical wired keyboards connect to the motherboard via a USB cable. Most modern-day keyboards are wireless, which connect to a computer via a Radio Frequency (RF technology comprises of an RF Transmitter and an RF Receiver), Infrared or Bluetooth (a Bluetooth keyboard is a wireless keyboard that communicates with a computer via Bluetooth protocol). Some popular wireless keyboard manufacturers include HP, Logitech and Anker. Smartphones and tablets do not come with a physical keyboard; they come with a thumb keyboard or on-screen keyboard. Notebooks and laptops have integrated keyboards, but an external keyboard can be attached to these portable devices through USB.

Spotlight Tip
All types of keyboards need a device driver in order to function properly. Standard keyboards normally don't need a driver to be downloaded as it is already included in the operating system.

6.1.1 Keyboard Keys—Numeric, Control and More

As the use of computers in the business world increased, so did the need for speedy data entry; hence the introduction of a numeric keypad. Apart from the standard keys, some keyboards also have keys for volume control and to power down the device. Modifier keys like *Control*, *Shift* and *Alt* also are important keys; they are called modifier keys as they modify the function of another key. The regular function of the *numeric* key 4 is to input the number, but if a user holds down *Shift* and 4 simultaneously, the dollar ($) sign is the result. Another common example of modifier keys is 'Ctrl-Alt-Del' combination, which is a keyboard command to either terminate a task or reboot a system. There are several non-alphanumeric keys, which can be quite confusing for non-tech people.

Standard keyboard settings like blink rate, repeat delay and repeat rate can be changed through the control panel. For advanced changes, one can use third-party programs. These third-party utility programs also come in handy for remapping keys, for example, if a particular key is not functioning or missing, its functionality can be mapped to another.

Table 19: Description of Keys

Keys	Description
Numeric Keypad/ Number Pad	Usually a 17-key keypad found on the far right side of a typical keyboard. It can be activated or deactivated through the Num Lock key.
Function Keys	There are usually twelve function keys that are arranged in a row at the top of the keyboard, labeled F1 through F12. Each function key is for some specific purpose, for example the F1 key is often used as the default help key in many programs.

Contd...

Control Keys	
Ctrl + A	Select all text or other objects.
Ctrl + B	Bold effect on highlighted characters, words or text
Ctrl + C	Copy any selected text or other object.
Ctrl + I	Italics effect on highlighted characters, words or text
Ctrl + N	Create a new page or document
Ctrl + P	Open print window
Ctrl + S	Save a file or document
Ctrl + U	Underline effect on highlighted characters, words or text
Ctrl + V	Paste any text or other object that has been copied
Ctrl + X	Cut selected text or other object
Ctrl + Y	Redo any undo action
Ctrl + Z	Undo any action
Symbols Keys	
~	Tilde
`	Acute, Back quote, grave accent, left quote
!	Exclamation mark or Exclamation point
@	Asperand or At symbol
#	Number, Pound or Hash
£	Pound
€	Euro
$	Dollar
¢	Cent
%	Percent
°	Degree
^	Caret or Circumflex
&	Ampersand or And
*	Asterisk
(	Open parenthesis
)	Close parenthesis

<table>
<tr><td>-</td><td>Hyphen, Minus or Dash</td></tr>
<tr><td>_</td><td>Underscore</td></tr>
<tr><td>+</td><td>Plus</td></tr>
<tr><td>=</td><td>Equal</td></tr>
<tr><td>{</td><td>Open Brace or curly bracket</td></tr>
<tr><td>}</td><td>Close Brace or curly bracket</td></tr>
<tr><td>[</td><td>Open bracket</td></tr>
<tr><td>]</td><td>Closed bracket</td></tr>
<tr><td>|</td><td>Pipe or Vertical bar</td></tr>
<tr><td>\</td><td>Backslash</td></tr>
<tr><td>/</td><td>Forward slash or Solidus</td></tr>
<tr><td>:</td><td>Colon</td></tr>
<tr><td>,</td><td>Semicolon</td></tr>
<tr><td>“</td><td>Quotation mark, or Inverted commas</td></tr>
<tr><td>’</td><td>Apostrophe or Single Quote</td></tr>
<tr><td><</td><td>Less Than or Angle brackets</td></tr>
<tr><td>></td><td>Greater Than or Angle brackets</td></tr>
<tr><td>.</td><td>Full Stop or Period</td></tr>
<tr><td>?</td><td>Question Mark</td></tr>
</table>

6.2 Mouse—Most Popular Pointing Device

A mouse is used to input the movements of a cursor as they are captured when the mouse is rolled over the mouse pad. It is the most popular pointing device. Moving a mouse along a flat surface or mouse pad can move the on-screen cursor to different icons or items on the screen. This device apparently got its name as it about the same size and color as that of a mouse, even the cable attached to a mouse resembles the tail of a mouse.

A mouse can perform several operations: it can select or click on files, folders or icons. It can be used to open or run applications by either clicking or double clicking the required icon. It is also used to scroll up or down to view a long webpage or document. A mouse can also be used to perform drag and drop operations; this operation describes the action of selecting an object or text, then moving it (dragging), and then finally placing it (dropping) into an alternate area, to a new location.

How to Perform Drag and Drop
A drag and drop operation involves moving the mouse cursor over an object or text, selecting it, and moving it to a new location. A user can perform this operation by clicking the mouse button to select an object or text, then moving the mouse while keeping the mouse button pushed down. This action is called "dragging". Once the user has moved the object or text to desired location, the user can lift up the mouse button to place the object or text in the new location; this is called "dropping".

The mouse was originally known as the "X-Y position indicator for a display system" and was invented by Douglas Engelbart in 1963. The first prototype was built in 1964 and the patent application for this "X-Y position indicator for a display system" was filed in 1967, and all this occurred two decades before it would ship with the first Apple Macintosh. This invention was a simple wooden box with one button and two wheels that rolled directly on a hard surface. In 1972, Bill English developed the design further by inventing what is known as the "Ball Mouse" that we all know today.

The mouse is one of the most important breakthroughs in computer ergonomics because it provides a hassle-free operating to the users. It is important for graphical user interface because one can simply point to icons or options and click a mouse button to perform a certain action.

There are three basic types: optical, mechanical and opto-mechanical. An optical mouse contains a laser or LED to detect the mouse's movements. An optical mouse has no moving mechanical parts and it responds more quickly and precisely than the other two types, but is more expensive. Since an optical mouse has no mechanical parts, it eliminates mechanical fatigue and failure. An optical mouse takes microscopic snapshots of the working surface at a rate of more than 1,000 images per second. A mechanical mouse uses a ball and rollers to detect the mouse's movements. This ball rolls in a socket and the ball then scrolls two optical encoding wheels on their X and Y axis. These wheels have sensors that send this X and Y movement information to the software that directs movements of the cursor. Although a mechanical mouse is cheaper than its optical counterpart it has some problems; dirt and dust can cause it to malfunction. An opto-mechanical is the same as a mechanical one, but uses optical sensors to detect motion of the ball.

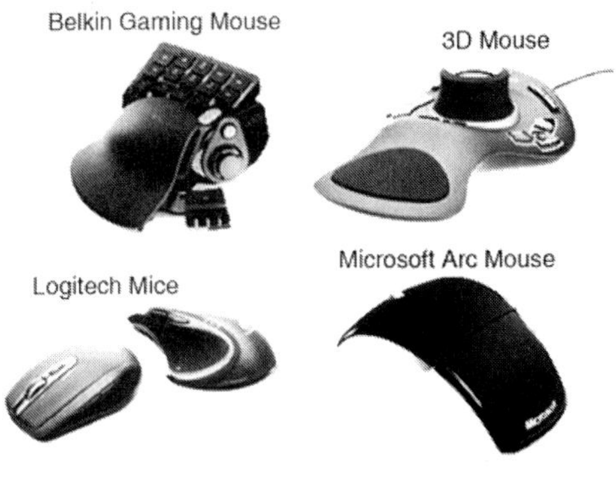

Image 15: VARIOUS MOUSE TYPES

Image Source: http://www.what-is-my-computer.com/what-is-a-computer-mouse.html

There are several other types like Computer Aided Design mouse, gaming mouse and 3D mouse. The IntelliMouse is an optical mouse that has a wheel between the left and right mouse buttons. This is the most popular style of a mouse device. Although it is a Microsoft product, it has become the standard mouse model used by most computers. Most modern models also have a scroll wheel that allows the users to scroll up and down webpages or documents.

There are several other examples of pointing devices: light pen, leap motion joystick, footmouse, etc. Some mouse manufacturers also provide a version for left-handed people. Popular mouse brands are Razer, Logitech and Corsair.

6.2.1 Components of a Mouse—Casing, Buttons and Much More

A mouse consists of a plastic or metal casing, one or more buttons on the top of the casing, a cable (connection interface) that connects this device to a computer, and a ball that sticks out of the bottom of the casing and is rolled on a flat surface, and battery in case the mouse is wireless. Each mouse has its own brain in form of a driver.

They come in many shapes and sizes. A standard mouse has two buttons toward the front—*left-click* and *right-click*. However, a computer mouse can have anywhere from one to six or more buttons to provide additional functionality. While older models use a small ball on the bottom to control the cursor movement, newer ones use a laser. In older models, the ball is held in place by a support wheel and two shafts. Modern models have a light source like a light-emitting diode and a light detector such as an array of photodiodes to detect movement relative to a surface. There are different types of clicking: single-click, double-click, triple-click and right-click.

Today, most computer mouse models connect to a computer system using a USB port or even wireless options are available. Examples include USB, Serial Port, Bluetooth and Infrared. Latest models have lost their tails; they have gone wireless and transmit their data through infrared or radio waves.

6.3 Microphone—Inputs Audio Data

A microphone also called mic is an instrument that allows users to input audio into their computers. It is a device that converts sound vibrations into electronic signals. It can be used for various purposes like music, gaming, voice recognition, communication, sound recording, etc.

There are several types of microphones but all work in almost the same fashion. Inside the microphone is a diaphragm composed of film or foil, and a screen which is sensitive to pressure waves. When one makes a sound, it creates waves of pressure in the air, which push onto the screen. When the diaphragm moves, it produces an electric signal, which is sent to a computer's sound card. An internal microphone is in-built whereas an external microphone is a peripheral device that is plugged into the computer through the sound card. Another type is that of USB microphone and USB headsets or a combination of computer headset with microphone that connects directly to a USB port. The latest type is a wireless microphone.

Depending on the purpose of using a microphone, the form factor needs to be considered while buying one. If the user is an ardent computer gamer or into Internet phone conversations then a desktop microphone is good enough. For more intense uses like audio recording or creating podcasts, a professional microphone is the best buy.

The three most common types of microphones are:

1. Condenser uses a capacitor to convert acoustical energy into electrical energy. In this capacitor, there are two plates with a voltage between them, and one of the plates acts as a diaphragm, which when hit by sound waves, generates vibrations. These vibrations produce changes in the distance between the plates and hence a change in electrical energy.
2. Dynamic converts sound into an electrical signal by means of electromagnetism. It uses a wire coil

and magnet to create the audio signal. This coil is positioned in the magnetic field of a permanent magnet and is attached to a diaphragm. When sound enters through the microphone, the sound waves move the diaphragm. When the diaphragm vibrates, the coil moves in the magnetic field, and this produces a varying current in the coil through electromagnetic induction. There are two types: ribbon and moving coil.

3. Ribbon uses thin duraluminum, aluminum or nanofilm of electrically conductive ribbon placed between the poles of a magnet to produce a voltage by electromagnetic induction. The ribbon's vibration in the magnetic field generates the electrical signal.

Another aspect to be considered while buying a microphone is what is being recorded and this is dependent on another factor called directionality. Examples include directional, bidirectional and shotgun microphones. A directional microphone is suitable for use in a hearing aid or in an assistive listening device (ALD is used to improve hearing ability for people, specially hearing impaired people), as it can be used to enhance specific sound that needs to be heard and to diminish background noise. A bidirectional microphone picks up sound well or with high sensitivity from the front and back, but poorly or with low sensitivity from the sides, and is suitable for presentations and lectures. A shotgun microphone focuses on the sound coming from directly in front of it while ignoring sound from the rear and sides, and it is suitable for interviews. An omnidirectional microphone picks up sound evenly from all directions. Whether a speaker speaks into the microphone from the back, front, right or left side, an omnidirectional microphone will record the signals all with equal gain. In a cardioid microphone, the area in front of the mic is most sensitive, but to a lesser extent from the sides (the sides are less sensitive), and the rear is ignored, and it is suited for events and documentaries. The term cardioid means "heart-shaped," which is used to describe the type of pick-up pattern this type of a microphone uses.

How To Locate a Microphone

Whether the microphone is internal or external, it is listed in the devices list. For Windows machine, one can find out whether a microphone is attached or not through the search box->System information->click the + sign next to Components, then Sound Device. For laptops, one can consult the device documentation or manually examine the edges for a small hole labeled "mic" or has a microphone icon.

6.4 Scanner—Scans and Converts into Digital Data

A scanner works like a Xerox machine. It is a device that captures images from posters, photographic prints, documents, book and magazine pages, and other similar sources for editing, storing and displaying purposes. It optically reads/scans an image, printed or written text, etc., and converts it into a digital signal/format. Whenever something is scanned, it is converted into a digital format and this creates an electronic version that can be viewed and edited on a computer.

Most scanners include basic scanning software that facilitates users to configure, initiate, and import scans. Scanning plug-ins can also be used that allow various software programs to import scanned images directly. These days, smartphone apps like FineScanner, CamScanner and many more for scanning are also available. A scanner is normally attached to a computer with a Small Computer System Interface (SCSI) or USB. SCSI refers to a set of interface standards for connecting devices; refers to the types of ports and cables used to connect devices.

A scanner requires both scanning software and machinery. The choice of scanning software depends on the user or business requirements. The image quality depends on various factors like density range, color depth and optical resolution. The scanner software can produce various patterns. Scanning helps large offices to transform paper files and documents into digital format for better office management and time saving, and this in turn helps to save natural resources like trees. Some of the popular manufactures of scanners include Epson, Xerox, Microtek and HP.

6.4.1 Types of Scanners—From Flatbed to Drum

The most popular type of scanner is the flatbed scanner that has a flat surface on which documents and other objects are placed to be scanned. A flatbed scanner, also called a desktop scanner, has a cover that lifts up so that papers, books and other bulky objects can be scanned. A flatbed scanner is available as a standalone unit or it can come integrated with other print hardware such as a printer or photocopier. A handheld scanner is based on the same basic technology as a flatbed scanner, but relies on the user to move it instead of a motorized belt. The image quality of a handheld scanner is much lower in quality. A sheetfed scanner, also referred to as an automatic document scanner, is smaller than a flatbed scanner and it closely resembles a compact laser or inkjet printer. In a sheetfed scanner, paper documents are drawn from a sheet feeder and passed across the device's imaging sensor, which then end up in an output tray. A sheetfed scanner is good for scanning memos and invoices, but it is not suited for bulky documents, thick objects and bound books. A drum scanner spins the image that is wrapped around a drum/cylinder at high speed while it is scanned pixel by pixel by a detector head, and the result is a high-quality image. These scanners are often used in graphics production and commercial printing.

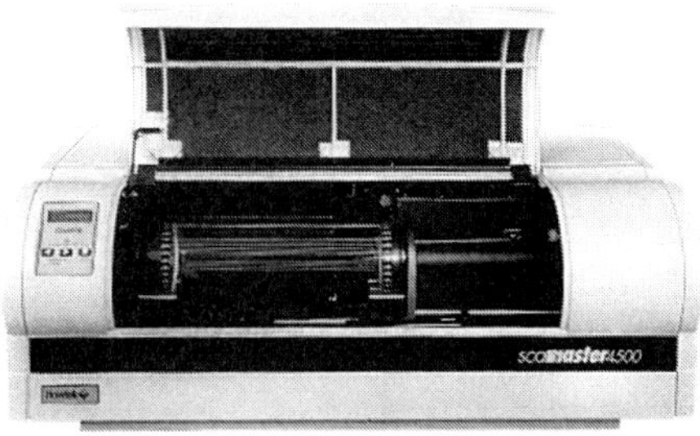

Image 16: DRUM SCANNER

Image Source: http://www.circuitstoday.com/working-of-scanner

6.5 Optical Character Reader—Enables Conversion of Documents

Optical Character Reader, also called Optical Character Recognition (OCR), is a device that enables the conversion of different types of documents such as PDF files, physical copies of books, handwritten material, scanned paper documents or images captured by a digital camera into editable and searchable data in the form of Word documents, Excel spreadsheets, etc. OCR can also be used for machine translation and text mining purposes. With the help of OCR, people no longer need to manually retype important and lengthy files and documents when entering them into electronic databases.

As you read these words in your book, your brains and eyes are in a way carrying out an optical character recognition process. Your eyes are recognizing the patterns of light and dark that form the characters, symbols, numbers, etc., and based on this recognition, your brain is trying to help you process what you are trying to read. The OCR functionality also works in a similar manner. The OCR functionality involves photo scanning of the text character-by-character, analysis of the scanned-in image, and then translation of the character image into character codes that a computer can understand, for example ASCII codes. It is currently the best way of digitizing typed material.

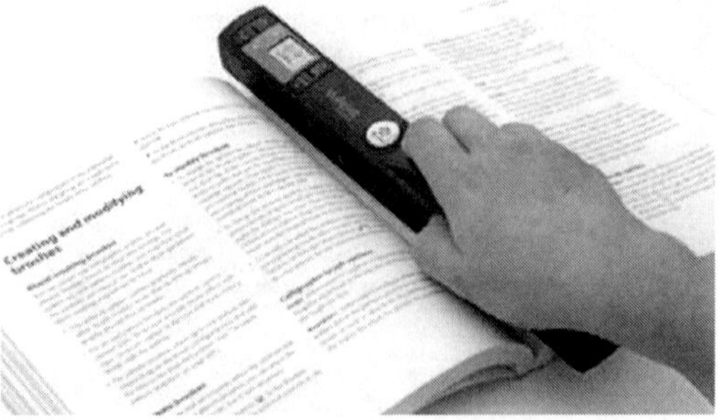

Image 17: OPTICAL CHARACTER READER

Image Source: http://generalnote.com/Basic-computer/OMR-OCR.php

The main components include a scanner for reading the text and software for analyzing the images. Before OCR can be used, the source material must be scanned using an optical scanner or any other appropriate scanner software, in order to read in the source material as a bitmap (a pattern of dots). In the case of images, appropriate software to recognize them is needed. The scan is then processed by the OCR software to distinguish between images and text and to determine what letters or numbers are represented in the light and dark areas. Most OCR devices use a combination of specialized circuit boards (hardware) and software to recognize characters, and this recognition is carried out on the basis of set of pattern images and numerous hypotheses. Patterns that cannot be identified are rejected.

OCR is used in a number of industries like retail, education, banking, etc., where it has helped to simplify data and information collection, analysis and sharing. Digitization of libraries is easily done by this technology. In the retail sector, OCR and barcode recognition are used. In the education industry, OCR has made numerous texts of knowledge available to a large number of learners and students across the globe in an affordable manner. In the banking industry, OCR is used to process checks and the correct amount of money is transferred after scanning the written contents of a check. Though at times, manual intervention and confirmation are required, the OCR technology for checks is quite accurate; hence reduces wait and processing times.

Spotlight Tip
Modern-day OCR technology offers the blind and visually impaired people the advantage of scanning printed documents and text, and then these can be spoken back to these people using synthetic speech.

6.6 Barcode Reader—Capture and Read Barcode Information

A barcode reader/barcode scanner, also called a point-of-sale (POS) scanner or price scanner, is a stationary input device or hand-held input device used to capture and read information from a barcode. A barcode is referred to as optical Morse code; it is a series of black bars and white spaces (black-and-white zebra stripes) printed on labels to uniquely identify items and products. This is a linear barcode and is seen on most products known as the Universal Product Code (UPC), which can hold any type of text information. In contrast to the linear barcode, a 2D (two-dimensional) barcode is more complex as it can include more information including web address and image. A barcode is used for several purposes like tracking products, prices and stock levels.

A barcode reader merely captures and converts the barcode into numbers and/or letters. This data must be sent to a computer so that it can make sense of the data. A barcode reader consists of a scanner, a decoder (either built-in or external), and a cable used to connect the reader with a computer. The scanner shines laser light or LED on the barcode and by directing this beam of light across the barcode, it measures the amount of light that is reflected back. The light reflects back off from the barcode into a light detecting component. Black areas reflect the least light and white areas the most. As the scanner moves over the barcode, a pattern of on-off pulses is generated by the cell. The scanner converts the light energy into electrical energy, which is then converted into data by the decoder and forwarded to a computer.

There are five kinds of barcode readers/barcode scanners—charge-coupled device reader/scanner (CCD reader/ scanner), image reader/scanner, pen wands, slot scanner, and laser scanner.

1. A CCD reader/scanner is silicon-based integrated circuit consisting of photodiodes. It has hundreds of tiny LED lights arranged in one row that function by converting light energy into electronic charge.
2. Image reader/scanner (camera scanner) uses digital camera technology and processing to capture an image of the barcode for processing; for decoding the barcode. It is used in manufacturing, retail and industrial warehousing.
3. Pen wand or pen-style barcode reader consists of an LED light and a photodiode in its tip. When this tip moves over a barcode, the LED light illuminates the black and white bars. Because of their small size, pen wands are suited for portable devices and for low volume scanning applications. It is also durable and affordable. A pen wand contains no moving components and due to this fact, it must be held at a certain angle, and it has to remain in direct contact with the bar code, and has to be moved over the bar code at a certain speed.
4. Slot reader/scanner is a stationary device and the item with the barcode is pulled by hand through the slot. It is usually used to scan identification cards.
5. Laser reader/scanner uses a system of lenses and mirrors to facilitate the device to read the bar code regardless of orientation and distance. Specialized laser scanners are capable of reading a barcode up

to 30 feet away. To reduce the error rate, a laser reader/scanner may perform up to 500 scans per second.

6.7 Monitor—The Most Common Output Device

A monitor, also known as video display terminal (VDT), screen, video screen or display unit, is the most common output device of a computer. It displays pictures and images in real time. Even though the monitor is placed outside the main computer system, it is an essential part of the complete system. It usually consists of a display device, buttons to adjust screen settings, circuitry, power supply and casing that holds all of these components. It is that hardware component that renders video and graphics information generated through the video card or video adaptor. It acts as an interface between CPU and a user.

A monitor is an external device and connects to a port on the video card or motherboard via a cable. It can be connected to the computer via DVI (Digital Visual Interface), HDMI (High-Definition Multimedia Interface), VGA (Video Graphics Array), LVDS (Low-voltage differential signaling) or other proprietary connectors and signals. In portable computer systems like tablets, laptops, and all-in-one desktop machines, monitors are built-in as part of the computer system.

While older monitors used cathode ray tubes (CRT) and a fluorescent screen, the modern-day computers use liquid crystal display (LCD) and thin film transistor liquid crystal display (TFT-LCD) display devices with a flat panel display technology. The flat panel display makes modern-day monitors much lighter and thinner in comparison to traditional monitors. The modern-day monitors are easy on the eyes and use less electricity than their CRT counterparts.

Monitors are usually considered as an output device as they serve the purpose of showing the output on the screen, but there is yet another type of monitor called the touchscreen, which acts both as an input and output device. Some examples of touchscreen include bank ATMs and information kiosks.

The main components that determine the quality of a monitor are resolution, dot pitch, power consumption, refresh rate, contrast ratio, aspect ratio, viewing angle, response time and luminance. Some of the common problems that arise are blurred screen, dead pixels, etc. Some of the popular monitor manufacturers are LG Electronics, Acer and Dell.

6.7.1 Types of Monitors—CRT, LCD and LED

Cathode Ray Tube (CRT) Monitor—is the traditional glass-screen, TV set-like monitor. A cathode ray tube is a vacuum tube containing an electron gun at one end and a fluorescent screen at another end. In a CRT monitor, a stream of intense high energy electrons is used to form images on a fluorescent screen. What happens is that a process called thermionic emission generates a strong beam of electrons. This beam then travels through a narrow path within the tube with high speed using various electro-magnetic devices and finally it strikes the phosphor points on the fluorescent screen thereby creating an image.

Liquid Crystal Display (LCD) Monitor—is a super-thin display unit that is used in laptops and flat panel monitors. Smaller monitors are used in portable devices like personal digital assistant. This type consists of a layer of monochrome or color pixels arranged schematically between a couple of transparent electrodes and two polarizing filters. The pixels are switched on or off electronically using liquid crystals to rotate polarized light. This type of monitors consumes much less power than other display types because they work on the principle of blocking light rather than emitting it.

Light Emitting Diode (LED) Monitor—is a flat screen, a flat panel computer monitor, and it consists of a number of LED panels that, in turn, consist of several light emitting diodes. It is efficient and has low-energy consumption, and these attributes are especially needed for chargeable devices and handle devices.

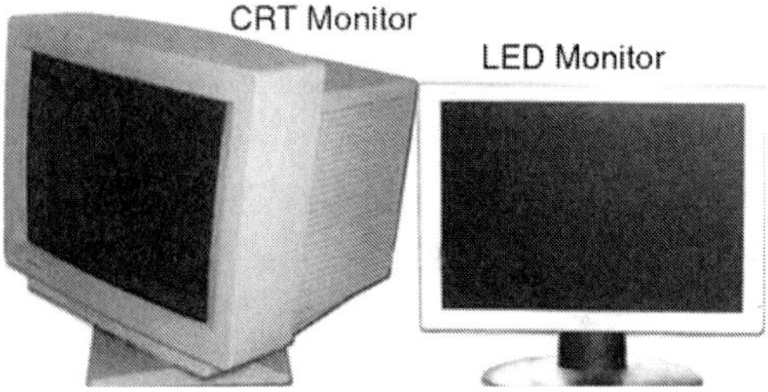

Image 18: TYPES OF MONITORS

Image Source: http://www.computer-hardware-explained.com/computer-monitor.html

6.7.2 How does a Monitor Work—Video Card, Colors, Signals and Output

The CPU sends instructions to the video card or video adaptor telling what needs to be displayed on the screen/monitor. Thereafter, the video card or video adaptor converts the instructions into a set of corresponding signals. These are then sent to the monitor and the monitor contains a circuitry that generates the output on the screen from these set of signals.

A monitor generates three colors of light (red, green and blue) and the different colors we see are due to different combinations and intensities of these three primary colors.

6.7.3 Monitor-related Terms—Resolution, Dot Pitch and Many More

1. Resolution tells how densely the pixels are arranged on the screen. It is expressed by identifying the number of pixels on the rows (horizontal axis) and the number on the columns (vertical axis) such as 800 × 600 pixels or 1024 × 768 pixels.
2. Dot Pitch is a specification that describes the distance between dots (sub-pixels) on a display screen. It indicates how sharp the displayed image can be. It is

measured in millimeters (mm) and a smaller number means a sharper image. Most monitors have a *dot pitch* between 0.25 and 0.28 mm.

3. **Contrast Ratio** is the difference between the darkest blacks and the brightest whites a given monitor can produce, or in other words, it is the ratio of the luminance of the brightest color (white) to that of the darkest color (black). A high contrast ratio is always better.
4. **Luminance or brightness** is measured in candelas per square meter, also referred to as nits.
5. **Screen Size** is usually measured in inches from one corner to the corner diagonally across from it. For a LCD monitor, screen size is measured diagonally from the inside of the beveled edge and the external casing is not included in measuring screen size. For a CRT monitor, screen size is measured diagonally from outside edges of the display casing and the exterior casing is included in measuring screen size.
6. **Aspect Ratio** is the ratio of the horizontal length to the vertical length. Monitors usually have the aspect ratio 4:3, 5:4, 16:10 or 16:9. Two measures describe the size of a monitor: aspect ratio and screen size.
7. **Refresh Rate** is the maximum number of times the image can be refreshed or renewed per second. For example, a monitor with a refresh rate of 85 Hz means the screen is going to redraw 85 times per second.
8. **Dead Pixels** are pixels that remain unlit or black when they should be activated and displaying a color. All the three RGB (red, green, blue) sub-pixels are permanently turned off, which creates an unlit or black spot on the display.

6.8 Printer—Converts Electronic Data into Text or Images

A printer is an output device that takes electronic data stored on a computer or other devices, and generates a hard copy of it in the form of reports, text, images, etc. Some printers can print only text. Other printers can print both text and images. Printers are connected to a computer either through USB cable or through WiFi.

A computer stores data in electronic format and a printer's job is to convert this electronic data back into words and images, i.e., to turn electricity into ink. The speed of a printer is measured in characters per second (CPS) or pages per minutes (PPM). The output generated by a printer is classified into these categories: *letter quality* (as good as a typewriter), *near letter quality* (not as good as letter quality, but better than draft quality) or *draft quality*.

Impact printers make contact with the paper. Examples of impact printers include dot matrix, line, daisy wheel and drum. Non-impact printers print without striking the paper. Examples of non-impact printers include inkjet, thermal wax transfer, laser and solid ink. Non-impact printers are quieter than impact printers and also have better speed as they do not have any moving parts in the print head.

6.8.1 Types of Printers—Dot Matrix, Inkjet and Laser

There are three main types of printers: Dot Matrix, Inkjet and Laser. Apart from these three main types of printers, there is also what we call hybrid printers. These are printers that can do many different tasks as one device, right from printing to photocopying and from scanning to faxing.

1. **Dot Matrix**—it generates the output by striking pins against an ink ribbon to print closely spaced dots. Each pin makes a dot and then this combination of dots form the text and images. In a dot matrix printer, the image quality is determined by the number of dots per inch. The more dots that are used, the more clear and accurate the output will be. This type was first introduced by Centronics in 1970.

2. **Inkjet**—uses ionized ink that is sprayed to the sheet of paper. In this type, ink guns are operated electrically, which fire precise streams of ink on the page from tiny nozzles through an electrical field. The droplets are then guided to the paper by electrically charged deflecting plates: one plate has positive charge (upper plate) and the other plate has negative charge (lower plate). When a droplet is not needed for the character or image being formed, it is recycled back to its nozzle.
3. **Laser**—uses non-impact, photocopier technology. Printing is done by directing a laser beam at a mirror, which bounces the beam onto a drum. Before any new printing commences, this type of printer removes prior image information and toner from the drum. Then applies a uniform negative charge to the drum. A light source such as LED or laser writes to areas on the drum discharging the negative charge where it hits. The toner is ionized with a negative charge and is attracted to the areas previously written on the drum. Then this toner is transferred to the paper by positively ionized field. At this stage, the toner is not yet permanently set on the paper; hence the last stage is that of fusing where pressure and heat are applied to the toner and paper and this causes the toner to melt, which then is pressed onto the paper. A hot roller bonds the toner to the paper.

Spotlight Tip

Laser printers are usually larger than inkjet printers. Larger laser printers have additional ongoing costs in comparison to inkjet printers. Laser printers use toner to produce the output, whereas inkjet printers use ink. Laser printers are less wasteful when compared to inkjet printers.

4. **Other Types of Printers**—a line printer prints output a line at a time rather than character by character.

A line printer can typically print in the range of 1,200 to 6,000 lines per minute. There are two types of line printers: chain and drum. A chain printer uses a chain with raised characters and the values of all the characters are stored in a printer buffer. When a particular character needs to be printed then printer sends this information to the buffer. Thereafter, this chain is rotated and when a match is found, the character is printed by striking a hammer on a ribbon which then leaves an impression on the paper. In a drum printer, instead of a chain, a drum with raised characters is used.

A daisy wheel printer has a metal or plastic disk containing letters, numbers and other characters it supports. When something needs to be printed, the printer rotates the disk to the required match and then using a hammer strikes it into an ink ribbon to create the output on paper. This type of printer was popular in the 1970s and 1980s. It is no longer in much use as better printers have entered the market.

Image 19: TYPES OF PRINTERS
Image Source: http://www.typesof.com/types-of-printers/

A thermal wax transfer printer uses heat to transfer an impression onto paper. This type of printer is used on surfaces that can't absorb ink or on surfaces to which toner won't stick. It uses heat to bond a wax-based pigment to paper. This wax-based pigment is on a thermal transfer ribbon and when heat is applied to this ribbon using a thermal print head, this results in the melting of ink, which is then transferred to the paper where it becomes permanent after it cools.

A solid ink printer uses solid wax ink that is melted into a liquid before being used. It jets the ink onto a drum before it is transferred to the paper.

6.9 Speaker—Converts Electrical Signals into Sound Waves

A speaker is a hardware device that connects to a computer to generate sound. It converts electrical signals into sound waves. A speaker receives audio input from a computer's sound card and produces audio output in the form of sound waves. A speaker is a transducer that converts electromagnetic waves into sound waves. It receives audio input that may be either in analog or digital form. An analog speaker simply amplifies the analog electromagnetic waves into sound waves, whereas a digital speaker must first convert the digital input to an analog signal, and then generate the sound waves. Some of the uses include internet phone service and web conferencing.

Spotlight Tip
Many computers come with a speaker as a part of the motherboard, which means there is no sound card included, but one can still hear low-quality sounds and beeps from this onboard speaker or through headphones.

Stand alone speakers that come with computers are generally enough for movies, games and other entertainment needs. When a user wants to upgrade the sound quality, volume and tone, the user will need to attach additional speakers. Advanced speaker systems include features like subwoofers and surround sound. Subwoofers enhance bass output. Laptops come with built-in integrated speakers, which are usually small and have a restricted sound quality.

Image 20: Advanced Speaker System
Image Source: http://www.computerhope.com/jargon/s/speaker.htm

How to Generate Sound from a Speaker
A speaker is usually made up of an electromagnet, an iron coil, cone and a case. This device makes use of electromagnetism. In a speaker, a coil of enamel insulated wire is wound around a thin tube, and this tube is placed around a magnet, and held in place by a membrane called a spider. When a fluctuating electric current flows through the coil, it becomes a temporary electromagnet, attracted and repelled by the permanent magnet. As the coil moves, it moves the cone back and forth, creating sound waves.

6.10 Plotter—Prints Vector Graphics

A plotter is like a printer used for printing vector graphics [large scale images or drawings like computer-aided design (CAD)]. It can draw continuous point-to-point lines directly from vector graphics files or commands. A vector graphic is made up of points, lines, angles and curves related to one another using a sequence of commands or mathematical statements. A plotter can be used for drawing large scale maps, building or engineering plans. The term "plotter" actually describes the original technology in which the plotter pens plotted across the paper to create drawings. Instead of a toner, a plotter uses a pen or any other writing tool to draw multiple, continuous lines onto a paper.

Plotter pens and papers are the two main deciding factors of plotter performance. Depending on the purpose, a variety of papers and pens are available. Types of plotter paper—Vellum slightly more expensive than most other types and the output produced on it is classier in look and feel; Bond is long-lasting and water-resistant; Translucent is lightweight, suited for transparent printing, and can be used as a substitute to Vellum. A plotter can print on a wide variety of materials like fabric, card, paper, film, plastic, etc. It can maintain the resolution even while working on very large sheets of paper or any other material.

Spotlight Tip
Though a typical plotter was once widely used in various applications like CAD, now its modern-day counterpart called a wide-format printer is used. A wide-format printer (large format printer) is a printer that prints on large paper, which can range from 2 to more than 15 feet in width.

6.10.1 Types of Plotters—From Flatbed to Inkjet

The different types of plotters are: flatbed plotter, electrostatic plotter and drum plotter, and they are explained as follows:

1. A flatbed plotter (also known as table plotter) draws on paper placed on a flat surface; the paper remains stationary on a flat surface while a pen moves across it horizontally and vertically. It is used with many CAD programs. This mechanical movement makes this plotter slow in producing the output, but modern flatbed models are much faster. Older mechanical models have been replaced by electrostatic, thermal and inkjet plotters. Modern flatbed plotters are used in making large colorful prints found on maps and posters.

2. A drum plotter wraps a sheet of paper around a drum with a pin feed attachment and the plotter uses this drum revolver to move the paper during printing. In a flatbed plotter, the plotting is done by moving an arm that in turn moves a pen over paper rather than having paper move under the arm as in the case of a drum plotter. There are two types of drum plotters: internal and external. In the internal drum plotter, paper is wrapped around its internal surface, whereas in the external drum plotter, paper is wrapped around its external surface.
3. An electrostatic plotter draws on negatively charged paper with positively charged toner and it is used in Computer-Aided Engineering (CAE). It produces a raster image by charging the paper with a high voltage. This voltage then attracts the toner which is then melted into the paper with heat. This plotter is fast but the image quality is generally lower than that of pen-based plotters. It produces the images using either the liquid toner or dry toner model. A liquid toner model uses a positively charged toner to draw on a negatively charged paper.
4. An inkjet plotter creates a digital image by spraying small droplets of ink onto paper or other substrates. A popular choice for advertising agencies and graphic designers, inkjet plotters are used generally for large outputs, such as banners and billboards and large signs often seen along roadsides. They are available in thermal or piezoelectric models. Thermal inkjet plotters use heat to apply droplets of ink, while piezoelectric plotters use charged crystals to apply the ink. Inkjet plotters typically produce better quality graphics than other plotter types.

6.11 Input/Output Devices—Two in One

Some devices perform both input and output operations and are referred to as I/O (input/output) devices. Some of the common I/O devices are network card, CD burner, DVD burner, audio/sound card, modem, disk drive, headset and facsimile.

A network card is an electronic device that connects a computer to a computer network such as a local network or the Internet using an Ethernet cable with an RJ-45 connector. It provides a computer with a dedicated, full-time connection to a network. A CD burner is a device that can record data to a recordable compact disc. There are two types of writable CDs: CDs that can only be written one time (CD-R) and CDs that can be written and rewritten multiple times (CD-RW). A DVD Burner is either an internal DVD drive or an external add-on that can read and write data and store it on a blank DVD disc. An audio/sound card is an expansion card for generating sound on a computer that can be heard through headphones or speakers. A modem (short for modulator-demodulator) is a device that enables a computer to transmit data over telephone or cable lines. A disk drive is a rewritable storage device that reads and/or writes data to a disk. A headset is a device that combines a pair of headphones with a microphone. While headphones can only be used as a listening device, a headset can be used as a listening device and a recording device through its microphone component. Facsimile is a device that transmits and receives documents over a telephone line.

6.12 Questions for Reflection

1. What is a wireless keyboard?
2. List three I/O devices?
3. How does a flatbed scanner work?
4. Identify the various types of monitors?
5. List the most common types of microphones?
6. How does a laser printer function?
7. What operations does a mouse perform?

Part 3
THE INTERNET, THE FUTURE AND MORE

7

Programming Fundamentals—Languages, Loops and More

Similar to human languages, computer programming languages are also made of several elements like keywords, syntax, data types, etc. A programming language is used to create commands, which can be interpreted into a code understood by a machine. It is usually used to write computer programs like applications, utilities, etc. The process of writing programs is called programming.

What is programming—it is the process of writing a specific set of ordered instructions and operations for a computer to interpret and execute. These instructions are called computer programs. People who write these programs are called programmers.

There are lots of ways of thinking about programming. The different ways lead to different kinds of programming languages. There are five main fundamentals or stages of programming: defining the program, planning the solution, coding the program, testing the program, and documenting the program.

There are a number of ways of developing a program and these ways help to define the problem and plan for the solution. One method is a graphical technique called flowchart. Another method is the definition of the problem in pseudocode. The coding stage is the translation of the program from flowchart or pseudocode to a programming language of choice. The testing stage starts from test planning then moves on to designing test cases, preparing for execution and evaluating status till the test closure is achieved where all bugs and errors have been resolved.

A lightweight programming language is one that is designed to have a very small memory footprint. It is easy to implement as it has only a few rules, practices, features and syntax, and porting such a language becomes easy. Some examples of lightweight programming languages are newLisp and JavaScript. A heavyweight programming language tries to plan out the project in great detail over a long span of time, and this involves a lot of plans, specifications, schedules and reports. This heavyweight approach works well only until things start changing. The heavyweight approach may be more predictive than the lightweight one, but it is not change-oriented.

Behind every key press and mouse click, there is a computer program. There are hundreds of programming languages out there, but the popular programming languages include: Java, Perl, Ruby, C++, C#, etc.

7.1 Algorithm—A Dry Run

In the earlier days of programming, it was a common practice to prepare flowcharts for programs that needed to be run on a computer. These days, an algorithm is a popular way of performing a dry run of the program. Before one can get on to programming languages, one needs to learn how to write efficient and logical algorithms. Efficient implies using the minimum resources such as memory and CPU cycles. Logical implies ensuring everything makes sense and the required results are achieved.

The first step to programming is to define, outline and analyze the problem. Thereafter, one needs to expand the outline of a problem into an algorithm. An algorithm is a self-contained sequence or step-by-step procedure of unambiguous instructions for solving a problem. When you are telling the computer what to do, you also get to choose how it is going to do it, and this is where algorithms step in. It is like a road map for accomplishing a given problem or task. An algorithm expects a defined set of inputs and it produces a defined set of outputs.

An algorithm has a definite start and a definite end, and a finite number of steps. It is used for data processing, automated reasoning and calculations. A particular problem can usually be solved by more than one algorithm. Each algorithm has advantages and disadvantages. Optimization is the process of finding the most efficient algorithm for a given task or problem.

Spotlight Tip
Test data is a necessary step to see if an algorithm successfully solves the problem or performs the task. Thereafter, the algorithm can be translated into a computer program using any programming language.

An algorithm can be expressed in any language, from natural languages like English to programming languages like FORTRAN. An algorithm can also be written using pseudocode. A pseudocode, also called p-code, is an outline of a program written in a form that can easily be converted into real programming statements. A pseudocode is an informal language that helps programmers to develop algorithms.

An algorithm can be designed using a flowchart too. A flowchart, also called business process mapping, process map or process flowchart, is a diagrammatic representation of an algorithm. It is a series of steps depicted as boxes of various types and their order is shown by connecting them with arrows. Some of the common purposes where flowcharts are used are data management, managing workflow, modeling a business process, planning a new project and auditing a process. To design efficient and effective flowcharts, there are some tips that one needs to keep in mind—keep everything on a single page for flowcharts can range from simple, hand-drawn charts to comprehensive, computer-drawn diagrams. A flowchart uses some standard symbols. The following table depicts these symbols and their descriptions.

Table 20: Flowchart Symbols and Their Descriptions

Name	Symbol	Meaning/Usage
Start or Stop	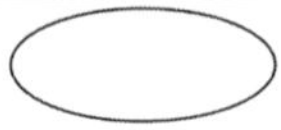	An oval represents the beginning and end-points in a sequence
Process	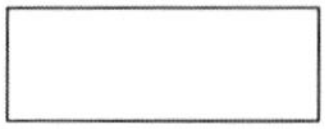	A rectangle represents a command or instruction
Decision	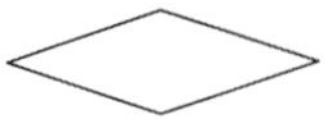	A diamond represents a decision (either yes or no)—questions asked or conditions tested
Input or Output		A parallelogram represents input or output
Direction of Flow		An arrow represents a connector that shows flow and sequence relationships between the representative symbols
Connector		A connector symbol indicates a jump from one point to another in a sequence
Document	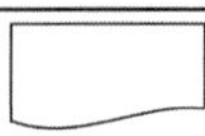	Represents a printed document or report

7.2 Program—A Well-defined Set of Instructions

A computer program is a well-defined set of instructions that when executed make a computer perform in a predetermined manner. In current times, most programs are written in high-level languages like Java, COBOL, etc. They can also be written in low-level languages called assembly languages. Eventually, all programs must be translated into a machine language that the computer can understand.

Any program should be documented very carefully. Describing each line or major code snippets in details helps the team to update and maintain the program in an efficient way. Any new programmer can easily pick up pace when she or he needs to access the program for future changes or corrections. Perhaps a day will soon come when one can ask a computer to do the desired tasks or run specific programs by speaking into the computer. But until such time, programs need to be written and instructions need to be given in order for the computer to do its job.

Before writing a program, one must decide what data (input) is needed by the program and what information (output) one wants the particular program to produce. For example, if we were to write a program to calculate the average marks of three subjects for each student, then the first step of the program is make provision to acquire inputs (marks) for the three subjects, the next step would be to save them somewhere like temporary storage, thereafter the actually processing or math operation would be carried to arrive at the average figure, which is the output. This output can be presented to a user in several ways like in table format on a computer screen, or as a printout, etc.

The main aspects of a good computer program are discussed as follows:

1. **Readability**—refers to the ease with which other programmers or new programmers are able to read and understand a program. The program should be written in such a way that it enables other programmers or users to follow the logic of the program without much effort.
2. **Efficiency**—is another important aspect of a good program. It is the degree with which a program fulfills its purpose without waste of resources.
3. **Flexibility**—refers to that aspect of a program where it is able to incorporate all the changes and future updates without having to reconstruct or rewrite the entire program or application.
4. **Portability**—is the ability of a program to run on different platforms with minimal changes.

5. **Structural**—refers to breaking down of a program into subtasks whereby each subtask can be performed without any dependency on the other subtasks. A program developed in such a manner is more readable, and the processes of documentation and testing also become manageable.
6. **Debugging**—is another important aspect of a good program. The process of ensuring that a particular program runs correctly without any coding errors, bugs and runtime exceptions is call debugging.
7. **Reusability**—refers to the use of an existing program or program knowledge to build new programs.

Table 21: Program and Program Category

Program	Program Category
Microsoft Word	Word Processor
Microsoft PowerPoint	Presentation
Microsoft Excel	Spreadsheet
Google Chrome, Mozilla Firefox	Internet Browser
Outlook, Gmail	Email Client
Adobe Dreamweaver, Microsoft Expression Web	HTML Editor
Microsoft Visual Studio, PHPEdit	Source Code Editor
Adobe Photoshop	Photo Editor

7.2.1 Basic Types of Programs

A computer performs a myriad of programs. Each and every operation that a computer performs has instructions that a programmer or a team of programmers has to write in a programming language. The basic types of programs are:

1. **Input**—is one of the most important aspects of programming concepts and fundamentals. All applications require some type of input. Each and every program needs an input for it to execute. Input could come from a variety of sources, another application, another program, a user, etc.

2. **Output**—once the input/data is in fed to a program, one wants the system to output the results. The output may take the form of output to a monitor, output to another program, printed documents, etc.
3. **Conditional Execution**—this type of program causes variable flow of execution of the same program, each time the program is run, based on a certain condition to be true or false.
4. **Math**—a program used for solving mathematical problems; performs calculations like addition and multiplication.
5. **Repetition, Sequence and Selection**—a repetition lets a code snippet or a certain part of a program to be executed any number of times dependent on some condition being met. An occurrence of repetition is generally known as a loop. A sequence involves simple steps which are to be executed one after the other. These steps are executed in the same order in which they are written. A selection is used to determine which particular step or set of steps need to be executed. A selection statement can be used to choose a specific path of execution dependent on a certain condition. There are two types of selection: binary selection (two possible paths) and multi-way selection (many possible paths).

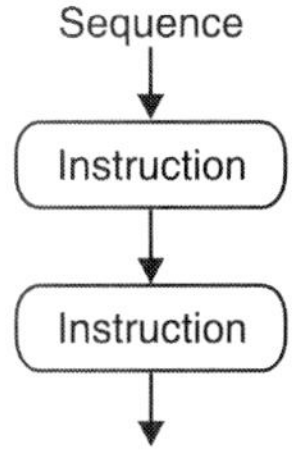

Figure 27: SEQUENCE FLOWCHART

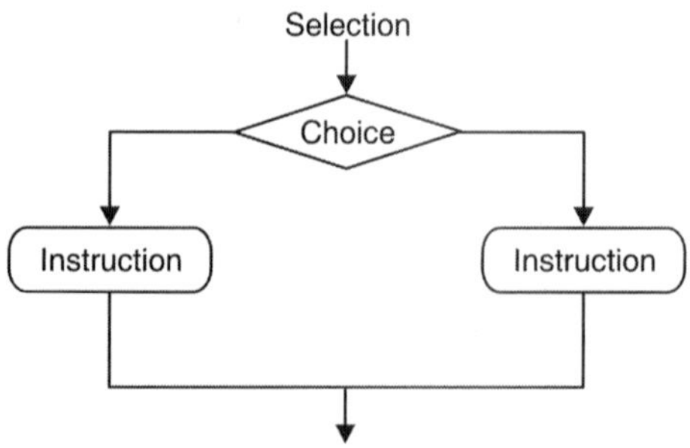

Figure 28: SELECTION FLOWCHART

7.3 Basic Elements of Programming—Values, Variables and More

To develop programming instructions, there are some basic elements needed and these are explained as follows:

1. **Values and Data Types**—a value is a piece of information, such as a number, like the value 16, or a string, like the value "Greetings to all". A "string" data type indicates a container that can hold a value of string of characters.
   Each value belongs to a specific data type, where a type is a set of possible values that are related by the fact that they are defined by the values they can take, the operations that can be performed on it, or the programming language used. A data type can be numeric, decimal, alphanumeric, etc., and it specifies the size and type of values/information that can be stored in an identifier. Most languages have two types: primitive data types like boolean, character, integer and floating type; non-primitive are usually defined by a programmer and examples include array, stack, queue, etc.
2. **Variables and Constants**—a variable is a data container that stores information and the value inside may change at any time during the course of a program. In other words, a variable is a name that refers to a value. A constant is a data container that stores information and the value will never change at any time during the

course of a program. Most programming languages support two types of variable initialization: variable initialization at the time of variable definition (static initialization) or dynamic initialization in which the variable initialization is done at run time. At run time a variable can be initialized using expressions at the place of declaration.

Variables tell how data is represented that can range from something very simple such as the name of a person to something very complex like the employment record of employees holding their name, address, qualifications, etc.

Character variables are letters of the alphabet, ASCII characters, or numbers 0-9. Numeric variables can either be of the type integer (int) or of the type real (float). Integer (int) values are whole numbers like 0 or -1. Real values can have a decimal point in them like 2.3 or -11.22. Boolean variables can only hold the values true or false.

How to Declare a Variable
Declaration of a variable involves declaring the type-name and after the type-name, the name of the variable is stated. Declaration of a variable associates a type and an identifier (or name) with the variable.

A constant is a value that never changes. The value stored in a constant is locked for the duration of the program. A constant can be a character string like "this is a good" or a character like b, or a number like 16. Typical examples of compile-time constants include mathematical constants, internal configuration values or values from standards. Generally there are four types of constants: numeric is further divided into real constant and integer; character is further divided into single character constant and string constant.

Table 22: Differences between Variables and Constants

Variables	Constants
Value can be changed anytime during the course of the program	Value remains constant and it cannot be changed during the course of the program
Variables can be initialized dynamically	Dynamic initialization of constants is not possible
Example: a=15 means associating the value 15 to the name a and this value can change anytime during the course of the program	Example: const float PI = 3.1415927 this value will remain constant throughout the program

3. **Loops**—a sequence of instructions, or a specific block of code, or a statement, or a group of statements that is continually repeated until a certain condition is reached. All high-level programming languages provide various forms of loops, which can be used to execute one or more statements repeatedly. Loops allow us to "code once" and then "execute many times". Usually programming statements are executed sequentially, i.e., the first statement in a function is executed first, followed by the second, and so on. But at times loops are needed to fulfill certain requirements, for example in a payroll program, a loop could be needed to calculate the salary and bonus for all employees in a certain company.

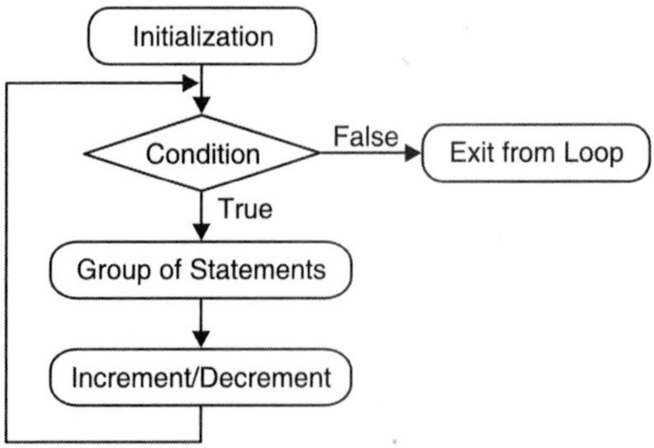

Figure 29: GENERIC LOOP FLOWCHART

In a loop, usually three basic operations are performed: initialization, condition check and increment/decrement. Variable initialization allows to either declare a variable and give it a value, or to assign a value to an already existing variable. Second, the condition tells the program that while the conditional expression is true the loop should continue to repeat itself.

The most common types of loops are: *while loop* and *for loop*. *While loop* is used when we do not know how many times the loop will be executed, but want to continue until a certain condition is met. In the *for loop*, we know how many times the loop will be executed. *For loop* statement defines the start and end-point as well as the increment/decrement for each iteration. Another example of loops is *do...while* loop which executes a block of code at least once and then repeatedly executes the block or not, depending on a given Boolean condition at the end of the block. A *do...while* loop is similar to a while loop, except for the fact that it gets executed at least one time and the test for condition check is performed at the end of the do...while loop.

There are also nested loops where the code for one loop is placed inside the code of another loop. In this case the inner loop is executed one time in its entirety for every time the outer loop executes. While all types of loops may be nested, the most commonly nested loops are for loops.

Other types of loops are *Goto loop* and *infinite loop*. Goto loop performs a one-way transfer of control to another line of code. The jumped-to location is usually identified by a label or line number. At the machine code level, a Goto is a form of branch or jump statement. Infinite loop, also called an *endless loop*, is a piece of code that lacks a functional exit and this makes it repeat itself indefinitely. Usually, an infinite loop results from a programming error. If the presence of the specified condition cannot be determined, the next instruction in the sequence tells the program to return to the first instruction and repeat the sequence, and this typically goes on until the program terminates automatically after certain duration of time or the operating system terminates the program with an error. But at times, infinite loops are used deliberately in certain cases like embedded system or a demo program.

A Word of Caution
Goto loop makes it difficult to trace the control flow of a program, making the program hard to understand and hard to change.

Table 23: Types of Loops

Loop Type	Description

For	Used to repeat a section of code for a known number of times.
	for (variable initialization; condition; variable update)
	{
	Code to execute while the condition is true
	}

While	Allows code to be executed repeatedly based on a given Boolean condition
	while (condition)
	{
	Code to execute while the condition is true
	}

Do...While	Executes a specified statement(s) until the test condition evaluates to false do { statement(s) } while(condition)

Nested	The first pass of the outer loop triggers the inner loop, which executes to completion. Then the second pass of the outer loop triggers the inner loop again and this process repeats until the outer loop finishes
	for (init; condition; increment)
	{
	for (init; condition; increment)
	{
	statement(s);
	}
	statement(s);
	}

The *break* statement is like an emergency exit for a while loop or for loop. It causes an immediate jump to the commands after the end of the loop body. The break statement allows exiting a loop from any point within its body, bypassing its normal termination expression. The *continue* statement skips the rest of a loop and then repeats the body from the next round or iteration. In while and do-while loops, a continue statement will cause control to go directly to the test condition and then continue the looping process. In the case of for loop, the increment/ decrement part of the loop continues. The continue statement is the opposite of the break statement.

Loops execute programming tasks faster and in an accurate manner. They help programmers to develop programs that are efficient and effective in meeting business needs.

4. **Conditionals**—they specify execution of a group of statements depending on whether or not a particular condition is satisfied; perform an action depending on whether a specified Boolean condition evaluates to true or false.

Spotlight Tip
We can combine more than one condition into a single condition using AND or OR as long as in the end, the expression only produces one value: true or false.

If statement is a programming conditional statement that, if proved true, performs a certain function. Often a computer program must make choices on which way to proceed. If this condition is true then do this task or else do that task. These tasks are called conditions and these conditions are usually expressed in the form of a mathematical statement using equal to, less than, or greater than. For example: if (myvar < 5) {print "value is less than 5"}, in this example, if the variable myvar is less than 5, the program prints "value is less than 5" on the screen.

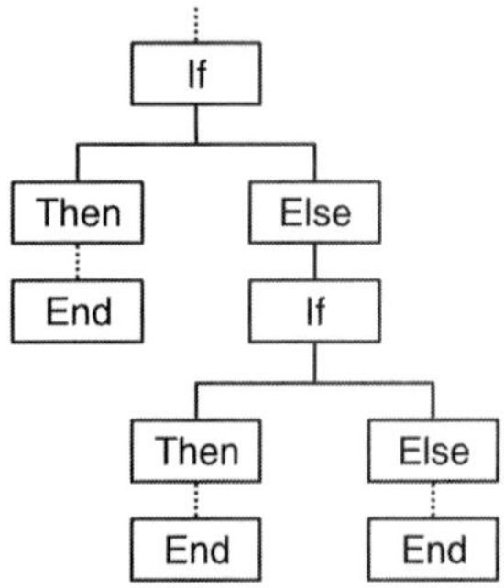

Figure 30: IF-THEN-ELSE FLOWCHART

5. Subroutines and Functions—they allow us to put frequently used snippets of code into one location that can then be accessed over and over again.

   A subroutine is a reusable section of the software. It is a group of instructions that usually performs one task that is stored in memory once but can be used often. A subroutine with a private scope can only be called from the source file from where it was defined. A subroutine with a public scope can be called from anywhere in the program. A subroutine is normally invoked by a call statement. We can pass values to a subroutine by placing them in parentheses after the name of the subroutine in the call statement; these are called arguments.

A function is like a mini-program. A function is the same as a subroutine but usually returns a result/value in the function name.

The general form of a function:

Function Name (arguments)
declarations
subprogram statements
Return
End

Table 24: Differences between Subroutines and Functions

Subroutine	Function
Works directly with the values of the caller or code segment which invoked it	Takes parameters, works locally and does not alter any value or work with any value outside its scope
Subroutine may or may not return a value; it need not contain return statement.	Normally returns a value to the program that references it
Subroutine return values via arguments	Function return values via the function name
A subroutine is normally invoked by a call statement	Referenced by using its name in an expression

Parameters are used in subroutines and functions, and they are a way of passing data to be used with the subroutine or function. The most common methods of passing a parameter are to pass the value of the actual parameter (call by value) or to pass the address of the memory location where the actual parameter is stored (call by reference). A parameter is a variable declared in the declaration whereas an argument is the actual parameter value that is passed to a function or subroutine by the caller.

6. **Control Structure**—is a block of programming that analyzes variables and chooses a direction in which to go based on given conditions and parameters. These initial conditions and parameters are called preconditions; these are the state of variables

before entering a control structure. Based on these preconditions, a computer runs the control structure to decide what to do. It is the basic decision-making process. There is a way in programming to 'select' which lines of code to execute and which lines to skip, and that will all depend on the state/value of the variables inside of a control structure. The result is called a postcondition (state of variables after the control structure is run).

When a program is executed it is read line by line and this is called code flow. As this code flow is being read, it may come to a point where it needs to make a decision. And this decision could make the flow jump to some another point in the program, or repeat a code snippet or just skip a certain section of the program. This decision will in turn affect the flow of code and this concept is known as a control structure.

In the If-Else control structure, when the "if" condition is true then the set of statements enclosed in if body get executed, otherwise when the condition is false, the else statements gets executed. If-Then statement is a simple control structure that tests whether a condition is true or false. If a condition is true, then a particular action occurs and if the condition is false, nothing is done. If-Then-Else is another control structure, in which the flow of action can be in more than one way, and it can take a secondary course of action. If the condition is true, then an action occurs. If the condition is false, then an alternate action occurs. A control structure placed inside another control structure is said to be nested.

7.4 Types of Languages—Low-level and High-level

A programming language is a special language programmers use to develop software programs or other sets of detailed instructions for computers to process and execute. Although there are 2,000+ programming languages, relatively few are widely used. From the first generation to the current generation of computers, there is a plethora of programming languages used to communicate with the computer. There are two basic types of languages: low-level languages and high-level languages.

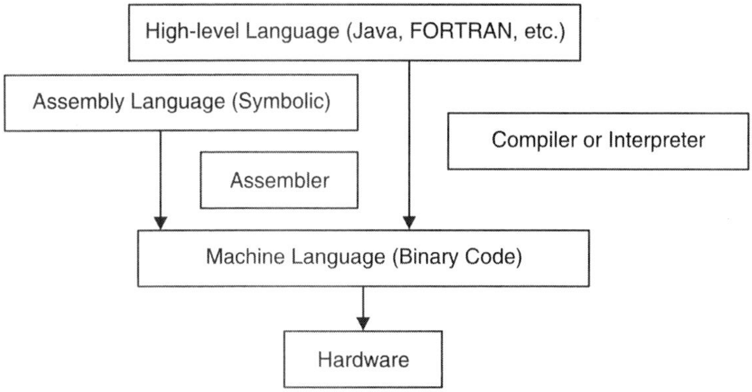

Figure 31: LOW-LEVEL AND HIGH-LEVEL LANGUAGES

7.4.1 Machine Language—Elemental Language

Machine language, also called machine code or object code, is the elemental language of a computer that consists of the numeric codes for the operations that the computer can execute directly. It is the native language directly understood by the computer's central processing unit.

Machine language instruction has two components: operand and operation code. Operand tells a computer where to find or store the data and operation code tells a computer what function is to be performed. Operation codes differ from one machine model to another.

Machine language is a collection of binary digits or bits that the computer reads and interprets. It is almost impossible for humans to read and write as this language does not resemble normal human interface languages or conventional mathematical notations, and its codes vary from computer to computer. Each instruction performs a very specific task, such as a jump, load, or an ALU operation on a unit of data in a CPU register or memory.

Spotlight Tip
Each type of CPU has its own machine language. It is written in binary code of 1s and 0s, and they represent electric impulses or on and off electrical states respectively. This code or instructions are organized in various lengths such as 16 bits, 24 bits, 32 bits, etc.

Machine language is created by conversion programs called assemblers, compilers and interpreters. These conversion programs convert the programmer's source code into binary-coded machine instructions. A programmer understands and presents data input and output in a logical manner, for example, "add this and that," whereas for the computer to perform this operation, machine language is needed to tell the computer where precisely this and that are located.

The main advantage of machine language is that there is no need of a translator or interpreter to translate the code; the computer can directly understand this language. The disadvantages include error debugging is difficult, remembering the operation codes is a herculean task, and moreover as it is machine dependent only a single type of computer can work with it.

7.4.2 Assembly Language—One Level Above Machine Language

Assembly language is a low-level programming language used to interface with the computer hardware, microcontroller or any other programmable device. Assembly language is one level above machine language. It is almost similar in structure and has a similar set of commands as that of a machine language but instead of bits, assembly language uses short alphanumeric mnemonic codes for instructions. It is symbolic and non-binary in format.

Each and every assembly language is hardware dependent and is specific to a particular computer architecture. An assembly language program can be written from scratch or it may be produced by compiling source code from a high-level programming language. Programming in assembly languages requires extensive knowledge of computer architecture.

The main types of assemblers: one-pass and multi-pass. A one-pass assembler scans a program only once and creates the equivalent binary program. A one-pass assembler is used when it is desirable to avoid a second pass over the source program, but the disadvantage with this assembler is that it cannot forward reference in the program. Forward referencing means reference to an instruction which has not yet been encountered by the assembler. In order to handle forward reference, a program needs to be scanned twice, and this is where a multi-pass assembler comes in the picture. A one-pass assembler goes through the source code once assuming that all symbols will be defined before any instructions that references them. A multi-pass assembler performs two passes to resolve the forward references, as it creates a table with all symbols and their values in the first pass. Thereafter, it uses this table in a second pass to generate code and the length of each instruction on the first pass must be determined so that the addresses of symbols can be calculated.

Assembly language code needs to be converted into executable machine code by a utility program referred to as an assembler. The conversion process is referred to as assembling the source code. Examples of assemblers include GNU Assembler, FASM Assembler, etc. The translated program is called as object program. The assembly language program is fed to the assembler via an input device, then the assembler produces the object code in machine language, and finally the program is executed.

Each instruction is represented by one assembly language statement. Some of the basic elements of an assembly language are directives, comments, labels and orders. A directive provides directions to the assembler in order to carry out the assembly process; a directive is used to issue commands to the assembler itself. Examples of common directives are ORG (origin) and EQU (equate). A comment is used to facilitate proper documentation of a program. A comment comes in two forms: endline comment (appears at the end of a source statement) and standalone comment (appears on a line by itself). A label is a special type of symbol used to represent textual version of an address in RAM or ROM. A label is always placed at the beginning of a program line. During the process of compiling, the assembler automatically replaces such labels with appropriate addresses.

The advantages of assembly language are that it is suitable for time critical jobs, it is used for optimizing programs for speed or size in small embedded systems, it provides easy access to system registers, hardware, etc., and it requires fewer instructions to accomplish the same result. The disadvantages are that an assembly program written for one computer might not run on other computers with different hardware configuration as assembly language is machine dependent and platform-specific (portability becomes difficult), it has difficult syntax to remember and coding time is longer than coding time in high-level languages.

Assembly language programs are challenging to develop as they require a great deal of experience and knowledge. Code written for assembly language might not run on another computer with a different hardware configuration. As assembly language code is nearer to machine code, it is fast to process and returns the output immediately. Assembly language programs are used for developing firmware codes for micro-controllers, interrupt service routines or for new operating systems. Earlier programs like database managers, operating systems, etc., and many other applications were written in assembly language to maximize the machine's performance, but these days C or C++ is widely used instead.

7.4.3 High-level Language—Closer to Humans

These days, most programs are written in high-level languages such as Java, FORTRAN, Prolog, Visual Basic, Ruby, C++, etc., and they are used for several purposes, right from scientific applications to general uses and from business applications to artificial intelligence. The first high-level programming languages were designed in the 1950s. Several specialized high-level languages like Simulation Language (SIMAN) and List Processing Language (LISP) are very popular. A program written using a high-level language is called a source code. They follow a strict syntax that facilitates the conversion of source code into accurate machine code. A single instruction in high-level language is equivalent to several instructions in machine language.

Spotlight Tip
High-level languages are referred to as "closer to humans" as they are designed to make programming easier and less error-prone.

Programs written in high-level languages are easier to write, read, modify and maintain. They are user-friendly as they are written in English-like language. They are problem-oriented rather than machine-based; they let the programmer to concentrate on the logic of the problem rather than the intricacies of the machine architecture. A program written for one computer can generally be run on many different computers with a little or no change.

A high-level language enables programmers to write programs that are more or less independent of a particular type of computer or hardware architecture. However, as with assembly languages, every single high-level program written in a high-level language must be interpreted into machine language before it is executed by a computer. Every single high-level program has to be processed by passing it through a program called a compiler or interpreter, which translates it into machine code before it can be executed.

The basic purpose of a complier and an interpreter is the same—translate a code written in high-level language which humans can understand to executable machine language which computer systems can understand, but there is a slight difference. A compiler translates high-level language programs directly into machine language programs. It first checks a computer program and lists all the errors found, and after all errors are corrected, the compiler then converts this error-free source code into machine code or object code. Examples of programming languages that use compilers include COBOL, C and C++. An interpreter works line-by-line and this is how the high-level language is read and then executed as it goes line by line, with no compilation stage. Examples of programming languages that use interpreters include Visual Basic, Ruby, Basic and PHP.

Table 25: Compiler versus Interpreter

Compiler	Interpreter
A complier works on the complete program at once. It takes the entire program as input.	An interpreter works line-by-line. It takes input as one statement at a time.
Generates intermediate object code which further requires linking, hence requires more memory. A complied program takes more memory because the entire object code has to reside in memory.	No intermediate object code is generated; hence an interpreter is memory efficient.
Executes conditional control statements and logical constructs faster than an interpreter.	Executes conditional control statements and logical constructs at a much slower speed.
Errors are reported after the entire program is checked.	Checks for errors in a program statement by statement.
A compiled program does not need to be compiled every time. Compile once and run anytime.	An interpreted program is interpreted line-by-line every time it needs to be run.
Debugging is comparatively hard as a compiler generates a list of errors only after scanning the entire program. Compiled languages are more efficient but difficult to debug.	Debugging is easy because an interpreter stops and reports errors as soon as it encounters them. Interpreted languages are less efficient but easier to debug.

A high-level language allows for the development of programs to occur at a high level of abstraction, both computation abstraction and data abstraction, in order to insulate the programmer from low-level complexities like memory management and provide a more user-friendly programming experience. Abstraction allows the programmers to focus on solving the problem and not deal with details that are not part of the problem.

When high-level languages are standardized by international bodies then the manufacturers can develop compilers to compile programs that conform to a specific standard into their own internal machine language. This makes it easy to take a program which conforms to the standard and implement it on many different computers merely by re-compiling it. The main advantage of a high-level language is portability of programs.

7.4.4 Other Types of Languages—Visual, Scripting and More

There are also other types of languages which are as follows:

1. **Visual language**—a visual programming language (VPL), also known as executable graphics language, is a language that uses graphical images and elements to develop programs. The textual software code is replaced with a series of visual graphics elements like animation, graphics or icons, partially or completed. In an increasingly digital world, we are communicating more with images and less with words; hence these languages are becoming popular day by day. Visual languages are suitable for applications in the field of system simulation and scientific visualization.

   The main elements of a visual language are: any system that involves writing of programs using two or more dimensions, and it allows programming with visual expressions or manipulates visual information. Conventional text-based languages are not considered two-dimensional since the compiler or interpreter processes them as one-dimensional streams of characters.

Spotlight Tip
A visual language can be classified based on the type and extent of visual expressions used like diagram languages and icon-based languages.

Languages like Visual C++ and Visual Basic are partially visual in nature; they are primarily textual languages with a graphical GUI environment (only the user interface portion is visual to make programming interface easier). Authentic visual language examples include: Pict, CODE 2.0 and Prograph. Prograph is an entirely graphical visual programming language and environment based on iconic symbols to represent actions to be taken on data.

2. **Scripting language**—a scripting or script language is one that supports scripts. It is often a simpler language and much easier to learn in comparison to other languages, as it uses relatively simple syntax and semantics. It is language that is interpreted or translated on the fly rather than compiled ahead of time. It is a series of commands within a file that is capable of being executed without being compiled. This type of language is easy to port between different operating systems.

   The difference between a scripting language and programming language is that a scripting language is less code intensive as compared to a traditional programming language. Scripts facilitate the development of content-rich and functionality-rich websites. In the case of scripting an application, a scripting language is also known as an extension language.

A scripting language may be a general purpose language or it may be used for specific functions to support the running of an application or a system program. Many applications have their own limited purpose scripting languages, for example, Visual Basic for Applications (VBA) is a subset of Visual Basic and it is used to automate Microsoft Office applications, another example is of macros used in spreadsheets.

Another type of scripting language is command language or command script. It is a language composed mainly of a set of commands, through which a user specifically communicates with the operating system. For example, the DOS command language includes commands like DIR, DEL, etc. The part of an operating system that responds to operating system commands is called the command processor. A command language usually has stronger coupling to the underlying OS.

There are two main types of scripting languages—server side scripting and client side scripting. Server side scripting languages usually manipulate and process data at the server end like a database. Client side scripting languages usually process and affect data that a client sees usually in a browser; they are commonly embedded in HTML pages and deal with user interface components. Client-side scripting languages include JavaScript. PHP, Ruby and Python are examples of server side scripting languages.

Advantages of scripting languages include easy portability between different operating systems as they are open source, they allow users to view and edit the script, they are easy to grasp and write, they facilitate complex tasks to be performed in relatively few steps, and they are much faster to develop than actual programs. Disadvantages include: they may not be supported by all browsers, as they are text-based they can be rendered broken by modifications, and they can be used for malicious purposes.

Some of the applications of scripting languages include extracting information from a data set, graphic displays and automating certain tasks in a program.

Table 26: Advantages and Disadvantages of Scripting Languages

Advantages	Disadvantages
The code file may not require compilation	In some cases, a script may be slower than complied code
Much faster to develop than an actual program	Requires the user to install an interpreter before the script can be executed
Open source allows users to view and edit the script	Some companies may prohibit users from viewing or editing the script

3. **Markup language**—a language that consists of keywords, names, or tags that help format the overall view of a page and the data it contains; its aim is to structure information in a specific format. Some examples of a markup language are Hypertext Markup Language (HTML), eXtensible Markup Language (XML) and Extensible Hypertext Markup Language (XHTML). HTML is the basic language used to create documents for the World Wide Web. XML is a text-based markup language derived from Standard Generalized Markup Language and it is used for representation and transfer of structured data on the web or between different applications. XHTML is almost identical to HTML 4.01 with only few differences and it helps web developers make the transition from HTML to XML. Most markup languages are human readable. Markup is also used to indicate special characters to display or print, including those that are not available on a standard keyboard.

Markup languages specify code for formatting, both the layout and style, within a text file. The code used to specify the formatting is called tags. For example, with HTML, XML and XHTML, the markup tags are enclosed between < and >. Any text that appears within these signs is considered as part of the markup language and not part of the annotated text. For example: Example of <i>italics</i> in HTML. As can be seen in this example, the <i> tag is just one of many HTML tags that can be used to control or change the look of a web page. Here is the output of this example: Example of *italics* in HTML. <i> and </i> indicate that the enclosed text will be rendered in italics.

Markup languages are different from programming languages. A markup language does not usually have any functional properties or does not have any programming logic, whereas a programming language does.

4. **System language**—a language used for system programming; for writing system software. The earliest system software was written in assembly language. System software is the interface between the user applications and hardware. Operating system is the best known example of system software; other examples include device drivers, linkers, runtime libraries and compilers.

   System language programming requires some level of hardware knowledge and is machine dependent. In contrast to application languages, a system language can access the hardware. Some application languages can also be used to write system programs, although some routines may still need to be written in assembly language.

   The basic difference between a system language and application language is that a system language is used to write software which provides services to a computer system whereas an application language is used to write software which provides services to a user. Over time, this difference between system programming languages and application programming languages has become blurred with the widespread popularity of PL/I, C and Pascal.

7.5 Questions for Reflection

1. What is programming?
2. Describe the main aspects of a computer program?
3. What is a flowchart?
4. What is the difference between variables and constants?
5. Are computer games programs?
6. Describe the various types of loops?
7. Differentiate between machine-level and high-level languages?

8

The Internet—The Super Network

The Internet has revolutionized the world communication scenario like never before. Its reach touches all points on the world compass. Geographic location does not affect its information dissemination capacity. It is a worldwide system of a super network of computer networks and other electronic devices. Anyone who connects to the Internet through a computer or any other electronic device can access any sort of information, can download all types of material and can connect to anyone who is on the internet. This is called 'going online', which also indicates a state of connectivity. The Internet is a vast array of interconnected networks and devices that entails services far beyond just web pages.

The Internet first started being developed in the late 1960s and began in 1969 as the US Department of Defense's Advanced Research Project Agency (ARPA) to provide immediate communication within the Department in case of war. As more and more scholars began to go online, this network expanded its focus from military use to scientific use too. As this project grew, more and more people gained access to the Internet and began shaping it to what we know it as today.

Today, the Internet is a public service accessible to hundreds of millions of people worldwide. As much as it has changed our lives, in the process, the Internet itself has changed too. The Internet's exceptional success continues to thrive because the Internet model is open, unique, transparent and collaborative. It provides shared global ownership and freely accessible processes for technology and policy development. One can connect to the Internet through cable modems, smartphones and other mobile devices, WiFi, etc.

Just as the postal service enables people to send each other envelopes containing messages, the Internet enables computer users to send each other small packets of digital data. Just like postal envelopes can contain different types of data like documents, letters, photos, etc., similarly, the Internet data packets can contain several types of data like files, graphic images, etc.

According to the report by Internet World Stats, here are the figures of World Internet Usage and Population Statistics as of March 2017.

Table 27: World Internet Usage and Population Statistics (as of March 2017) (Source: http://www.internetworldstats.com/stats.htm)

World Internet Usage and Population Statistics as of March 2017						
Regions	**Population (2017 Est.)**	**Popula-tion % of World**	**Internet Users 31 Mar 2017**	**Pene-tration Rate (% Popu-lation)**	**Growth 2000-2017**	**Users % Table**
Africa	1,246,504,865	16.6%	345,676,501	27.7%	7,557.2%	9.3%
Asia	4,148,177,672	55.2%	1,873,856,654	45.2%	1,539.4%	50.2%
Europe	822,710,362	10.9%	636,971,824	77.4%	506.1%	17.1%
Latin America/ Caribbean	647,604,645	8.6%	385,919,382	59.6%	2,035.8%	10.3%
Middle East	250,327,574	3.3%	141,931,765	56.7%	4,220.9%	3.8%
North America	363,224,006	4.8%	320,068,243	88.1%	196.1%	8.6%
Oceania / Australia	40,479,846	0.5%	27,549,054	68.1%	261.5%	0.7%
World Total	7,519,028,970	100.0%	3,731,973,423	49.6%	933.8%	100.0%

8.1 History of the Internet—From Government-Run to Global

The Internet has evolved from a small government-run network of researchers to a network of networks that practically runs the whole world now. The Internet today is a widespread information infrastructure developed from the initial prototype, Galactic or Global Information Infrastructure.

J.C.R. Licklider of MIT first proposed a global network of computers in 1962 and then moved over to the Defense Advanced Research Projects Agency (DARPA) in late 1962 to head the work to develop his proposed idea. He envisioned a globally interconnected set of computers through which everyone could quickly access data and programs.

1960s-1970s—ARPANET—Leonard Kleinrock of MIT and later UCLA developed the theory of packet switching, which formed the basis of Internet connections. Lawrence Roberts of MIT connected a Massachusetts computer with a California computer in 1965 over dial-up telephone lines. This demonstrated the feasibility of wide area networking, but also showed that the telephone line's circuit switching was inadequate. Kleinrock's packet switching theory was confirmed. Roberts moved over to DARPA in 1966 and developed his plans for ARPANET.

The Internet (then known as ARPANET) went online in 1969 and it was mainly used by engineers, scientists, computer experts and librarians. It initially connected four computers of UCLA, Stanford Research Institute, UCSB and the University of Utah. In the next two years several other institutes were plugged into the Internet like Harvard, MIT, Carnegie-Mellon and more. Computers were added quickly to the ARPANET during the following years and work on finishing a functionally complete Host-to-Host protocol and other network software was also done side by side.

The Internet developed at a matured rate in the 1970s due to TCP/IP architecture. TCP/IP architecture or protocol suite is the conceptual model and set of communication protocols used to interconnect network devices on the Internet. It implements layers of protocol stacks and each layer provides well-defined network services to the upper layer protocol. This architecture was a result of the joint work of Bob Kahn at ARPA and Vint Cerf at Stanford. Ethernet was developed in 1974 and it is a link layer protocol in the TCP/IP stack, commonly used in local area networks (LAN), metropolitan area networks (MAN) and wide area networks (WAN).

Unix to Unix Copy Protocol (UUCP) was invented in 1978 at Bell Labs. Usenet was started in 1979 based on UUCP. Usenet is a collection of newsgroups where users can post messages and these messages are distributed via Usenet servers. Though Usenet was not a part of Internet as it does not use TCP/IP, it linked Unix systems across the globe, and this helped many Internet sites to access the newsgroups. This development was a significant step in online community building.

BITNET was an early world leader in network communications for the research and education communities as it provided a network of academic sites. Its name was originally taken from the phrase "Because It's There Net," but later changed to "Because It's Time Net". It laid the groundwork for the current Internet's introduction, especially to areas outside the US. Listserv software was developed for this network and later on used for other networks as well. Listserv and other email discussion lists enhanced online community building.

As the standards for FTP, E-mail, and other aspects of the Internet became established, it became easier for non-technical users to join the Internet. Other departments besides computer science, engineering and libraries, also started communicating with their counterparts around the world and started sharing resources.

As more and more universities and organizations joined the Internet bandwagon, keeping track of resources became difficult. Archie, an application created in 1990 by Alan Emtage while he was still a student at McGill University in Montreal, was used for indexing *FTP* archives, allowing people to find specific files. It is considered to be the first Internet search engine. Then in 1991, Gopher protocol was introduced, it represented an early alternative to the World Wide Web.

Spotlight Tip
The emergence of a commercially-based Internet became possible due to the significant event that took place in 1989, where Tim Berners-Lee and others at CERN, proposed a new protocol for information distribution. This protocol eventually became the World Wide Web.

The Internet was initially funded by the government National Science Foundation (NSF is United States government agency that supports fundamental research and education in all the non-medical fields of science and engineering); hence it was limited to education, research and government uses. But from the early 1990s, independent commercial networks began to grow and this growth made it possible to route traffic across various locations without needing the support of the government funded NSFNet Internet backbone. Microsoft's entry on the horizon of the Internet led to its tremendous growth. The release of Microsoft Internet Explorer added more value to the Internet.

Wireless (WiFi) networking has grown rapidly in the last few years. It allows users to connect to the Internet without the wires. WiFi is already connecting the Internet of Things applications. Another trend that is rapidly growing on the horizon of the Internet is more and more WiFi "hot spots" are made available to enable universal wireless access. All sorts of smart devices like smartphones, tablets, smartwatches, etc., are beginning to tap into the Internet on the go. From our computers to our smartphones, most devices today are equipped to use WiFi.

The Internet has become faster, accessible and universal to both technical and non-technical communities, and this has enabled both technical and non-technical communities to share their common interests, and this has led to the building of a global social community.

The Internet in its modern-day avatar has become a ubiquitous tool and a worldwide phenomenon facilitating both technical and non-technical communities to coexist and enabling people from all walks of life to exchange information and communication. This proliferation of the Internet and its services has led to an unprecedented growth in collaborative services and social networking opportunities.

8.2 Topology of the Internet—Arrangement of a Network

A topology is the arrangement of a network, including its nodes and connecting lines. Network topologies are categorized into the following basic types: star, bus, tree, ring and mesh. The basic topologies can be implemented simply or in a combination with each other to create hybrid networks.

A Word of Caution
There are many different ways a network can be designed, connected, and accessed. Organizations need to assess all aspects before deciding on the type of topology or else there could be a mismatch between the topology and their business needs and goals.

8.2.1 Star Topology—Central Point of Communication

Star topology is the most commonly used network topology. All the network nodes are individually connected to a central switch, hub or computer which acts as a central point of communication to pass on the messages. The central point acts as a server and the peripheral devices act as clients.

Advantages include easy addition of nodes to the network, even if one node fails, the rest of the network can continue functioning, and centralized management is possible due to the central node. Disadvantages include complete network failure when the central node fails, and this topology can be costly to implement, especially when using a router or switch as the central node.

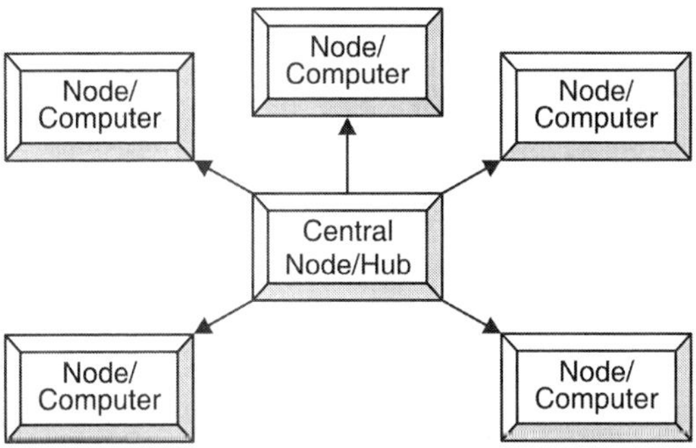

Figure 32: STAR TOPOLOGY

8.2.2 *Bus Topology—Single Cable or Backbone*

Bus topology, also called line topology, is a network setup in which each computer node and network device are connected to a single cable or backbone. Terminators are required for both ends of the cable. Taps and drop lines are used to connect nodes to this backbone. A tap is a connector. A drop line is a connection between the node and the backbone. Every device is connected to a single cable. It transmits data only in one direction.

Advantages include easier installation in comparison to other topologies, it is cost effective, and this topology requires less cabling as compared to tree and star topologies. Disadvantages include problem isolation becomes difficult when the whole network fails, it can be hard to troubleshoot individual devices, additional devices can slow down the network, cable has limited length, and this topology is not suited for large networks.

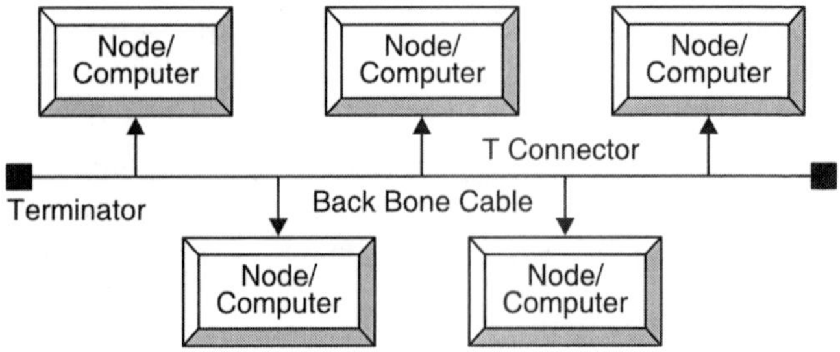

Figure 33: BUS TOPOLOGY

8.2.3 Tree Topology—Also Called Star Bus Topology

A tree topology is also called as a star bus topology. A single cable functions as a shared communication medium that devices attach with an interface connector. It integrates the characteristics of star and bus topology. In tree topology, star-configured computer systems are connected using a linear bus backbone cable. This main cable looks like the trunk whereas the other star networks resemble branches.

Advantages includes easy expansion and implementation of this topology, if one device becomes faulty then the other devices are not affected, and suitable for temporary setups. Disadvantages include maintenance becomes difficult as more devices are added, the data is visible to everyone on the network, and if there is problem in the main line, the entire network is rendered functionless.

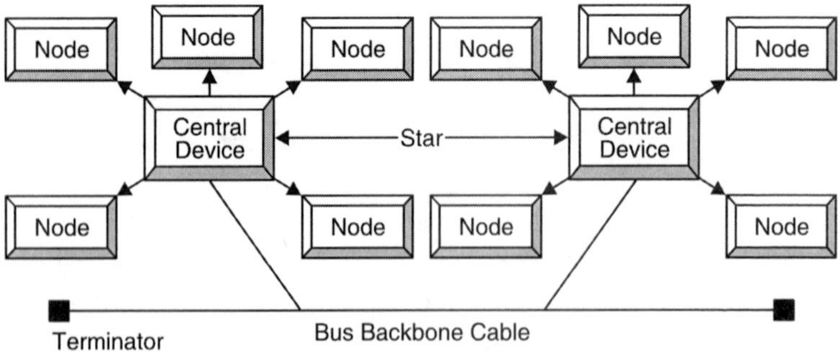

Figure 34: TREE TOPOLOGY

8.2.4 Ring Topology—Connected in a Closed Loop

A ring topology is a configuration in which each node connects to exactly two other nodes, forward and backward, thereby forming a single continuous path for signal transmission; devices are connected to each other in a closed loop. Every device has exactly two neighbors for communication purposes, with the last one connected to the first. Data travels from node to node. All computers in the network together form a ring. A ring topology has no beginning and no end.

There are two sub-types based on the data flow: unidirectional (handles data traffic in either clockwise or anticlockwise direction) and bidirectional (handles data traffic in dual direction). A bidirectional or dual-ring structure provides a backup option in case one direction fails; if one ring fails, the second ring can act as a backup to keep the network up and running.

Token passing is a major feature of the ring topology. A token is regularly passed from one node to another. If a node has some information to pass on the network, the node releases the information. If the node does not have any data to release on the network, then it transfers the token to the next node. At the start of transmission, a free token is circulating on the ring, and this is a data frame which is an empty vessel for transporting data. To use the network, a device first has to capture this free token and replace the data with its own message. One major benefit of token rings is that there is no danger of data colliding since only one token ever travels around the ring. In large ring networks, repeaters are used to prevent the loss of data.

Advantages include: it does not need a central hub in order to function, troubleshooting is easier, it is scalable, each device has equal access to resources, and all data flows in one direction thereby reducing the chance of packet collisions. Disadvantages include: failure in any device or cable breaks the loop and will render an entire segment functionless, it is slower than other topologies as each data packet must pass through all the computers between source and destination, and it is highly dependent on the wires.

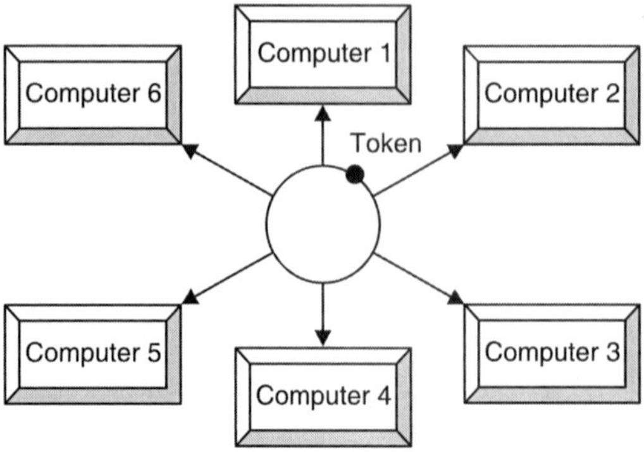

Figure 35: RING TOPOLOGY

8.3 Working of the Internet—Protocols, Hardware and More

How does the information move around the Internet? For example, if a user wants to access a particular image on a particular web page, then the user sends a request for this image, which is generally hosted on a particular web server. The user's computer sends this request to the required web server and the server returns the required resources. Thereafter the connection between the client and server is disconnected.

There are two main components of the Internet: protocols and hardware. Protocols are sets of rules that devices on the Internet follow to complete tasks. Without a common set of protocols that all devices connected to the Internet must follow, communication exchange between devices won't be possible. A protocol stack is set of network protocol layers that work together to provide networking capabilities. It is called a stack because it is designed as a hierarchy of layers, each supporting the one above it and using those below it. Each layer has a different function. This layered approach facilitates reuse and modularity. This approach facilitates allowing different protocols to be substituted for each other to accommodate new protocols and new network architectures.

Apart from the widely used TCP/IP model (4 layers) for network protocol architecture, another popular model is the Open Systems Interconnection (OSI) model (7 layers). The numbers of layers differ in both the models, but these two models share many common goals. The OSI model divides the functions of the Application layer into three layers: Application, Presentation, and Session. OSI divides the functions of the Network layer into two layers: Data Link and Physical.

The functions of the main layers of the Internet Protocol Stack are:

1. **Application Layer**—responsible for data formatting, creating sessions, process-to-process communication across a network and provides a communication interface and end-user services like chatting and email. This layer provides applications the ability to access the services provided by the other layers and defines the protocols that applications use to exchange data. This is done using messages. Some of the common application layer protocols are File Transfer Protocol, Hyper Text Transfer Protocol and Domain Name System. This layer is concerned with providing network services to applications and users.
2. **Transport Layer**—responsible for packaging data for host-to-host delivery. For long streams of data, data is divided into segments. It ensures the reliable delivery of messages and provides error checking mechanisms, data flow control and congestion control. The main protocols in this layer are Transmission Control Protocol (TCP) and User Datagram Protocol (UDP). TCP is a reliable, stateful and connection-oriented protocol whereas UDP is an unreliable, stateless and connection-less protocol. This layer is concerned with the transmission of data. Some applications

require reliable delivery of packets and this is where TCP is used, for example, applications like Telnet. Applications where reliable data delivery is not much of a priority then UDP can be used.

3. **Network Layer**—responsible for logical addressing, data encapsulation of messages received from the upper layers by placing them into packets, routing, error handling, and fragmenting and reassembling of large packets. This layer is concerned with constructing the packets of data. Some of the common network layer protocols are Address Resolution Protocol, Internet Control Message Protocol and Internet Protocol Version 4.
4. **Data Link Control (DLC) Layer**—if the network layer is the one that defines how interconnected networks work, the data link layer is the one that defines the boundaries of what is considered a network. This layer is responsible for identifying the network protocol, type of packets, error control, data flow control (controlling the rate at which the sender transmits so the receiver is not overwhelmed with data) and framing (putting delimiters around the packet to make a frame). This layer controls how data is placed onto the media and how it is received from the media using techniques such as error detection and media access control. Some of the common data link control protocols are Point-to-Point Protocol framing and Ethernet IEEE 802.2 framing.
5. **Physical Layer**—responsible for the transmission and reception of wire level data. This layer deals with the physical components (cables, wires, modem, Ethernet network card and electronics), signaling and data encoding. This layer deals with the how data is physically encoded and decoded. It defines the way in which data is physically converted into digital signals on the communication media.

Table 28: The Internet Protocol Stack

Protocol Layer	Purpose	Data Unit
Application	Provides network services to application programs	Message
Transport	Responsible for data segmentation, transmission, data flow control and error control	Segment
Network	Routes packets to their destination	Packet
Data Link Control	Responsible for identifying the network protocol, type of packets, error control and framing	Frame
Physical	Responsible for the transmission and reception of wire level data	Bit

8.3.1 Hardware—From Cables to Computers

The Internet includes several hardware components, everything from the cables that carry data every second to the computer sitting in front of you. Computers on the Internet include file servers, work stations, web servers, etc. Several end devices are also present like VoIP phones and printers.

Spotlight Tip
Depending on the type of network to be installed, some of the parts or components may not be needed. For example, in a wireless network, hubs and cables are not needed.

Communication across the Internet is carried through a network medium; physical channel used for transmission in the network. Common types of network media are coaxial cable, twisted-pair cable, fiber-optic cable and wireless. A coaxial cable is a type of shielded and insulated copper cable. A coaxial cable is the primary type of cabling used by the cable television industry and is widely installed for use in business Ethernet [Ethernet is a family of computer networking technologies commonly used in local area networks (LAN), metropolitan area networks (MAN) and wide area networks (WAN)] and other types of local area network also. A twisted-pair cable consists of two independently insulated wires twisted around one another, and this minimizes electromagnetic interference and crosstalk.

A twisted-pair cable is used in computer networks and to deliver cable TV services to end users. A fiber-optic cable uses glass or plastic threads (fibers) to transmit data; it transmits information as light pulses along a glass or plastic thread or fiber. A fiber-optic cable is the fastest form of broadband technology.

A host device is either the source or destination of a message/data transmitted over the network. In modern network setups, a host can act as a client, server or both. A network host handles user requests by offering services, information resources and applications to other nodes within a network.

Intermediary devices are also needed to interconnect end devices. These devices provide connectivity and work behind the scenes to ensure that the message/data flows smoothly across the network. These devices include switches, routers and firewalls. A switch acts as a controller, enabling devices to talk to each other. The Internet is not limited to merely two computers. One can connect as many computers as one wishes, but this setup can get complex quickly. To solve this problem, each computer on a network is connected to a special small computer called a router. A router is connected to at least two networks and it is located at a gateway, the place where two or more networks connect. Many routers are wireless, and this allows to create a wireless network. A switch creates a network, whereas a router connects a network. A firewall is a network security application or device that monitors incoming and outgoing packet requests, and blocks any request that may be from an untrusted zone.

A hub acts like a distribution center. It is a device that splits a network connection into multiple computers. A hub contains multiple ports. When a packet arrives at one port, it is copied to the other ports so that all segments of the network can see all packets. A hub deals with transmitting frames, whereas a router routes packet to other networks until that packet ultimately reaches its destination. Hubs are becoming obsolete and are being replaced by more advanced devices such as switches and routers. Several types of integrated routers are available that come with a wide variety of services; features of both a hub and a router are integrated in one device.

A modem is another crucial device to access the internet. It is a device that converts digital signals of the source computer to analog signals and passes them through the telephone line and again converts analog signals of the telephone line to digital signals and passes them to the destination computer. A router sits between a modem and computer. But it is not necessary to have a router but is beneficial to have one. A router adds another level of security to one's connection and also one can use it to operate a laptop in a wireless mode. Many modems include a built-in router. For a computer that does not have built-in WiFi connectivity, a WiFi adapter that plugs into a computer's USB port can be used to provide WiFi connectivity.

8.3.2 Protocols—Set of Communication Rules

Two of the most important protocols are the Transmission Control Protocol (TCP) and the Internet Protocol (IP). We often group the two together: TCP/IP. Every computer that connects to the Internet understands these two protocols and uses them to send and receive data.

1. **Transmission Control Protocol (TCP)**—is the protocol that figures out how to get the data from the source to the destination.

   The request is usually sent as a "data packet". It is a unit of data that is routed between an origin and a destination on the Internet or any other packet-switched network and it is formatted, addressed and sent using common Internet communication protocols such as the Transmission Control Protocol/Internet Protocol (TCP/IP). TCP/IP is the most prevalent protocol stack used to connect hosts to the network and networks to each other. It contains information such as the IP address of the intended recipient, source data and network information. The process of sending and receiving data packets is referred to as packet-switching.

TCP breaks down every piece of data into small chunks called packets. IP then figures out how the data is supposed to get from source to destination by passing it through a series of routers. Each router examines the destination addresses of the packets it receives and then passes the packets on to another router as they make their way to the final destination. If a piece of data is broken into five packets, then each of those may have traveled a completely separate route. But as each of the packets arrive at the final destination, TCP takes over again, identifying each packet and checking to see if it is intact. Once it has received all the packets, TCP reassembles them into the original data.

The information in the packet is composed of binary data so that it can be easily transmitted over the network. Each packet that arrives at the destination has some typical sections like header, message body and footer. The header section contains the packet origin (source address), packet number that identifies each packet within a sequence and packet destination information (destination address). The header section may also include additional instructions like packet size and protocols (on networks that carry multiple types of information and the protocol determines what type of packet is being transmitted, for example streaming video, email). The message body is also called the payload, and this represents the data that the packet is carrying. If the packet is smaller than the standard size then a filler needs to be added to reach the correct size. The footer section contains ending or termination instructions.

Once a packet arrives at its destination server, this server opens the packet and reads the request and then sends a response to the client browser. The browser then parses through the page and looks for other page elements it needs to complete the web page. In the case of applets, images or other embedded content, the browser makes additional connections and HTTP requests to appropriate servers for each of the element. Once the browser has finished loading all applets, images, etc., the page will be completely loaded in the browser instance.

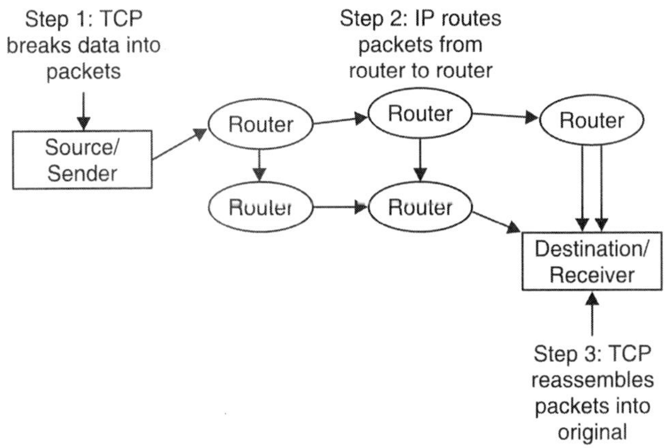

Figure 36: TCP/IP WORKING

2. **Internet Protocol (IP)**—is a set of communication rules by which datagrams are sent from one computer (source) to another (destination) on the Internet based on their IP addresses. It standardizes the way computers over the Internet route the packets based on their IP addresses. To achieve this transfer, IP uses the process of encapsulation, in which it puts tags or address information in the metadata within datagrams. Addressing and routing are the two main functions of IP. Internet Protocol version 4 (IPv4) was the first major version of IP. Another important protocol is the Internet Protocol version 6 (IPv6).

TCP and IP work in unison to transmit data over the internet, but at different levels.

Each computer connected to the Internet has a unique address. This address is known as IP address (IP stands for Internet Protocol). IP address is a 32-bit binary address and it is subdivided into four 8-bit segments called octets. IP is the Internet's addressing system.

Part of the IP address is used for network ID (N) and the remaining part of the address is used for the host ID (H). The segments are not equal as the address allotted to network ID varies. IP addresses fall into the following address classes: class A: the first 8 bits of the IP address are used for the network ID and the remaining 24 bits are used for the host ID; class B addresses: the first 16 bits of the IP address are used for the network ID and the 16 remaining bits are used for the host ID; class C addresses: the first 24 bits of the IP address are used for the network ID and the final 8 bits are for the host ID.

Table 29: Address Classes

Class	IP Address	Size
A	N.H.H.H.	Suitable for large size network
B	N.N.H.H.	Suitable for medium size network
C	N.N.N.H.	Suitable for small size network

IP address is expressed in the "dotted decimal" format. The four decimal values are then separated with periods (4*8 = 32). Eight binary bits can represent any whole number from 0 to 255.

If a computer is connected to a network as well as the Internet, then the computer will have an internal IP address which marks its location on the local network, and an external IP, which is the IP address of the Internet connection. Anyone who connects to the Internet is assigned an IP address by the Internet Service Provider.

There is a relatively simple system called DNS (Domain Name System or Domain Name Server) that enables a computer to look up the IP address for any given website. DNS maintains a directory of domain names and translates them to IP addresses. In other words, DNS is a distributed database that maintains internet domain names and their corresponding IP addresses. For example, if a user types www.justforexamplewebsite.com into a web browser's address bar, a server behind the scenes will map this name to a specific IP address.

How to Find IP Address

There are several ways to find the IP address and here are some of the ways of finding the same. For Windows, one can click the Start Menu and select Run. Then one should type "cmd" into the box and click the "OK" button. Finally, at the command prompt, one should type "ipconfig" and this will display the IP address. For finding the public IP address, one can simply type the search string "ip address" in the Google search bar. For Mac computers, from the Apple menu, one should select System Preferences. In System Preferences, from the View menu, select Network. In the Network preference window, click a network port and IP address can be seen under "Status".

3. **Message/data from source computer to destination computer**—it would start at the top of the protocol stack on the source computer and work its way downward. If the message is long, each stack layer that the message passes through may break the message up into smaller chunks of data called packets. These packets move through the application

layer and then continue to the transport layer. Each packet is assigned a port number. Ports help to find out which program on the destination computer needs to receive the message/data because it will be listening on a specific port. A port is necessary to differentiate between different IP services such as file transfer (FTP) and web service (HTTP). After going through the transport layer, the packets move to the internet layer and this is where each packet receives its destination address. Now that the packets have a port number and IP address assigned to them, they are ready to be delivered. The physical or hardware layer transforms the packets into electronic signals (a stream of 0s and 1s) over the wire and on the other end of the Internet connection, a router checks the destination address to determine where to send each packet. Often a packet gets routed several times before it reaches its destination. Finally, each packet reaches its destination computer. On this destination computer, all the packets start at the bottom of the destination computer's protocol stack and work their way upwards. As these packets travel upwards through the layers, all the addressing and routing data that the source computer's protocol stack had added is stripped. By the time these packets reach the topmost layer, they have been reassembled into their original form.

8.4 The Internet Ecosystem—Various Stakeholders

The Internet Ecosystem is the term used to describe the organizations and communities that help the Internet work and evolve. The Ecosystem stakeholders and players play an important role in shaping the development of the Internet and its policies. They are involved in the making of policy processes related to the progress of the Internet and the management of Internet resources. These organizations are responsible for coordination, administration, standardization and day-to-day management.

The Internet Ecosystem or the Internet Society has several sub-sections which are handled by specific organizations and communities, right from basic end-to-end communications to frameworks and policies required to ensure that the Internet model continues to provide open, transparent and flexible services, and from education and capacity building to reliable connectivity. All these components work in unison and are interdependent on each other so that coordination, administration and day-to-day management of Internet happen in a smooth fashion. These policies, services, technologies and resources are highly interdependent and require a significant amount of coordination. The Internet Society (ISOC) is US, non-profit organization founded in 1992 to provide leadership and direction in Internet-related standards, access, education and policies. Its mission statement: to promote the open development, evolution and use of the Internet for the benefit of all people throughout the world.

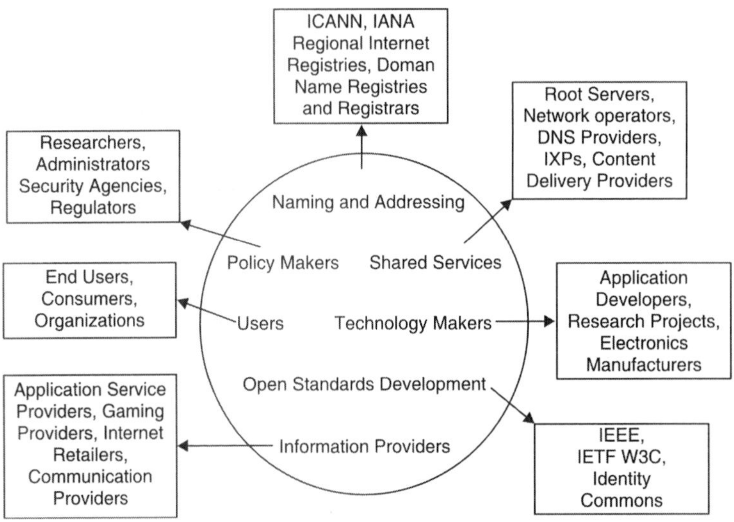

Figure 37: THE INTERNET ECOSYSTEM

The open, active and transparent approach of working together helps the Internet Ecosystem adapt to the Internet's rapidly evolving technology and to the changing needs of the Internet community. There is broad engagement and active participation from all stakeholders like governments, users, universities, business community, technical experts and civil society, due to which the development and working of the Internet becomes successful.

The main organizations that make up the Internet Ecosystem are as follows:

1. Organizations that manage resources for global naming and addressing capabilities such as the Internet Corporation for Assigned Names and Numbers (ICANN), including its operation of the Internet Assigned Numbers Authority (IANA) function, Regional Internet Registries (RIR), and Doman Name Registries and Registrars.
2. Organizations that provide education and build capacity for developing and using Internet technologies such as multilateral organizations, educational institutions and governmental agencies.
3. Technical standards bodies such as the Internet Engineering Task Force (IETF), the Institute of Electrical and Electronic Engineers (IEEE), Identity Commons and the World Wide Web Consortium (W3C).
4. Individuals and organizations that use the Internet to communicate with each other and offer services and applications.
5. Companies that provide shared global services and operations, and network infrastructure services such as root servers, network operators, Domain Name Service (DNS) providers, Internet Exchange Points (IXPs) and content delivery providers.
6. Consumers and users include individual end users and organizations that use the Internet to communicate with each other, and develop content or offer services and applications.

8.5 Future of the Internet—Virtual Reflection of Physical Diversity

Both utopian and dystopian visions of the future internet are hovering over its horizons. There will be twists and turns in the evolution of the Internet; some predictions will come true and some may not.

Data is an integral part of the Internet. According to research statistics, volumes of data are growing at a rate of 40% per year and industry experts estimate it to increase 50 times by 2020. Apart from the amount of personal data, even the amount of industrial data is growing, rather much faster than personal data. But with this exponential growth comes the challenge of security. Companies and organizations will need to come up with robust strategies for strengthening the security of their customers' data.

The Internet had and will continue to extend beyond political borders and now it has gone even beyond our planet through a prototype called Interplanetary Internet that already stretches between our planet and the International Space Station.

The current generation of mobiles and smartphones provide great Internet connectivity, but the next-generation devices will be capable of projecting the Internet, or even embedding it into the real environment through application of augmented reality.

With technologies like Worldwide Interoperability for Microwave Access (WiMAX is a wireless industry coalition dedicated to the advancement of IEEE 802.16 standards for broadband wireless access networks in an economical way) that provide the ability to access the Internet wirelessly opens up many more doors of growth for portable devices that will facilitate plugging into the Internet without the need for wires.

The Internet of Things (IoT) will become more prevalent in times to come. Currently IoT connects several home appliances, industrial equipment, cars, etc. According to industry sources, IoT will hit mainstream by 2020.

Some peace-building organizations and peace promoters hope that the Internet will provide a common ground that will let various people come together for bringing about an era of harmony and peace. And some others believe as the Internet grows, it will make the divide between haves and have-nots even wider; it will help the rich get richer and make the poor all the more poor and marginalized.

Messaging, and particularly instant messaging, are here to stay and are only going to get better. One thing that seems certain is that data transmission speeds will increase on a global level, and at the same time, the costs of producing ultra-high-speed networks will decrease.

The Internet connectivity will be constant, permanent and streamlined to the point where no individual "connection" is really required. This concept is slowly becoming a reality and as time goes by worries of outages will be minimized. More widespread Internet delivery will mean reaching a wider audience.

Smart services based on artificial intelligence algorithms will be able to help us manage our workloads and the online world will be more streamlined.

On the one hand, the Internet is bringing about profound changes in the lives of billions, but on the other hand, its rapid rise is also bringing a plethora of problems like cyber stalking and cyber-crimes; a rise in virtual nightmares.

The breakneck speed growth of the Internet needs up-to-date governance, regulatory frameworks and administration standards, and this is one area that all the Internet stakeholders need to focus on and gear up in bringing them in line with the Internet growth rate.

The Internet of the future will bring both good and bad things. It will be a virtual reflection of the diversity that we all represent in the physical plane.

8.6 The World Wide Web—Most Widely Used Part of the Internet

The Internet is often confused with the World Wide Web; they are considered to be synonyms. In reality, both are different. The Internet is much bigger than the World Wide Web. The Internet is a network of networks and the most widely used part of the Internet is the World Wide Web.

The origin of the World Wide Web dates back to as early as 1946 when Murray Leinster wrote a short story in which the idea of a vast information network available to everyone in their homes was presented, and also the initial concept that developed into the World Wide Web was given by Leonard Kleinrock.

Real work on this concept began almost forty years later. In the 1980s, Tim Berners-Lee was working on a project known as "Enquire," which was the predecessor to the World Wide Web. Enquire was a simple hypertext program and it forms the conceptual basis of the World Wide Web.

The World Wide Web, abbreviated WWW or the Web, is a collection of different websites you can access through the Internet. This definition is given by the World Wide Web Consortium (W3C). W3C is an organization that Web inventor Tim Berners-Lee founded and it is the main international standards organization for the WWW. In other words, WWW is a collection of public websites seamlessly connected to the Internet together with client devices like computers and smartphones that access it.

A Word of Caution
The WWW is different from the Internet. The internet is a giant network of computers all connected together. The WWW is a collection of web pages found on this network of computers. The WWW uses the Internet to pass over the information.

On 6th August 1991, the World Wide Web was first introduced to the world and it came online. After a few days, the WWW was made accessible to everyone. WWW has its foundation in the work that a British scientist, Tim Berners-Lee did in the 1980s at CERN, the European Organization for Nuclear Research. He invented the web in 1989 for helping scientists to easily share the data from their experiments.

WWW was originally developed to meet the demand for automatic information-sharing between scientists in universities and institutes across the globe. In 1990 the world's first website went live at the research lab of CERN.

WWW is a collection of billions of pages linked to each other that contain images, graphics, text, multimedia components and other interactive software programs. The web browser uses the Internet to access the WWW pages.

8.6.1 Evolution of the WWW—From the Dull Past to the Interactive Present

The initial websites were made up of simple pages. In the earlier days before Web 2.0, it was difficult to create web pages. After Web 2.0, the usage of the WWW became widespread. People started communicating and sharing more as designing web pages became easier with Web 2.0; it helps to deliver more with less—it is user-friendly, functional, interactive and dynamic, it is available at any time, any place, it provides a plethora of tools like discussion boards, blogs, etc., it provides a platform for building dynamic learning communities, and it provides ways of enhancing social, personal and professional promotional and branding activities. The WWW is continuously changing.

Before the WWW, the Internet provided dull pages full of text. Though the Internet was a great tool for accessing and exchanging information, it was not that appealing. Several companies began developing graphical user interfaces that added a bit of layout and a dash of color. But the real aspect that made the Internet appealing is the WWW, which is full of interactive content, multimedia, web apps, Uniform Resource Locators, etc.

Between the years of 1995–2000, businesses started to change their focus: they went from traditional marketing tactics to leveraging the web for increasing their returns. This was known as the internet boom or the dot com boom, which led to the commercial growth of the Internet since the advent of the World Wide Web. But the year 2001 witnessed the dot com bubble crash and only a few major players survived this downturn.

The next era is that of social networking. The WWW lets people share their experiences, values, thoughts and ideas through social networking sites, video sharing, blogs, etc. With the help of the WWW, the social networking landscape has revolutionized the way people socially interact on the web. Accessing the WWW through mobile phones is one of the major milestones of this period. From 2000s onwards more users began to access online content via their mobiles. It was in 2007 that the iPhone first became available to the world, revolutionizing the way we access the web from our phones and introducing the concept of mobile apps. Mobiles added another layer of accessibility to the already popular WWW. In the initial days, accessing the traditional WWW through mobiles was not a very pleasant experience due to incompatibility issues. But as more and more upgraded smartphones entered the scene, the WWW and the Internet quickly adapted to the needs of the smartphone age and users. These days, it is rare to find a website that is not smartphone or mobile compatible.

With more and more advances, web developers and web designers are able to provide WWW users with more immersive web experiences.

8.6.2 Core Components—Web Browser, Web Server and Protocols

The WWW is one of the many applications of the Internet and it is certainly the forerunner. The WWW is based on three core components or core technologies: web server and web browser, Hypertext Transfer Protocol (HTTP) and Hyper Text Markup Language (HTML).

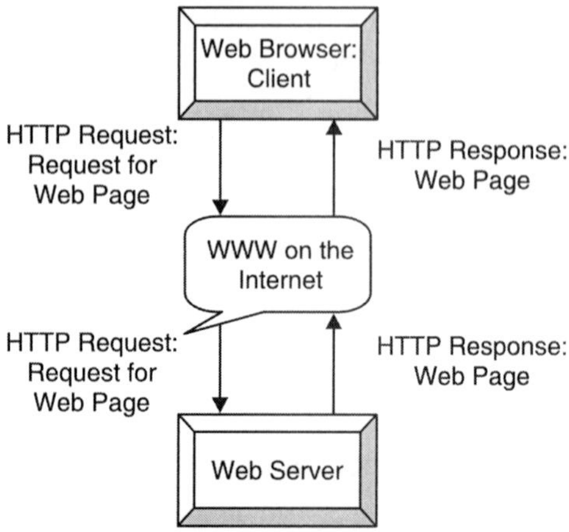

Figure 38: WORKING OF THE WWW

1. **Web Server and Web Browser**—a web server is a program that uses HTTP (Hypertext Transfer Protocol) to respond to HTTP requests in order to deliver content and services. It is used to host web sites; this is where the web content is stored. Apart from hosting websites, a web server can also be used for other purposes like FTP, gaming, etc.

   There are normally two ways in which a web server responds to a client request: generates a response by initiating a script and communicating with a database system or sends the file to the client linked with the requested uniform resource locator. A client sends a request to a web server by entering the URL of the web page in the address bar of the web browser. Then the browser requests the Domain Name Server for the IP address corresponding to the URL. After receiving the IP address, the browser sends the request for web page to the web server using HTTP protocol. The web server first searches for the requested page, if it is found then the server delivers it to the client with HTTP response and the browser interprets and displays the contents of web page in the web browser's window. In the case of a webpage not found, the web server will send HTTP response: Error 404 Not Found. An HTTP 404 error page appears when a webpage can't be found; the webpage simply does not exist with the URL entered.

In case a client has requested some other resource then the web server will contact the application server and data store to construct the HTTP response. An application server, also called an appserver, provides access to business logic for use by client application programs. An application server is designed specifically to extend a web server to support dynamic content. An application server can be used to develop and run web-based applications.

Table 30: Popular Web Servers

Web Server	Description
Internet Information Services	It is a flexible, general-purpose web server from Microsoft that runs on Windows systems to serve requested HTML pages or files.
Apache HTTP Server	It is a web server for UNIX/Linux and Windows operating systems
Lighttpd	It is a fast, secure and flexible web-server that has been optimized for high-performance environments
Nginx	It is open source software for web serving, caching, load balancing, media streaming, reverse proxying and more

A web browser, commonly referred to as browser, is used by the Internet, which can be used to access and view websites. It is application software used to find, retrieve and display content on the World Wide Web, including webpages, video and other files. The first web browser was invented in 1990 by Tim Berners-Lee. This browser was called WorldWideWeb and later on renamed to Nexus. NCSA Mosaic or simply Mosaic browser helped to popularize the WWW and was named for its support of multiple internet protocols. Mosaic was neither the first web browser nor the first graphical web browser, but it was the first to be widely used. Modern-day leading browsers are Mozilla Firefox, Microsoft Internet Explorer, Google Chrome and Apple Safari. A web browser can also be used to upload or download files from FTP servers.

The web address or uniform resource locator that a user types into the address bar tells the browser where to obtain a page or pages from.

Spotlight Tip
Several browsers have plugins/extensions that extend their capabilities so that they can display multimedia information or can be used to perform tasks such as designing webpages, videoconferencing, etc.

Table 31: Popular Web Browsers

Web Browser	Description
Google Chrome	Freeware, fast and secure web browser developed by Google
Mozilla Firefox	Free and open-source web browser developed by Mozilla Foundation and its subsidiary the Mozilla Corporation
Apple Safari	Graphical web browser and it is included as part of the Mac OS X operating system

2. **Hypertext Transfer Protocol (HTTP)** is the set of rules used by the WWW for transferring files (text, graphic images, video, sound and other multimedia files). This underlying protocol defines how messages and other data are formatted and transmitted, and what actions web servers and web browsers should take in response to various commands. The three main HTTP message types are GET, POST and HEAD. The browser is HTTP client and the web page server is HTTP server.

   GET messages sent to a web server contains only a Uniform Resource Locator (URL). Zero or more optional data parameters may be appended to the end of the URL. The URL is an address that is unique to each resource on the web; URL uniquely identifies a specific web page and it is composed of a communication protocol, a domain and a page. It could be the address of a webpage, video or an image file. POST messages place any optional data parameters in the body of the request message rather than adding them to the end of the URL. HEAD request works the same as GET request. The web server sends back only the web page header information contained inside the HTML <HEAD> section. The browser initiates communication with an HTTP server by initiating a TCP connection to the server. Web browsing sessions use server port 80 by default although other ports such as 8080 are sometimes used instead.

   Once a session is established, users of web browsers start the sending and receiving of HTTP messages by visiting web pages that have HTTP (or HTTPS) URLs. Tim Berners-Lee created the initial HTTP in the early 1990s. Three primary versions were widely deployed during the 1990s: HTTP 0.9, HTTP 1.0 and HTTP 1.1. The contents of HTTP requests and responses are easy to read and understand as they are quite similar in syntax to English.

HTTP is an application-level protocol for distributed, collaborative, hypermedia information systems. It is a stateless protocol because each command is executed independently, without any knowledge of the commands that came before it. The connection is maintained between the client and the server only for the immediate request, and thereafter the connection is closed. After the HTTP client establishes a TCP connection with the server and sends it a request, the server sends back its response and closes the connection.

When accessing any web page, the user enters the web site or URL by entering http:// in front of the address and this tells the browser to communicate using HTTP. By default most addresses are preceded by HTTP, but there are some other protocols also used at times such the File Transfer Protocol (FTP). FTP is a standard network protocol used to transfer files between computers on a network; used for the transfer of computer files from a server to a client.

Another version of HTTP is Hypertext Transfer Protocol Secure (HTTPS: the 'S' at the end of HTTPS stands for 'Secure'). It is the secure version of HTTP. It is a protocol which ensures all communication between the browser and the website is encrypted. HTTPS is used in cases where the information on the wire is highly confidential and needs to be protected from online theft like credit card transactions and online banking transactions.

HTTPS operates via Secure Socket Layer (SSL) and Transport Layer Security (TLS) encryption mechanisms. In order for a web server to process HTTPS requests, the computer at each end use a document called "SSL Certificate" containing character strings that are the keys to their secret "codes". SSL certificates contain the computer owner's "public key". SSL uses a technique called public key cryptography. This cryptographic method uses two keys; a public key known to everyone and a private or secret key known only to the recipient of the message. The public key is used for encryption and the private key is used for decryption. This method provides security benefits of integrity and confidentiality. Integrity—the decryption process involves verifying that the contents of the original encrypted message and the new decrypted one match, and even if there is a slight change in the original content, this would cause the decryption process to fail. Confidentiality—the message can be encrypted only with an individual's public key and it can be decrypted only by using the individual's private key, and these aspects ensure that only the intended receiver can get to decrypt and view the contents/ messages.

3. **Hyper Text Markup Language (HTML)** is the authoring language that consists of a set of markup tags, elements, symbols or codes and it is used to create electronic documents on the World Wide Web. These electronic documents are also called web pages. These tags, elements, symbols or codes form the building blocks of a website. The current version is HTML 5 version which is an extension and this version was published in 2012.

   Hypertext refers to the way in which web pages are linked together. In most websites, certain words or phrases appear in text with a different color than the rest of the contents; often this text is also underlined. This text helps the user to navigate through a series of collection of pages. This colored text is called hyperlinks.

Table 32: HTML Tags

Tag	Description
<!DOCTYPE...>	Defines the document type
<a>	Defines a hyperlink
<div>	Defines a section in a document
<embed>	Defines a container for external application or interactive content
<form>	Defines HTML form for user input
<html>	Defines the root of HTML document
<head>	Defines information about the document
<header>	Defines a header for a document or section
<h1> to <h6>	Defines HTML headings <h1> defines the most important heading and <h6> defines the least important heading
<title>	Defines a title for a document or section
<body>	Defines the document's body
<b>	Defines bold text
<abbr>	Defines an abbreviation or an acronym
<img>	Defines an image
<b>	Defines a single line break
<footer>	Defines a footer for a document or section
<img>	Defines an image
<main>	Specifies the main content of a document
<meta>	Defines metadata about HTML document
<script>	Defines a client-side script
<style>	Defines style information for a document

HTML ensures that the formatting of the components that need to be rendered on the pages is done correctly. Originally, HTML was developed with the intent of defining the structure of documents like lists, headings, etc., to facilitate the sharing of scientific information between researchers. Now, it is being widely used to format entire web pages.

HTML is a markup language and makes use of various tags to format the content. These tags are enclosed within opening and closing angular brackets (< >). Except a few tags, most of the tags have their corresponding closing tags. Tags are made up of two main components: attribute name and attribute value, for example, <p align=“right”>this is right aligned</p>. The attribute name is the property that one wants to set. For example, the paragraph element <p> element has an attribute that has the name align and the value as “right” (the value of the property to be set and it is always put within quotes). These two components provide additional information about elements. Within the opening and closing tags the content to be rendered on the page is included.

Everything one sees in a web page and on a website is a result of the combination of HTML and CSS. CSS is the short form for Cascading Style Sheet and it is used for describing the presentation of web pages (e.g., fonts, colors, spacing, layout, width, etc.). CSS is a design language intended to simplify the process of making web pages presentable. CSS allows the separation of document markup content (HTML) and the presentation/styling of it.

Example of internal CSS:

```
h1 {
color: red;
font-size: 4em;
}
```

In the above example, h1 is the selector and the selector is followed by a declaration block that includes two declarations. By using h1 as the selector, we are stating that every level 1 heading on the specific web page should follow the declarations contained in this CSS rule set. An external style sheet is stated as follows: <link rel=“stylesheet” type=“text/css” href=“extstyle.css”>

When one right clicks in the browser instance and selects “view page source” then what opens up is HTML source code—one will able to see hundreds of tags and web page source code—this is what makes up HTML.

8.7 Questions for Reflection

1. Define the Internet?
2. What is WiFi?
3. List the advantages of star topology?
4. What is the concept of token passing?
5. What are the functions of TCP?
6. Name the various stakeholders in the Internet Ecosystem?
7. Describe the core components of the World Wide Web?

9

Security—Protection Measures and Strategies

Computer and Network Security, also known as IT security or cyber security, refers to the measures that are taken for protection against or prevention of intentional but unauthorized modification or destruction of data and information, access of data and information by unauthorized users, and theft or damage to software and hardware components. Availability, Authenticity, Integrity and Confidentiality are the key aspects that need to be taken care of while designing a computer security strategy. A threat refers to anything that has the potential to cause serious harm to a computer or network system. There are several types of threats: interruption occurs when the availability of services and resources is attacked; integrity threat occurs when miscreants are able to alter or compromise the original data; and authenticity threat occurs when an imposter poses as an authentic user and accesses the resources in an unauthorized manner. At times, employees of an organization themselves can compromise their organization's resources and data. Unethical employees may break into their employers' computers and network system for a variety of reasons, right from selling data to venting out due to their disgruntlement. Hackers, identity thieves and spammers, also called the "bad guys" in colloquial language, constantly develop new techniques to pose new threats to computer security. The CIA: Confidentiality, Integrity and Availability triad is a model designed to guide policies and measures for computer and network security.

1. **Availability**—data should be available to authorized users when needed.
2. **Integrity**—ensuring that data and information is not modified by unauthorized users in a way that is not detectable by authorized users.
3. **Confidentiality**—protecting confidential and sensitive information from disclosure to unauthorized parties. Cryptography and encryption methods help to ensure confidentiality of data transferred from one computer system to another.

Authenticity—ensuring that users are the persons they claim to be; they are authorized users.

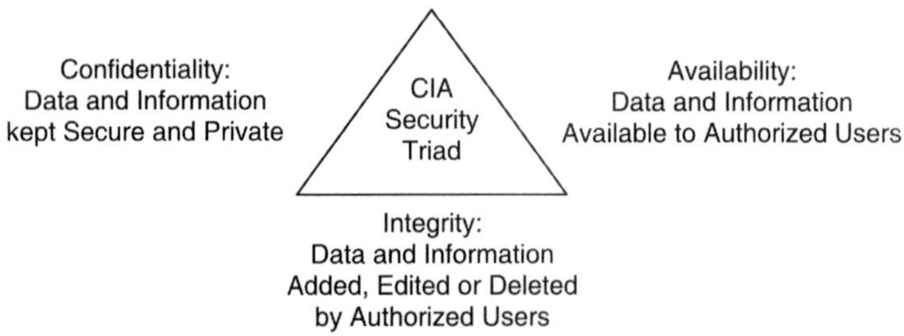

Figure 39: CIA SECURITY TRIAD

9.1 Importance of Security—Defense in Depth

Prevention of destruction of data or theft of sensitive information like credit card number, bank account number, etc., is extremely important in the modern age, as most of the population depends on computers and the Internet for their daily needs, be it personal or business. Business and home users must safeguard their computer systems and resources from breaches of security like software threat, information threat, data loss, hardware threat, etc.

There is no magic bullet for computer and network security. But by having a comprehensive security strategy and emergency action plan in place computer and network security threats and risks can be minimized. The security strategy should always have up-to-date anti-virus programs, security tools, adequate firewalls, detection measures and intrusion prevention tools to keep the computers and network safe from identity thieves, hackers and cyber-criminals. An anti-virus program scans for programs that attempt to modify the operating system, boot program and other programs that normally are read but not modified. Apart from this, an anti-virus program also scans downloaded attachments, files downloaded from websites, etc. Organizations can implement a firewall solution themselves or outsource their security requirements to a company specializing in providing firewall protection.

Table 33: Popular Anti-virus Tools

Anti-virus Tools	Description
Kaspersky Anti-virus	Protects from the latest threats of spyware, viruses, Trojans, malware and other threats
McAfee Anti-virus Plus	Provides quality digital security with features like anti-virus protection, WiFi network intrusion prevention, vulnerability scanner, etc.
Bitdefender	Anti-virus protection suite with many bonus features
Webroot Secure Anywhere Anti-virus	Lightweight anti-virus program along with added features like anti-ransom ware and anti-phishing

Table 34: Popular Security Tools

Security Tools	Description
Snort	An open-source, free and lightweight network intrusion detection system software for Linux and Windows to detect threats
TCPDump	A packet analyzer and command-line tool for monitoring (sniffing) network traffic
Kismet	An 802.11 layer-2 wireless network detector, sniffer and intrusion detection system
OpenVAS	A software framework of several services and tools offering vulnerability scanning and vulnerability management
Wireshark	A network analysis tool used for network troubleshooting

Often these intruders want to gain control of computer systems or networks so they can use it to launch attacks on other computer systems or networks. Proper training in regards to security issues and risks needs to be given to employees and users. They need to be trained in how to set strong passwords and keep their accounts and work data secure. They need to be made aware of the potential dangers of phishing, downloading information from unknown sites, opening attachments or web links that are sent by unknown senders. Apart from installing security software programs, the second level of security is internal/inner security. Different levels of access throughout the computer and network systems need to be set up. These access levels ensure that critical and sensitive information is only available to those who have the right level of access clearance.

A Word of Caution
Despite security measures and precautions, it is always possible that a computer system or network will be breached. Intruders and hackers always find new ways to disrupt systems. New attack methods are launched continuously.

9.1.1 Trusted System Evaluation Criteria

Trusted System Evaluation Criteria and Security Standards follow the "90 / 10" Rule: 10% of the security standards and safeguards are technical; 90% of the standards and safeguards rely on the users to adhere to good security and computing practices. It is a computer security evaluation methodology wherein organizations define the various levels of security and provide guidelines for their implementation.

These criteria are not just an information technology, computer or network issue. For example, "Ctrl+Alt+Del" is 10%: technical precautions, whereas users/employees remembering to implement and follow all the precautions and measures (90%) is what finally makes a security policy an effective one. Computer and network security is everyone's responsibility.

Trusted Network Interpretation and Trusted Computer System Evaluation Criteria provide standards against which computer and network systems can be evaluated with respect to security measures and characteristics. Assurance and functionality are some of the evaluation criteria that are used to test the overall strength of a security strategy.

9.1.2 Precautions—From Passwords to Patches

Each major technological advance in computing gives rise to new security vulnerabilities that require new security solutions. Therefore, a broad-spectrum security strategy is needed to minimize threats or to minimize the loss of resources or downtime caused after such threats have occurred.

1. **Second Line of Defense**—sometimes even the best security software programs have vulnerabilities. In spite of adequate security standards and measures, a malicious attacker can still get into a system. The basic goal of any security software is prevention of attacks, but the second line of defense kicks in when this prevention is not possible. The second line is that of making the attacks expensive in terms of efforts, time, research and money needed to bypass security measures.
2. **Awareness and Training**—employees and users need to be given training in various aspects of security management. They need to be made aware of which kind of emails to open and which kind of emails need to be ignored; how to secure computer equipment; and what resources to access on the Internet. Working people on the move should ensure that nobody is sneaking around them while they work on their portable devices in public places; shoulder surfing should be avoided. Employees and even normal users should be wary while disposing any computer related personal or professional information. Papers

containing such information need to be disposed of properly or else imposters can go dumpster diving to obtain sensitive and confidential information. People should be careful while opening attachments embedded in emails.

A phishing scam is an email or website that is designed to steal data from a user. Hackers will use this email or website to install malicious software onto the user's computer. These web entities are designed to look like trusted sources, which is how hackers convince their victims to hand over personal data and sensitive information. In order to avoid becoming a victim of such scams: one should never open attachments from unknown sources; one should delete spam and junk mails immediately; and one should avoid sending work-related or personal sensitive data through emails. Another security threat is that hackers will inform the users that they need to execute a certain patch in order to keep their system secure. But the patch link or attachment is really malicious code that loads on the user's computer infecting not only that particular computer but other computers on the network as well. Email filtering should be implemented as it allows or disallows emails from designated sources; it helps to reduce unwanted emails.

Apart from awareness and training, companies need to include in-depth security guidelines in the employee handbook. Timely brochures, voice reminders, instructional videos and newsletters need to be circulated in the office setup to keep everyone in line with the latest security policy updates.

3. **Secure Passwords**—passwords are an extremely effective method for improving computer and network security. Numbers, symbols and a mix of upper and lower case letters in the password makes it

harder for someone to guess the password. Password managers can also help you use secure passwords, which are reasonably long and ideally should contain some combination of letters, numbers, and symbols. Different password for each of the important accounts like email and online banking account should be used.

Longer and complicated passwords are better than shorter ones. In addition to user name and password, some systems require users to also provide personal information like a secret question, maiden name, date of birth, etc. The longer the password, the more effort is required to crack it.

How to Protect Passwords
Once a password is set, it needs to be changed periodically. Having too many passwords is not a good practice; it is difficult to remember so many passwords. Writing down passwords on a piece of paper and storing it under a keyboard or behind a monitor should be avoided under all circumstances. Sharing passwords with customer care representatives, direct marketing firms, or anyone else is another aspect to be avoided.

4. **Security Roles**—the following experts are needed to be on board for implementing the various elements of a computer and network security policy: chief information security officer, network security specialists, security architects, vulnerability analysts and security assessors. Further to this aspect, organizations need to also implement role-based or identity-based operator authentication in order to allow access or denial of services and resources. Moreover, each and every level user role should be trained to perform power-up tests of their system like critical function tests, cryptographic algorithm tests, firmware integrity tests, etc.

5. **Backup**—computer systems, hardware and other devices could be stolen or destroyed. Theft of valuable data can occur. An intruder can crash the whole network. Organizations need to make provisions for data backup on a regular basis. Most modern-day operating systems come with built-in backup programs. Backup devices also have backup programs. Several third-party backup utilities are also available. A full backup copies all the files and folders whereas a selective backup includes only selected files and folders. Sensitive data can be backed up in an encrypted format. Organizations can maintain backup of critical data in off-site locations too.
6. **Audit Trail (audit log)**—it is useful both for maintaining security and for recovering lost transactions. An audit trail helps to maintain a series of system activity and user activity records. These records can help a security auditor to perform intrusion detection. An audit trail in conjunction with access controls can help to pinpoint users who are considered as a suspect of unauthorized access or modification of data. An audit trail may record "before" and "after" versions of records and data. Any discrepancy in these versions can help to identify the source of the problem, whether unauthorized access or malware.
7. **Avoid Malware and Spyware**—one should be careful about the programs that are downloaded from the Internet. Malware protection is a must-have step in keeping a computer system virus free. Even without knowing passwords or without physical access to computers and networks, spyware can attack and infect computers and networks. Much of the spyware exists on the Internet and it is difficult to detect; hence spyware is notoriously difficult to detect and remove. It is always better to use top anti-spyware tools.

Scheduling daily scans of a computer system's hard drive is a good security practice; an additional protective feature. Anti-virus and anti-spyware programs require regular signature and database updates. These timely and critical updates help to protect computer systems from the latest threats.

How to Install Anti-virus Updates
A user will generally receive update notifications from the manufacturer in the form of an alert on the screen. The user can either install these updates immediately or later. Some updates may require the user to restart the computer for them to go into effect.

8. **Software Updates and Patches**—these are needed for a variety of reasons. They are needed to fix a bug in order to handle new security loopholes, or upgrade the software with the latest version/features, or upgrade the stability of the program. These updates are a good defense method against the most common spyware, viruses, cyber-attacks and malware online. The scanning software programs are only as good as their database. They too must be as up-to-date as possible.

Spotlight Tip
A user will generally receive update notifications from the manufacturer in the form of an alert on the screen. The user can either install these updates immediately or later. Some updates may require the user to restart the computer for them to go into effect.

9. **Codes of Conduct**—this aspect mainly applies to the internal users or employees of organizations. Personal codes of conduct for home users are also a critical aspect. Codes of conduct specify the guidelines

pertaining to the ethical uses of computer systems and resources. These guidelines help to determine whether a particular use is ethical or not.

Codes of conduct include guidelines related to the following areas: respect the privacy of others, give proper credit for intellectual property, honor agreements and assigned responsibilities, honor confidentiality, perform only authorized access to computing, network and communication resources, avoid harm to others, etc.

10. **Firewall**—a firewall should be always enabled. A firewall is a network security system designed to prevent unauthorized access. A correctly configured and enabled firewall blocks unsolicited incoming connections and requests thereby protecting the computer and its operating system from malware. A malware monitors user's computer activity without their permission, encrypting or deleting sensitive data, etc. Malware may include computer viruses, Trojan horses (a Trojan horse is a program that hides within or looks like a legitimate program), spyware programs or worms (a worm is a program that copies itself repeatedly thereby exhausting system resources). One should also configure the firewall correctly—when it pops up and asks the user whether you are on a Home, Work or Public network, the user should choose the appropriate answer. A firewall that leverages the power of the cloud for real-time countermeasure to the latest malware threats is a better way of handling threats.

    Some viruses are embedded in macros; hence it is necessary for users to ensure that the macro security level is set for the applications they use so that these applications warn the users that a program they are attempting to use contains a macro. Users should enable macros only when they are from a known and trusted source. Users should never start their computers with removable media inserted in the drives or plugged in the ports. Email attachments from an unknown or untrusted source should be immediately deleted.

As companies move their data and applications to the cloud, a comprehensive cloud-based malware database is needed to minimize both local and global threats. Cloud services or third-party tools to encrypt data that needs to be used are required. This encryption is necessary for both data in transit and data at rest. Several web browsers also use encryption, for example, protection level 40-bit or 1024-bit. A digital certificate is another way of ensuring security. A digital certificate is an electronic "identification card" or "notice" that guarantees that a website or user is legitimate. A digital certificate is often issued by a certification authority. This authority guarantees the validity of the information in the certificate.

11. **Up-to-date Operating System**—no matter which operating system a computer is running, it needs to be up-to-date. OS manufacturers are always releasing new security patches and updates that fix security loopholes. A patch is a piece of software designed to update a computer system in order to fix or improve it. Malware exploits flaws in a system; hence regular patches are a must to avoid problems in applications that one uses (email, image viewer, web browser, etc.).
12. **Digital Rights Management (DRM)**—is a strategy of managing the access to and control of digital data. DRM is used to protect from information misuse, privacy leaks and intellectual property theft. DRM prevents users from copying content or converting it to other formats.

Organizations need to very carefully formulate their DRM strategy. It allows organizations to enforce their own access policies on content like restrictions on sharing, viewing or copying. DRM is used by copyright holders and content creators to ensure that their work is not copied or duplicated, to ensure that their work is distributed in original form, etc.

To protect from software piracy, manufacturers can use techniques of product activation and license agreement. Also to protect from in-house software piracy, companies can ask their employees to sign an anti-piracy statement. Regular software inventories also need to be done. Along with regular software inventories, unannounced audits can also help to minimize this problem.

13. **HTTPS**—HTTPS is the secure version of HTTP. All communication exchange between a web browser and a website are encrypted. This protocol encrypts and decrypts user page requests as well as the pages that are returned (responses) by the web server with Secure Sockets Layer. HTTPS protects against man-in-the-middle attacks. It provides three layers of protection: data integrity, encryption and authentication. Sniffing attacks on all types of networks can be reduced considerably. While using WiFi hotspots, users should interact with only those websites that are fully encrypted. Mobile apps on unsecured WiFi should be used with caution. Changing the settings on a mobile device so that it doesn't automatically connect to nearby WiFi is also a good practice.

9.2 Cyber-Attacks and Cyber-Terrorism—Challenges in the Cyber Realm

As the Internet grows bigger day by day, it creates a whole set of challenges in the cyber realm; the two most important challenge areas are cyber-attacks and cyber-terrorism.

Cyber-attacks are offensive maneuvers or malicious acts (fake websites, malware, information/intellectual assets theft, denial of service, etc.) done by individuals, groups or organizations to exploit networking, computing or other digital resources. These attacks could be politically or socially motivated causing far-reaching damage.

Cyber-terrorism is a term that can erroneously include acts of "hacktivism" and "internet vandalism". The National Infrastructure Protection Center (Garrison and Grand, 2001) defines cyber-terrorism in the following ways: "as a criminal act seeking to influence a government or population to conform to a particular political, social, or ideological agenda; to be by the use of computers and telecommunications capabilities; and to be violence, destruction and/or disruption of services to create fear by causing confusion and uncertainty within a given population." A 2008 NATO document defines cyber-terrorism as: "a cyber-attack using or exploiting computer or communication networks to cause sufficient destruction to generate fear or intimidate a society into an ideological goal (source:http://resources.infosecinstitute.com/cyberterrorism-distinct-from-cybercrime). Cyber-terrorism includes attacks on critical infrastructure. Cyber-terrorism is the use of digital devices and the Internet to carry out acts of violence. Many cyber-criminals follow the "smash and grab" approach to carry out their attacks: get in, take what they can and get out before they can be caught. For handling such frequent threats, an in-house team of cyber security experts working round the clock is a must.

9.2.1 Countermeasures—Authentication, Digital Forensics, etc.

Day by day, the techniques and methods for cyber-attacks and cyber-terrorism are becoming more advanced (elusive), making it difficult to detect them; hence at the other end of the spectrum, countermeasures too have to gear up against such acts. The below given countermeasures will certainly help to minimize the damages caused by cyber-attacks and cyber-terrorism. An integrated surveillance platform with the following features is needed to combat such cyber crimes.

1. **Two-factor Authentication**—many organizations and services follow a two-factor authentication for allowing users to log into their accounts. Instead of simply accepting a username and password to log in, the service/website will prompt users to enter a code sent to their mobiles/smartphones to verify their identity. A dashboard system that provides the status of system authorization at all levels should be used to keep track of who logs in, uses the resources and then logs out.

   Apart from two-factor authentication, organizations can also design an acceptable use policy in which guidelines for using the various resources and systems can be clearly stated. It should outline the activities for a computer system or network that may and may not be used.

2. **Intrusion Prevention Service**—is a preemptive threat prevention technology that examines network traffic patterns and flows to detect and prevent known and unknown vulnerability issues. It helps to minimize application-level attacks as well. Detection techniques include generic pattern matching, traffic anomaly detection, address matching and connection analysis. If vulnerability is spotted, the system will log it, block it, and will report it based on the intrusion prevention service policy guidelines.

   Several companies also use a concept called honeypot to detect, deflect or neutralize intrusion and threats. They set up a vulnerable computer on purpose to attract intrusion so that they can keep track of such intruders and learn of their attack techniques. This honeypot appears as a real resource to the intruders but in fact this honeyspot is kept away from the network.

3. **Device and Hardware Security**—Hardware firewalls are always better than the software ones as they stop or counteract attacks before they attempt to compromise a computer system. Device and hardware stealing and destruction are acts of theft and of vandalism respectively. Physical locks and alarm systems can help to minimize the incidence of such acts. For critical, high-value, high-risk devices, organizations can also have real time location tracking systems and this can be done using radio frequency identification tags which are embedded in these devices.

   Implementing fault tolerance and redundancy protects from any downtime caused by cyber-attacks. These aspects need to be coupled with cyber security policies in order to have rugged computing and networking resources. Fault tolerance refers to the ability to continue to function despite of attack or failure. Provisions for redundant channels can make the entire security strategy resilient. Redundancy refers to building and maintaining multiple resources that serve the same function and can replace each other in the event of attack on or damage to primary system resources. Active defense in the form of fault tolerance and redundancy is necessary to build adaptable, resilient and recoverable digital resources.

4. **Digital Forensics (Cyberforensics)**—digital forensics is a subset of the field of forensic science. It is the process of uncovering and interpreting electronic data and evidence found in digital devices in relation to computer crimes. Organizations need to support digital forensics practices. Information security professionals now recognize digital forensics as a core skill area. Popular forensic suites like EnCase and FTK have moved into the network/enterprise environment. As enterprises move their services and

data into the cloud, they also need to look at this branch as an evidence-based knowledge management process and not merely another aspect of security management. In addition to cybercrimes, digital investigators also use digital forensics as an anti-terrorism tool to combat terrorism.

5. **DNS Protection**—As DNS servers are the middlemen between the browser and website content, there are susceptible to various web-based threats like a compromised DNS server that directs the users to an unauthorized web server, drive-by infections, reflection attacks, DNS cache poisoning, etc.

   Content filtering is for blocking out unwanted and dangerous content like adware, adult sites, etc., and protection against botnets. These are all ways to protect critical network infrastructure and data from network threats.

   DNS cache pollution is an increasingly common vulnerability; it involves spoofing. The term "spoofing" describes the sending of non-secure data in response to a DNS query. If the DNS server cache is "polluted" with scrupulous/bogus DNS entries, users can be forwarded to rogue/malicious sites. Most DNS servers have the feature of secure cache against pollution option, which prevents a hacker or attacker from polluting the cache of a DNS server with resource records that were not requested by the DNS server.

   Firewalls should to be used to gain access control over who can connect to the DNS servers.

6. **Proxy Server**—large enterprises often use a proxy server to protect their sensitive data and data centers from unauthorized intrusions. A proxy server may exist on the same machine as a firewall server or it may be installed on a separate server, which then

forwards requests through a firewall. A proxy server controls which data can enter into and leave out of a network; it carefully scans all incoming and outgoing communication flow. Home users can use a personal firewall.

7. **Three-Pronged Approach**—involving governments, nations and organizations is needed to keep in check these cyber-terrorism threats. Firstly, governments should approve and pass in-depth laws that provide a legal framework for law enforcement and intelligence agencies to follow and implement while dealing with cyber-crimes. Secondly, nations should maintain a centralized command that serves as the main organization responsible for the development of countermeasures.

9.3 Questions for Reflection

1. Are there any special considerations for securing services in the cloud?
2. Can we ever say a system is totally secure?
3. You receive email with an attachment that states that the attachment needs to be downloaded for maintaining the security of your computer. What will you do, choose your option: (A) download the attachment (B) delete the message (C) reply to the sender or (d) contact your company security help desk.
4. Can multimedia content be infected with a virus?
5. How to safeguard personal information?
6. Discuss techniques to prevent unauthorized computer access?
7. Should all network setups install a firewall solution?

10

Technology of Today and Tomorrow—Getting Smarter

Technology is getting smarter by the day. Over the past few years, technology has taken over the world by a storm. We have smart audio, smart video and a whole gamut of smart technologies. Yesterday's science fiction has become today's science reality. Computing capacity is on the rise. The largest storage devices currently measure in terabytes, i.e., millions of megabytes.

Everyone uses technology, right from children to teenagers and from adults to elders. Rapid advances in technology are giving rise to what is being described as the "buy-it-and-bin-it" generation. With these growing demands and expectations of people, tech companies always have to tailor new technologies which can meet people's demands and expectations.

The current technology is much more portable and a miniaturized version of old technology. For example, the smartphone of today is a miniaturized version of a personal computer. It is more like a mini computer in your hands. Essentially speaking, the size of the computer is getting scaled-down and becoming much more powerful than before. No-touch interfaces will also be big thing in the years to come.

The mesh app and service architecture (MASA) is a multichannel solution architecture that leverages cloud and server-less computing, containers and microservices as well as APIs and events to deliver modular, flexible and dynamic solutions. Corporations will continue to work on developing solutions that are integrated, agile and scalable. These solutions ultimately should be able to support multiple users in multiple roles using multiple devices and connecting over multiple networks. However, MASA is a long-term architectural shift that requires significant changes in order to deliver scalable distributed applications.

By 2018, Gartner predicts most of the world's largest 200 companies will leverage intelligent apps to upgrade their offers and improve customer experience. Autonomic computing is also a big trend to watch. Autonomic computing refers to the self-managing characteristics of a network. Such dynamic large-scale networks will be able to overcome problems of complexity of IT infrastructure and shortage of skilled administrators. Ubiquitous computing is also a new and emerging field—in the future it is possible for computers to use DNA and light in order to operate, instead of electricity and semiconductors. Such a development will create computers that can be anywhere and everywhere, but cannot be seen, will develop technology that will be embedded in our environment.

Silicon chips very soon will face limitations as they won't be able to keep pace with the exponentially growing data requirements of the world. This is where emerging fields of DNA computing comes into play. DNA computing is in its infancy and several obstacles are yet to be overcome. In the future, it is quite possible that computers will no longer have RAM or DRAM but rather use DNA as a storage medium.

10.1 Internet of Things—Real and Virtual Worlds Blend Together

Internet of Things (IoT), in theory, is supposed to connect all devices together in a synchronistic symphony enabling them to send and receive data. More and more companies are starting to realize how valuable IoT data is to supply chains and service capabilities, customer experience, partner relationships and more. As all the data-sprouting devices will be interconnected through the Internet, they will be able to upload data for further processing, download updated software and often be controlled from remote locations.

IoT refers to the ever-growing network of physical objects; it is about connecting devices over the Internet. More devices are being created with WiFi capabilities and sensors built into them, and this is definitely making things look bright for IoT. Everyday products are getting an intelligent upgrade to become smart objects. Embedded information technology is making everyday products intelligent and smart, which will possess functionality beyond their basic purpose.

Smart cars of the future, smart homes of the future, smart offices of the future, smart manufacturing units of the future, and so many more smart scenarios and smart solutions will be a part of our lives and provide us with continuous connectivity and distributed intelligence. Marketing will also be transformed as customers will be able to have seamless access to digital products from advertisements in the physical world.

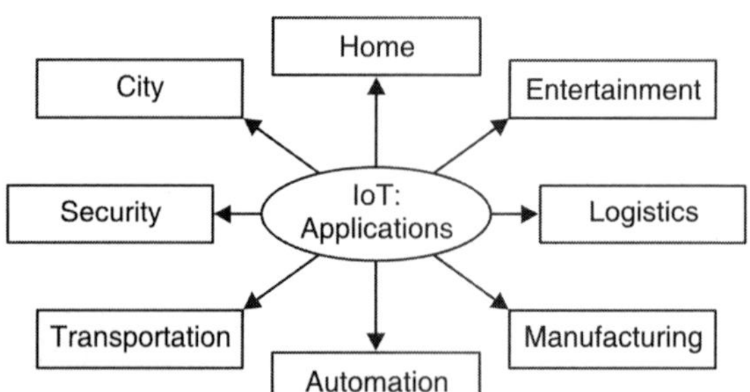

Figure 40: APPLICATIONS AREAS OF IOT

10.1.1 Future of IoT—The Next Internet

IoT shows a lot of promise in terms of improvement of business processes, and reduction of risks and costs, but it has two major downsides: privacy and security. According to Gartner (Gartner is an American research and advisory firm), by 2020 there will be over 26 billion connected devices (that is a lot of devices). According to industry research data, nearly $6 trillion will be spent on IoT solutions over the next five years.

Automated driving is still far away from reality, although it is implemented in a limited manner in some cities in the United States. Smart networking concepts is another trend that will catch on—all IoT devices (in office or at home) talking to each other, and they will know what we need, even before we need it—solving problems or making decisions on the fly.

As IoT devices proliferate, new ecosystems will emerge, and there will be more smart city and smart home setups mushrooming around the globe. The rise of IoT is making these devices to go from mesh connections to fully connected networks where each and every device is communicating with each other in some form or the other.

As IoT spreads across the globe, the gap between real and virtual will close. Companies are working to develop platforms for smart applications, so in the near future, users will be given options on their smartphones to overview their car applications, office environment applications or smart home applications.

IoT will significantly impact our everyday lives as well as the industrial sectors. Areas like logistics management will see a rise of IoT devices, especially for high-value goods where each good will be equipped by a tracking device that will monitor and inform about the condition and location of goods and containers so that nothing gets lost or damaged in transit.

Many industry experts have termed IoT as the next Internet or the next Industrial Revolution. But for this to happen, there are several challenges to overcome: IoT demands an extensive range of new technologies and niche skills that many industry players have yet to master. As

IoT becomes popular, there will also be more IoT-driven apps hitting the market and this will result in clashes between the app developers for acquiring a place in the mindshare. Security and privacy issues are another critical area which leads to problems like cyber-attacks and loss of control over personal information. Another challenge is that of interoperability standards. If devices from different manufacturers do not use the same standards, interoperability will be more difficult, requiring extra gateways to translate from one standard to another. The potential of IoT appears to be great despite these challenges.

10.2 Cloud Computing—Services Over the Internet

Cloud computing allows users to access data, information and applications through the online world rather than through the use of actual devices or hardware. It connects businesses and users to data everywhere they go in a cost-effective manner, and provides reliable data storage. The Cloud also facilitates creation, customization and configuration of the applications online. These applications can be offered as utilities and services over the Internet.

Spotlight Tip
Cloud computing is accessible and agile; no matter where one is located, one can continue to communicate and work by accessing the cloud and also share information through it. Cloud computing provides simplified and enhanced management and maintenance capabilities. Scalability is one of the key benefits of cloud computing.

Mobile-friendly cloud computing applications to manage business data are becoming popular day by day. Adoption of cloud computing community, public and private, will continue to grow rapidly. It is expected that as cloud solutions continue to be adopted, more developers will start to develop for the cloud.

The Cloud has made itself felt in the social communication field too. Social tools like microblogging are becoming popular and are preferred to traditional online communication tools like emails. Cloud software is and will continue to be integrated with these social tools so as to provide improved collaboration.

Another trend that cloud computing will impact in a major way is cognitive computing. Cognitive computing is the simulation of human thought processes in a computerized manner. Examples of cognitive computing include speech recognition, natural language processing and many more. "Cognitive on cloud" refers to cognitive services running in the cloud. The convergence of these two fields promises better return on investments and can provide actionable insight from historic data and real-time data. As this integrated approach will always be in a constant learning mode, the revenue streams too will always be in the flow. Such integrated systems will help users in various aspects like designing creative solutions to identifying unique market opportunities.

Apart from basic features of cloud computing, additional services like Analytics and Machine Learning will continue to grow and enhance business predictions based upon the data available. This will also further improve the core competencies of business setups in a cost-effective, scalable and productive manner. If programming is automation, then machine learning is a type of artificial intelligence that helps in automating the process of automation; getting computers to program themselves and giving them ability to learn without being explicitly programmed. The next level of machine learning will see the focus shifting from big data analytics to deep learning, and this trend will facilitate developers to focus on creating new applications without having to understand complex concepts like neural networks.

The future isn't just cloud—it is multi-cloud. A multi-cloud implementation reduces vulnerability and ensures that critical data is always kept safe and is accessible by all the stakeholders.

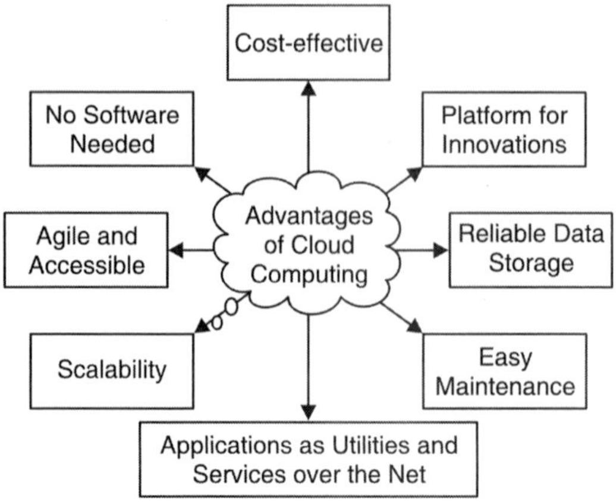

Figure 41: ADVANTAGES OF CLOUD COMPUTING

10.3 Virtual Reality and Augmented Reality—Immersive and Mixed Reality

Virtual Reality (VR) made a big comeback in 2016. Major steps have already been taken in the field of VR and Augmented Reality (AR). Both VR and AR provide the user with an enhanced and enriched experience. In the next few years, new and improved platforms for creating 3D VR and AR experiences online easily will be developed. VR and AR transform the way people interact with each other and with their environment. For example, VR can be used for training scenarios and remote experiences. AR, which enables a blending of the real and virtual worlds, means businesses can overlay graphics onto real-world objects. Over time AR and VR will expand beyond visual immersion to include all human senses.

VR is an artificial, computer-generated simulation or recreation of a real life environment or situation. Virtual Reality Modeling Language (VRML) is a popular language used for describing three-dimensional (3-D) virtual image sequences and possible user interactions to go with them.

VR provides an open and flexible platform for creating interactive three-dimensional scenes (virtual worlds). AR is a live direct or indirect view of physical, real-world environment whose elements are augmented by computer-generated sensory input such as video, graphics, GPS data, sound, etc.

Thousands of games and apps have already been released. Artificial intelligence beats a human expert at the highly complex, intuition-based game Go and this event has definitely set the stage for the rise of Intelligent Machines. The booming success of the Pokémon Go AR app has shown major companies that the users/gamers are ready for more. The next leap will lead to VR and AR versions of practically everything. VR and AR will drive new ways to engage and connect learners and will lead to new modes of education. Apart from gaming, other areas will also be more and more a part of the VR and AR landscape including concerts, travel, etc., and this will lead to the growth in non-gaming content.

VR is normally delivered to the user through a hand-held controller or head-mounted controller. AR is usually delivered through tablets, smartphones and tier mobile devices. Holograph headsets are also going to play a major role in the coming months and years.

Oculus Rift is a virtual reality headset developed and manufactured by Oculus VR, a division of Facebook. This device definitely gives us a glimpse into the future. Companies will begin to expand their focus on developing VR devices and systems that will be able to provide imaginative experiences to users wherein the users like what they can imagine that does not exist.

There are already VR programs to make virtual homes so people can plan out their interiors and furniture arrangements. Industry experts also believe that VR is an "empathy engine" and while developing systems based on *VR* + empathy, companies will need to be extra careful in avoiding the trap of commodification of the element of empathy.

AR technology is quickly coming into the mainstream. Industry analysts expect the augmented reality market will be three times larger than the virtual reality market. Microsoft's HoloLens is a forerunner in this area. This product interjects holograms with reality and this mixed reality enables people to visualize and work with computer content as a part of the real world. This mixed reality has a lot of promise in areas of collaboration, communication and creation.

VR content creation will increase in the years to come. In order to meet this increase, companies will also need to come out with accessible viewing devices. There will be more VR in the fashion sector to provide the consumers with a more immersive experience. Convincing replicas of the real world will no longer satisfy VR and AR users, instead embodied experiences is what the companies will need to offer to keep their VR and AR systems and products up and running.

Currently the VR headsets are bulky. The trend of smaller and user-friendly headsets will be a key trend in the next few years. Advancements in mobile VR will also pick up pace. Integration of VR and AR in the same headset will also be a big trend to track.

Alone or blended together, VR and AR are opening up new worlds—both real and virtual. VR and AR promise to change the way we perceive and experience the very world around us.

Spotlight Tip
Over time VR and AR will expand beyond visual immersion to include all human senses. True-to-life setting experiences and interactive online experiences will become highly popular in times to come.

Table 35: Differences between Virtual Reality and Augmented Reality

Virtual Reality (VR)	Augmented Reality (AR)
VR is an artificial, computer-generated simulation of real life environment	AR is a combination of real and virtual worlds; elements from the real world are augmented by computer-generated content
VR immerses users in a digital experience	AR creates a digital overlay on top of the physical world
VR experiences are usually delivered through a head-mounted or hand-held controller	AR experiences are usually delivered through laptops, smartphones and tablets

10.3.1 Challenges of VR and AR—Universal Standards, Health Effects, etc.

Most of the headset models currently available are just too expensive and bulky. Manufacturers will need to come up with cheaper and lightweight headsets equipped with more features. Powerful computers and smartphones will be required to render the effects that are anticipated from future VR and AR systems, only then they can cater to all application areas. High-resolution screens will be a challenging factor especially for AR technology.

Defining and adopting universal standards is a constant concern in the VR and AR segments. Corporations need to focus not only on their own products and services, but outward towards forming a workable standards ecosystem of collaboration and partnership with various industry players. The success rate does not merely depend on low-cost sensors, but also on bigger factors like uniform standards, value-added services and integration capabilities.

VR and AR systems and knowledge about them is needed to educate the broader market. Although there are several types of VR and AR experiences, customers are not aware as there is no extensive exposure to them. Also early exposure to these technologies is needed for the student community so that a talent pool can be developed that can handle the complexities of upcoming trends in VR and AR.

A Word of Caution

Without well-designed, thoroughly tested hardware, a user could experience cybersickness with symptoms like disorientation, blurred vision, etc. The long-term health effects of VR are still unknown. There is a lack of health research about these effects.

10.4 Wearable Technology—Body-borne Gadgets

Wearable technology also called wearable gadgets is technology that can be worn on the user's body as clothing or as an accessory. The wearable technology market is still relatively young. 2017-2018 will be a period of advances in wearable technology and devices and apps that will cater to real-time notifications, improved design, intelligent experiences, etc. Wearable devices are like tiny computers that users wear on their bodies as a watch, shoes, glasses, etc. The current industry has a lot of wearable devices on the market that cater right from fitness tracking to safety. Early prototypes and devices developed in the early 1980s were important steps in getting to where we are today in regards to wearables.

Spotlight Tip

One of the main features of wearable technology is its ability to connect to the Internet, facilitating data to be exchanged between a network and the devices, and thereby allowing people to access data hands-free from WiFi networks by using Bluetooth.

Miniaturization of hardware, advanced sensor technology and smart artificial intelligence algorithms will help bring wearable technology in the picture in the fight against chronic health conditions. Health and fitness wearables will continue to grow in popularity. Heart-rate monitors, pedometers and activity monitors are the most common devices that are embedded in healthcare wearables.

What comes first to our minds when we hear the terms wearables—wristwatches and glasses. In order to expand the reach of this market, companies have already started to focus on sensors and wires embedded in shoes, clothing, jewelry and headphones, and this trend will gain traction in the next few years. Many types of smart materials are in the process of development to measure a range of parameters such as muscle contraction and skin temperature. In the next few years, wearable technology will see a growth in opportunities related to energy management at home, in office, and personally.

According to industry analysis, by 2020, the global demand for wearable devices is expected to grow to around $34 billion. Although this is a promising forecast, currently this market faces a lot of challenges. Current devices often need to pair up with a smartphone or tablet in order for users to access their functionality. As this technology becomes more widespread and affordable, companies will be able to design the wearables that will reflect individual personality and style.

Small devices with inexpensive computers and low-power sensors that work along with your smartphone will gain traction in the coming period. Experts and researchers continue to research and explore the ways in which wearable technology will improve and enhance the lives of the users.

Wearables present an important opportunity for businesses. Retailers can ping wearable devices to determine which sections of a store a consumer visits, advertisers can target consumers based on location and the nature of the application associated with the device, and information uploaded to a website dedicated to the device can provide marketers with information specific to an individual consumer.

Wearable technology will generate market potential for IoT systems too. Wearable technology is capable of data collection and data configuration. It is natural for IoT to tie up with wearable devices in order to provide a more interconnected experience, and what could be more convenient to have such experiences through something that one can wear. Wearable IoT will see tremendous growth in areas of employer wellness programs, industrial processes, fitness trackers, smartglasses, etc. The main trend will be that of blending the best features of both worlds: wearable and IoT; the trend will be that of enabling sensor-equipped devices or "things" to communicate with one another in a more connected human-environment interface. This trend will be helpful in boosting smart city and smart home projects. Such a blend will give rise to potential privacy or copyright issues, which the organizations will need to handle in order to implement such systems successfully.

There will be more and more seamless integration of sensors into devices, clothing, footwear, watches and other accessories—hands-free design is the way forward.

10.5 Closing Words—What's Next!

These tech trends indicate that concepts, services, devices and applications that emerged within the last few years are ready to take off and become mainstream in the coming few years. With these huge future-based opportunities come concerns and challenges. Nearly every aspect of a future computer technology system is going to require big leaps in software programs, hardware components, apps, and many other aspects.

It may be a few years before the general population opens up to some of these path-breaking trends. Newborns of today will grow up in a highly customized, personal, electronic, sensory stimulation-based world of their own. There is always something new on the horizon, but anything new comes with a mixed bag of advantages and disadvantages. While the users and consumers will use all these tools and technologies to simplify their lives, they will also need to sacrifice some level of privacy as the connected world around them learns more about their personal preferences.

The future of computers promises to put nearly everything we can imagine right in our palms. We can't wait to see what else is in store for us!

10.6 Questions for Reflection

1. What are the forces driving these trends and changes?
2. Will we have the top-notch skills needed to match these tall trends?
3. Will VR technology really take off among non-gamers?
4. How wearable technology will fuel the growth of IoT?
5. What is a Cognitive Cloud platform?
6. Will VR and AR bring about more social empowerment or vulnerability?
7. What other significant trends can you spot?

Author Information

Chitra Lele is a young award-winning poet, world record holder, research scholar, record-setting author and software consultant. She is a double postgraduate: Master in Computer Management and Master of Science in Software Engineering. She holds several professional certifications in the field of software project management (CompTIA Project+ Certification in Project Management, Microsoft Certified Technology Specialist and many more). *She has an excellent academic record.* Her publications include scholarly articles and research papers, poetry anthologies, novels, and academic and reference books. She is the associate editor of the *Eternity* journal.

Chitra has been conferred with the title of "A Versatile Writer" by the India Book of Records. She set this record by penning maximum number of books in a short span of 18 months. The books belong to various genres, right from poetry to business management and from personal transformation to social studies. Her books have set a string of world records, received positive reviews, and garnered praise from world leaders, award-winning poets, best-selling authors, management gurus and business experts. Some of Chitra's titles are—*Corruption in India: Causes, Effects and Reforms, Ignite the Inner Spark: A Maiden Anthology of Profound Poems, Organizational Democracy, Call Center Essentials: A Practical Guide to Real-Time Results, English*

Language: The Gateway to Global Growth, The 6 Spheres of Life: Unlocking the Door to Success and Happiness, Waltz to the Future: A Divine Dance of Perfumed Poems, and many more. Her books certainly will be a valuable addition to your home as well as office library, and will help you to reach your goals and conquer new frontiers.

For more information about Chitra's professional management career, academic and reference books, literary awards, media mentions, poetry books, world records and much more, please visit her creative and academic blog: http://chitrathesavvysynergist.blogspot.in/p/about-me_20.html

BOOKS BY THE SAME AUTHOR

Title	Pages	HB/PB	Year of Publication	Price (₹)
Corruption in India: Causes, Effects and Reforms	160	HB	2015	450.00
Call Center Essentials: A Practical Guide to Real-Time Results	248	HB	2013	695.00
English Language: The Gateway to Global Growth	240	PB	2012	195.00
English Language: The Gateway to Global Growth	240	HB	2012	595.00
Organizational Democracy: Collaborative Team Culture—Key to Corporate Growth	304	HB	2011	595.00
The 6 Spheres of Life: Unlocking the Door to Success and Happiness	208	PB	2010	195.00